D0454911

DATE DUE

The Recalcitrant Rich

The Recalcitrant Rich

A Comparative Analysis of the
Northern Responses to the Demands
for a New International Economic Order

Edited by

Helge Ole Bergesen
Hans Henrik Holm
Robert D. McKinlay

St. Martin's Press, New York

ISBN 0-312-57912-8

Library of Congress Cataloging in Publication Data
Main entry under title:

The Recalcitrant rich.

1. International economic relations--Addresses,
essays, lectures. 2 Bergesen, Helge Ole.
II. Holm, Hans-Henrik, 1951-   . III. McKinlay,
Robert D.
HF1411.R416   1981   337'.09'048   81-9127
ISBN 0-312-57912-8

CONTENTS

Preface   x

PART ONE: INTRODUCTION
   The Origins of the NIEO Debate   1
   H.O. Bergesen, H.H. Holm, R.D. McKinlay

PART TWO: THE COUNTRY STUDIES
   Austria: Economic Egoist, Diplomatic Activist
   and Political Conciliator   22
   A. Skuhra

   Britain: Prisoner of Principle and Poverty or
   Parochial Pragmatist   37
   R.D. McKinlay and M.G. Naraine

   Denmark: Bridge-Building over Widening Gulfs   91
   H. Holm

   European Community: The Attrition of
   Negotiation and the Negotiation of Attrition   85
   U. Steffens

   Federal Republic of Germany: The Knights of
   the Holy Grail   98
   J. Betz and M. Kreile

   France: Egoism bien temperé   122
   M.C. Smouts

   Norway: The Progressive Free-Rider or
   the Devoted Internationalist   148
   H.O. Bergesen

v

Soviet Union: The Reluctant Participants   170
C.W. Lawson

Sweden: The Janus Face of Progressiveness   188
B. Nygren

United States: Who Pays the Piper?   205
G.C. Abbott

PART THREE: CONCLUSION
The Outcome of the NIEO Debate   223
H.O. Bergesen, H.H. Holm, R.D. McKinlay

Tables   251
Abbreviations   258
Index   260
List of Contributors   266

TABLES

Table 1 - Net Official development assistance from DAC countries and multilateral agencies.   251

2 - Comparative aid-giving performance in 1979   252

3 - Comparative ODA volume performance of major donor groups   253

4 - Comparative ODA terms performance of major donor groups   254

5 - The evolution of CMEA ODA flows to developing countries. Total net disbursements   255

6 - Capital flows and debt of the developing countries: oil importers and oil exporters, 1975-90   256

7 - Direction of merchandise trade, 1970 and 1977   257

PREFACE

The Third World demands for a New International Economic Order (NIEO) illustrate the synthesis of a number of important changes that have been taking place in the international political and economic system in the post-war period. The NIEO demands have been one of the most visible and vocal political slogans of the last decade, and as such have caught the attention of the media, have preoccupied diplomats, encroached on the time of decision-makers, and have intrigued academics of various persuasions.

The most general objective of this book is to analyze the responses of the North to the demands from the South for those political and economic changes that collectively constitute the NIEO package. To this end the book is organized into three sections.

Part One, titled Introduction: The Origins of the NIEO Debate, has two main objectives:
1. to outline the major demands of the NIEO package, and
2. to explain the emergence of the NIEO debate.
This chapter is designed to be read as a common introduction to each of the chapters that constitute the second section of the book.

Part Two, titled The Country Studies, consists of ten chapters each devoted to an examination of the response of a particular developed country to the NIEO demands. The sample of countries is not random. Short of being encyclopedic, it is impossible to cover all the developed countries. The selection has been made in an attempt to maximize the diversity of developed countries. In this way we hope not only to cover the whole gamut of responses but also better to be able to evaluate the generality and relative importance of different explanatory variables. Thus, the selection of countries covers: super, major and small powers; so-called 'hardliners' and 'progressives'; countries belonging to a variety of different groupings (including OECD, COMECON, EEC, 'like-minded'); countries having, both traditionally and currently, different forms and intensities of associations with the Third World; and, countries displaying a variety of different economic and political systems. Each of the country study chapters has two main objectives:

1. to describe that country's response to the major NIEO demands, and
2. to isolate the main factors that underlie and explain the response.

In much the same way that Part One acts as a common introduction to each of the country study chapters of Part Two, Part Three, titled Conclusion: The Outcome of the NIEO Debate, is designed to act as a common conclusion. It has two main objectives:

1. to evaluate the degree of Third World success or failure in satisfying the major NIEO demands, and
2. to isolate the main factors that explain this success or failure.

The book as a whole, by dint of the common Introduction and Conclusion and the common format of each of the country study chapters, has been expressly designed to read as a single extended study. In this way we hope to achieve the advantages of an edited work, i.e. the expertise of a wide number of people, without incurring, however, some of the costs common to many edited works, i.e. a rather disparate and unconnected set of contributions.

The rationale underlying the organizing objectives of this volume is set by four propositions. First, the actual scale of the NIEO demands, calling essentially for coordinated intervention by the North and the South to achieve a number of fundamental changes in the structure and working of the international economic and political system, makes the general subject matter of the NIEO demands effectively self-evidently important.

Second, within the general subject area of the NIEO demands, a systematic comparative analysis of the response of the North becomes extremely important. Although the NIEO demands themselves were initiated by the South, the NIEO debate could not take place until the North responded. Furthermore, since the success of the NIEO demands hinges almost entirely on the Northern response, then a systematic examination of that response becomes vital for an understanding and evaluation of the NIEO issue as a whole.

Third, although there is a substantial literature on the general subject matter of the NIEO debate, there has been little systematic or comparative analysis of the all-important topic of how and why the North responded as it has. Much of the literature tends to deal with the background to the demands, or with rather technical discussions of particular demands, or with 'grand designs' for the solution of the 'plight' of the developing countries.

Finally, a sufficient amount of time has now elapsed since the initiation of the NIEO debate that it is now possible to make a considered evaluation of the Northern response. In this context there is an even more important and enduring reason for making such an evaluation. It is now clear that the NIEO demands have met with a generally unsympathetic response. Furthermore, it seems unlikely that any major new initiative will be forthcoming from the North in the near future. Since the NIEO demands, however, constitute a major development initiative having potentially far-reaching ramifications for the structure and working of the inter-national system as a whole, it becomes all the more import-ant to explain why they failed.

The work that has resulted in this volume started as a Workshop directed by the editors during the Joint Sessions organized by the European Consortium for Political Research in March 1980. Many of the contributors to this volume par-ticipated in that Workshop. We are grateful for their con-tinued cooperation in this effort and to the other partici-pants in the Workshop for their valuable comments. We should also like to thank the other country experts who joined the project later. Without their contributions the coverage would have been too limited.

We gratefully acknowledge financial support from the Norwegian Ministry of Foreign Affairs and the Nordic Co-operation Committee for International Politics. We also appreciate the practical support offered by our own academic institutions.

PART ONE:
INTRODUCTION

THE ORIGINS OF THE NIEO DEBATE

H.O. Bergesen, H.H. Holm and R.D. McKinlay

In 1974 and 1975 the United Nations convened two extraordinary meetings, respectively the Sixth and Seven Special
Sessions. At the opening of the Seventh Special Session,
US Ambassador Daniel Moynihan, speaking from the perspective of the developed world declared:
'Let us put aside the sterile debate over whether a new
economic order is required or whether the old economic
order is adequate. Let us look forward and shape the
world before us.'
At the close of the same Session, Garcia Robles, speaking as
Chairman of the Group of 77 from the perspective of the
developing world, replied:
'The Seventh Special Session has convincingly proved
that this international economic order is something which,
although still in its infancy, is far from being a mere
point of dogma or a rhetorical figure. On the contrary
it already constitutes and will every day become more and
more the pivot on which the economic relations of states
will turn.'
Although a development dialogue between the North and
the South had been going on for some years, the two UN
Special Sessions introduced a major qualitative change in
this dialogue. This change was effected because the Special Sessions started a debate on a subject that potentially
had very far-reaching consequences. That subject was the
creation of a New International Economic Order (NIEO).

The main objective of this chapter is to analyze the origins of the NIEO debate. This analysis is divided into four
sections.

The immediate stimulus for the NIEO debate was a set of
demands that had been aggregated by the South. The first
section of our analysis is concerned to profile these demands.

The NIEO demands as a whole constituted a very extensive package. Such a wide embracing set of demands could only be formulated on the basis of a substantial degree of political mobilization by the South. The second section examines how and why the Third World achieved such a high level of mobilization. While many of the NIEO demands are on the one hand rather general, they do on the other hand manifest a very explicit content. Premised on a substantial degree of disaffection with the existing economic order, the NIEO demands presented both the strategies for achieving and the goals of a new order. The third section is concerned to examine the factors that account for the particular substantive content of the NIEO demands. Although the NIEO demands unequivocally originated in the South, the NIEO debate as such could not begin until a commitment was elicited from the North to become involved in the discussions. The final section confronts the question of why the North became involved in the NIEO discussions.

THE NATURE OF THE NIEO DEMANDS

Over a number of years prior to 1974, the developing countries had collected and refined a broad and loosely related set of demands that became organized under the heading of the NIEO. This package of demands formed the initial focus of the NIEO debate that began in 1974. In the ensuing debate, new statements, negotiations, expansions or modifications of earlier positions have resulted in some loss of clarity in the precise meaning of the NIEO. This loss can, however, be rectified by differentiating between the inclusive and exclusive conceptualization of the NIEO.

   The inclusive conceptualization of the NIEO is derived from a focus on the outcome of negotiations among the North, the South and international organizations. As such, the content of NIEO is defined by international resolutions contained in internationally approved documents produced from major international meetings. The exclusive conceptualization, on the other hand, focuses on Third World output. As such, it comprises the demands, in turn a composite of goals and strategies for achieving those goals, that have been produced and agreed upon by the Third World as a group. While the inclusive conceptualization is defined by the product of interaction between the demands of the South and the responses of the North, the exclusive conceptualization provides a more precise and undiluted statement of Third World demands. (1)

Since the main aim of this book is to examine the developed countries' responses to the NIEO demands, it would be logically inconsistent to use a conceptualization of NIEO that was already in part defined by such responses. In following, therefore, the exclusive conceptualization, we can more specifically define NIEO as that set of demands which is contained in three major Third World statements: 1. the Economic Declaration, Economic Resolutions and Programme of Action, adopted at the Conference of the Heads of State or Government of Non-Aligned Countries in 1973; 2. the Manila Declaration and Programme of Action, adopted by the Group of 77 at their Third Ministerial Meeting in 1976; and 3. the Arusha Programme for Collective Self-Reliance and Framework for Negotiations, adopted at the Fourth Ministerial Meeting of the Group of 77 in 1979. (2) Although these three documents do not cover the totality of the Third World demands, they do represent the most comprehensive policy statements from the Third World during the NIEO debate.

The substantive content of these documents can be ordered into three main clusters of demands:
— demands for changes in the structure and distribution of world production;
— demands for changes in the structure of market systems and for increased financial transfers; and
— demands for changes in the structure of international decision-making.

The first cluster profiles a set of demands designed to effect a more equitable distribution of global productive capacity with an overall goal of the Third World having a twenty-five per cent share of world industrial production by the year 2000. (3) More specifically the demands cover:
1 The transfer of productive capacities from developed to developing countries;
2 the diversification of production in the developing countries, the development of an indigenous technological base, and the increased processing of local commodities;
3 the promotion and protection and sovereignty over natural resources and domestic economic activity;
4 the harmonization of raw material production in the developing countries with the production of synthetics in the developed ones;
5 the restraint by developed countries of the use of subsidies for their ailing industries;
6 the adoption in developed countries of policies that encourage food production in the Third World; and developed country support for the creation of Third-World-

based multinational production enterprises.

Although the basic demands remained essentially unchanged over the period 1973 to 1980, there was some increase in the specificity of the demands and some change in the relative priority attached to different elements. In 1973 the major emphasis was on control over commodity production and the regulation of transnational corporations. The dominant theme, by 1980, was structural changes in world production location, and an increased stress on the need for collective self-reliance. (4)

While the first cluster of demands pertains primarily to a set of goals for the Third World, the second cluster - demands for changes in the structure of international market systems and demands for increased financial transfers - relates mainly to the means of or strategies for achieving these goals, symbolically expressed by the goal of attaining a Third World market share of thirty per cent of world industrial trade, and by the demands for one per cent official development and (percentage of GNP). (5) The demands for changes in market structure cover a wide range of issue areas, of which the main ones are:

1   Commodity trade - A Common Fund and a series of commodity agreements should be established in order to stabilize prices and boost developing countries' export earnings. (6) One of the proposed stabilization measures is the indexation of the price of Third World commodity exports to the price of manufactured imports from the developed countries.

2   Manufactured goods - The expansion and diversification of developing country exports should be promoted through technological and financial support from the developed countries, through easier access to developed country technology and through the elimination in developed countries of obstacles to developing country manufactured exports.

3   Financial support - Both official and unofficial transfers should be expanded. Furthermore, new types of official transfers are needed, e.g. the establishment of a development tax. Already existing official debts should be cancelled and private ones renegotiated. The international monetary system should be reformed in order to increase the availability of short- and long-term financing, for example through a subsidized expansion of special drawing rights.

4   International trade - Existing practices that discriminate against developing countries should be removed, both in the form of technical trade restrictions and by direct

control: quotas, orderly market arrangements etc.
Transport services generated by Third World trade
should be controlled by the Third World through cargo-
sharing in the shipping area and through regulation of
the international aviation system.

Demands for changes in international market structures
have been and still are the central elements in the Third
World conception of NIEO. Priority has shifted over time
from a focus on commodities to the fight against protectionism and financial aspects of North-South trade.

The third cluster of demands relates to changes in the
structure of international decision-making as a means of
achieving greater international influence. The establishment
in the 1960s of some new international institutions such as
UNCTAD or the IDA, had demonstrated to the Third World
the importance of the structure of international decision-
making. A final important component in the NIEO platform,
therefore, was proposals for institutional reform designed
to 'increase participation in the adoption of decisions concerning the future of international economic relations'.

1 Principally the demands have centred on two organizations: the International Monetary Fund (IMF) and the
   United Nations Conference for Trade and Development
   (UNCTAD). UNCTAD should expand its scope and
   strengthen its implementation machinery even to the
   point of being converted into a World Trade Organization.
   The IMF should be reformed internally by changing the
   voting system and allocating more decision-making power
   to developing countries, and externally by extending its
   authority *vis à vis* the developed countries.

2 The creation of new Third-World-controlled international
   regimes - e.g. the demands for codes on Restrictive
   Business Practices and on Transnational Corporations,
   but also the new decision structures built up in the Common Fund and in the Seabed Authority.

Collectively these demands have introduced into the
international agenda a development debate that is qualitatively different from earlier development discussions. In the
first place, the type of structural changes constitute a set
of demands that call for rather fundamental changes in global economic organization. (7) Furthermore, these fundamental changes are not to be implemented in one or two
relatively isolated issue areas. On the contrary, the NIEO
package profiles a collection of interrelated and comprehensive demands. (8) Thirdly, the structural changes present
a development strategy for the South that is premised not
only on substantial concessions from the North, but also

assumes a high level of coordinated action by the North and South. (9) Finally, the NIEO demands have not only a self-evident economic, but also a political content. On the very simple grounds that economic power is one of the bases, albeit not the only one, of political power, then the type of structural changes envisaged in the NIEO demands would automatically induce some rather important international political changes. Furthermore, the third cluster of demands are very directly oriented at a number of changes in major international decision-making bodies that more immediately would alter some features of the distribution of international political power.

THE MOBILIZATION OF THE SOUTH

Such a comprehensive set of demands could only be produced on the basis of a substantial degree of political mobilization by the South. This mobilization was the product of the conjunction of three interrelated factors. First, the developing countries became progressively more aware that they constituted a distinctive grouping confronting common problems and as such possessing a common identity. Second, this identity both stimulated and was stimulated by the progressive politicization and political organization of the Third World. Finally, based at least in part on successful political organization, the South came to realize that it possessed a degree of political power that enabled it to promote these interests.

While the structural preconditions for the creation of a Third World identity lay originally in the waves of European colonization that culminated in the nineteenth century, it is more useful to date an emerging identity from the Second World War. Since the territories that were to become the Third World were either by-standers or merely battlefields for the major protagonists of the Second World War, they did not become immediately involved in the post-war 'global' reconstruction. This reconstruction, necessitated by the collapse of the Euro-centric system, was quickly followed by the Cold War and the confrontation between the two worlds of the East and the West. Against this background, the Third World was created as the great residual of territories not immediately caught up in the Cold War confrontation.

The great residual did not remain passive. The first issue that began to galvanize an emergent consciousness or identity in the Third World was decolonization. One of the earliest formal manifestations of this was the Bandung

Conference of 1955 at which twenty-nine African and Asian countries gathered to discuss how the independence of the colonial territories could be hastened and how the newly independent countries should be located in the international system. This second preoccupation led to the non-aligned movement. While non-alignment respresented in principle a good focus for the development of a distinctive political identity, the independence issue was not so useful. The decolonization problem did not embrace much of Central and South America and also lost much of its force as more countries became independent.

Towards the end of the fifties a new issue appeared largely on the initiative of a number of Latin Americans. This issue was the weak structural location of developing countries in the world economy, and in particular the unfortunate consequences that this had for their trade. With the 1961 decision to hold a conference on trade and development, with the publication of the Prebisch Report and with the subsequent establishment of a formal organization of UNCTAD, a Third World identity was forged. (10) The significance of the preoccupation with economic development was that it provided a common denominator that could run through all developing countries irrespective of their geographic location and to some extent of their political complexions. What the establishment of UNCTAD essentially succeeded in doing was defining a Third World identity that was not based on their residual status from the first two worlds but was founded on their economically underprivileged location in the world. With the division of the world into the economic 'haves' and 'have-nots', the North-South division was created.

The Third World identity both stimulated and was enhanced by a concomitant politicization and political organization. From a relatively early stage the developing countries demonstrated a willingness and ability to organize to promote their interests. Thus within the context of international organizations developing countries discovered the advantage of collective action. Perhaps the most dramatic illustration of this was the victorious vote in the 1961 UN General Assembly which led to the 1964 UNCTAD Conference. As UNCTAD became a permanent organization, the UNCTAD Secretariat and leaders of the Group of 77 have become a type of think-tank, producing reports, documents and statements defining Third World causes and interests. As such UNCTAD came to act as a rallying point for the Third World. The merger within UNCTAD of the Afro-Asian and Latin American countries (the Group A and C countries) forced the industrialized countries to some extent also to act as a bloc. In this respect the political organization of the South has, rather curiously, forced a degree of political organization of the North.

The political organization of the Third World has not been confined to their collective action within the multitude of intergovernmental organizations. In addition to a large number of regional groupings, Third World countries have formed a number of producer organizations and have promoted their own more general organizations and conferences. Outside the meetings of the Group of 77, probably the next most important political forum has been the series of Non-Aligned Conferences meeting at Belgrade (1961), Cairo (1964), Lusaka (11970), and Algiers (1973).

The heightened identity or awareness of common interests together with increasing politicization and political organization coalesced to produce an even more important political development, the realization that the Third World possessed some political influence. Initially this political influence took the form of pressure group power.

This power has been manifested in two main ways. First, the Third World has been successful in defining certain areas of debate, i.e. breaking down certain non decision-making areas, and in structuring to some extent the agenda for international discussions. The first major achievement in this context was the success of the Group of 77 in calling for the first UNCTAD Conference of 1964. This was the first major illustration of the Third World being able to define certain discussion areas. This lesson has never been lost on the Group of 77 which ever since 1964 has continued successfully to define areas for debate. In this respect it is no coincidence that the Group of 77 prior to both UNGTAD II and UNCTAD III produced comprehensive sets of recommendations in the Charter of Algiers and the Declaration and Principles of the Action Programme of Lima. This same ability of using collective pressure to keep certain items on the international agenda was also seen in December 1973 when the 28th UN General Assembly decided to call a Special Session in 1975 to consider new options for solving world problems especially as these bore on developing countries.

A second manifestation of the use of a kind of pressure group power through collective action has been the ability of the Third World to extract a number of concessions from the industrialized countries. Certainly the first UNCTAD Conference and the establishment of a permanent organization illustrate this. Or again the UNCTAD II negotiations on a Generalized System of Preferences, which achieved some fruition at the end of the sixties, illustrates a concession won from the high-income countries that assuredly would not have been forthcoming without collective and organized Third World pressure.

While the significance of pressure group power through collective action should not be denigrated, it is a relatively limited form of power. In the early 1970s, however, the developing countries discovered that they had a much more effective weapon in the form of commodity action. The producer organization, OPEC, had relatively little direct control over the distribution of oil but had acquired substantial control over production both in terms of volume and price. In 1971, with the Tehran Agreement, OPEC demonstrated that it had the ability to increase prices in a concerted manner. It was, however, the dramatic price increases combined with restricted supplies during the Arab-Israeli War of 1973 that suddenly convinced the North and South alike that the South had a means of coercion that potentially could deal a devastating blow to the economies of the North.

By 1973 the progressive development of a Third World identity, political organization and political power reached fruition. The long learning process of collectively articulating and aggregating Third World interests and demands that had developed through the Charter of Algiers and the Declaration and Principles of the Action Programme of Lima produced in 1973, at the Fourth Conference of the Heads of State of Governments of Non-Aligned Countries, the Economic Declaration and the Action Programme for Economic Co-operation. The final piece in the jigsaw was provided by the newly found coercive power of the OPEC commodity action. The monetary and energy crises that followed in the wake of the OPEC price rises led to the convening of an interim Special Session before the one scheduled for 1975. This, the Sixth Special Session, was the first ever to be convened on the initiative of the Third World and the first not to be concerned with security.

THE CONTENT OF THE NIEO DEMANDS

In the context of the NIEO debate, the mobilization of the Third World led to the production of a very extensive set of demands for changes in the structure and working of the international economic system. In this respect the NIEO demands, despite their generality, have a very explicit substantive content. We turn now to consider the range of factors, of which there are three, that explain the particular content of the NIEO demands

In the first place, there had been a decline in the salience of the traditional issues. Thus, by the early sixties, most of the former colonies had either achieved independence or were scheduled to do so. There were of course a number of notable exceptions, particularly Portugese territories, to which were added also the issues of Rhodesia, South Africa and Namibia. Nonetheless these issues were of relatively minor importance. The issue of non-alignment also proved to have a limited life-span. Quite apart from conceptual difficulties in understanding the exact connotations of non-alignment, it was quite clear that the majority of non-aligned countries very clearly had ties, or alignments, with either the East or the West from which it was rather difficult to escape. Furthermore, non-alignment as an issue did not elicit in the early stages any substantial support from Latin America. Finally increasing signs during the 1960s of some general relaxation of tension between the East and West further eroded the rationale of the salience of non-alignment. It is certainly the case that Conferences of the Non-Aligned Nations continued both to meet and to recruit new members. It is noticeable however that the agendas of these conferences changed rather dramatically during the 1960s. The 1961 and 1964 Conferences in Belgrade and Cairo focused mainly on security issues and only secondarily on development ones. By the 1970 meeting in Lusaka, the emphasis had changed, while by the 1973 meeting in Algiers the agenda was almost exclusively devoted to economic and development problems.

The decay in the salience of the traditional concerns was more than compensated by the ever increasing preoccupation with economic and development issues. The changing emphasis on the Non-Aligned Conferences had been anticipated by UNCTAD which in turn had been anticipated by the the ECLA. Since the appreciation of their status of economic 'have-nots' was, as we have already argued, an important factor fostering a Third World identity, it is not surprising to discover that the developing countries should manifest a preoccupation with economic or development issues. Third World countries were, however, not only highly sensitized to their economic performance, but more importantly were becoming increasingly disillusioned both with their actual development and their prospects for future development. Relative to the developed countries, many Third World countries perceived themselves to be stagnating if not actually deteriorating. The preoccupation with development concerns combined with a growing disillusionment

about performance prospects provides the second factor
explaining the content of the NIEO demands.

   In general over the 1960s the real per capita growth
rates of the developing countries deteriorated against those
of the developed. This in turn increased the ratio of the
income level of the developed countries to that of the
developing ones, thereby giving rise to the idea of the
'widening gap'. Domestically the low or even declining per
capita growth rates of the developing countries were displayed in high unemployment, widespread poverty, woe-
fully inadequate public welfare and chronic hunger, spilling
over all too frequently into famine and starvation. Externally the picture was equally gloomy. Balance of payments
deficits were growing, debt was increasing and exports were
subject to substantial fluctuations. In global terms the
developing countries appeared to be caught in a position of
stagnation. The structure of their trade either in terms of
commodity or destination had not changed, their share of
global trade was essentially frozen, their share of world
industrial production or world research and development
expenditure had stagnated, and patterns of official and private capital flows were relatively fixed. Since the share or
contribution of the developing countries to these flows were
small, then there was a growing realization on the part of
the developing countries that they were ossified in a global
economy over which they had little control.

   This stagnation, if not actual decline, was all the more
poignant when set against the optimism of the First UN
Development Decade. There had certainly been a general
level of optimism in the early sixties when it was thought
that the Third World's development problems, though substantial, were far from intractable. Certainly in Western
eyes it was thought that through a certain degree of economic engineering the type of economic recovery that Western
Europe had experienced after 1945 could be repeated.
Thus, increased investment was seen as the main level that
could be used to get the developing countries through the
all-important take-off stage into self-sustained growth.
The developed countries for their part would assist the
priming of the investment pump through economic aid in
much the same way that the US had assisted the economic
recovery of Western Europe through the Marshall Plan.
Thus, even the Pearson Report, after cataloguing the failure of the first Development Decade, still clung to the idea
that increased aid would provide the panacea. (11)

   There is no doubt that the Western ideas of a development strategy had been disseminated to the South and

indeed they showed up in numerous development plans. Progressively, however, rather different explanations for the depressing performance and widening gap were beginning to appear in Third World forums. Increasingly the Third World was voicing the idea that it was not investment problems but rather their particular location in the global economy that was responsible for many of their economic difficulties. It is this explanation of Third World economic problems that provides our third explanatory factor for the content of the NIEO demands.

The idea that the particular location of the developing countries in the global economy was responsible for many of their economic ills was not a new one. Prebisch in 1962, and indeed during the 1950s while working at ECLA, had widely publicized the argument that the terms of trade were loaded against the primary producers of the South. The only remedy was through Third World industrialization which could combat the concentrations of technical advantage of the centre, overcome unemployment problems faced by the collapse of the export base, and reduce balance of payments problems by replacing imports. In short, the Third World could only escape its economic difficulties by pursuing a number of important structural and relational changes in the world economy. It was not difficult to generalize the argument from the terms of trade to suggest on an even more broad plane that the developing countries were the weak parties in an international economic system in which the structure of production and the rules of the game were determined by the developed countries. This type of explanation seemed to be highly consonant with the picture of stagnation outlined above.

Rather different explanations, which nonetheless reached an essentially similar conclusion, were made by a variety of other writers. Thus, the dependency theorists argued that economic penetration from the industrial countries created a centre-periphery in Third World countries whereby a modern industrial sector, controlled by foreign capital and repatriating profits back to the metropole, was imposed on the indigenous economy. Since the industrial sector sucked in all local capital and skill without producing any spill-over effects, then foreign penetration not only brought exploitation but also systematically underdeveloped Third World economies. Though the reasoning was different, one general message was much the same, namely that it was the peculiar structural position of the Third World that accounted for their economic ills. Furthermore since many of the major international economic institutions, such as GATT, the IMF

and World Bank, were both controlled by the developed
countries and therefore supportive of their dominance, then
major changes in decision-making control would have to be
effected in these organs.

These types of argument, i.e. of Prebisch or the dependency theorists, led to the conclusion that formal or *de jure*
independence was something of a chimera. *De facto* political
independence was increasingly seen to be contingent on economic independence. Without economic independence the
developing countries were open to foreign economic penetration and domination and were trapped in an international
economic system over which they had little control. In such
a condition their economic difficulties would be both com-
pounded and perpetuated. Furthermore the lack of economic independence, and therefore of *de facto* political independence, also left the developing countries open to overt
or covert foreign political intervention. Not only were they
easy prey but also there were a large number of temptations
for the developed countries to intervene politically in order
to support or protect their economic interests.

Given the decreasing salience of the traditional issues
and the obvious need and attraction of economic development,
it is not surprising that the Third World moved rapidly to a
position where the latter issues became its first international
priority. It is also not surprising that their relatively disappointing performance during the 1960s should underscore
this preoccupation. What is rather more contentious, though
nonetheless important, was their growing conviction, in contradiction to the West, that the major source of their difficulties lay in the structure and working of the international
economic and political system. Against this background it
was entirely consistent for the Third World to articulate a
set of demands oriented to radical structural and decision-
making changes in the international system.

Although this line of argument does explain why the
Third World would articulate a comprehensive set of economic
demands requiring fundamental structural change, one piece
of the jigsaw is still missing. It is true that the NIEO demands fit these criteria, but the NIEO demands are also premised on concerted action by the North and South. On the
basis of the argument thus far it would have been entirely
consistent for the Third World to posit other development
strategies, particularly those that involved breaking from
the North and pursuing autonomous development. The NIEO
strategy is not, however, an autonomous development strategy for the South but rather a development strategy for the
South within an integrated global economy. Why then did

the Third World wish to remain within the global economy?

The single most important factor explaining the continuing commitment to a single global economy was that many of the governing élites of Third World countries had come to internalize many of the same economic goals as the West. Furthermore they had come to realize that without the North many of these goals would be unattainable. Thus, the North, though perhaps creating a number of severe problems, also provided an enormous reservoir of several highly desired goods, such as technology, capital or skills. Given a choice between terminating or changing the conditions under which such flows were made, it is not surprising, given a general commitment to Western economic goals, that the Third World should choose the latter option. Moreover, a number of Third World élites were clearly benefitting from interaction with the North to the extent that trade and foreign investment were being used as successful mechanisms to promote growth. Finally, the majority of Third World countries have much more extensive economic ties with the North than they do with each other. In the short run, breaking such ties was perceived by the élites as being not only very disruptive but also very costly.

Thus, Third World countries were faced with a dilemma. Their interactions with and position *vis à vis* the North were generally perceived to be a major source of their economic ills. On the other hand, not only did many developing countries want to achieve exactly the same economic standard of living as the developed ones, but they also realized that they could not do so in a closed world of their own. Thus, while development strategies, such as self-sufficiency or basic needs, would be consistent with the argument that the North caused many of the economic and political problems of the South, such strategies would clearly lead to a form of Third World development radically different from that found in the North. Third World governing élites did not want this. What they wanted rather was a development strategy that, while keeping them within the global economy, would change rather fundamentally a number of important parameters such that they could more rapidly achieve the income and standard of living levels enjoyed in the North. This is precisely what they considered the NIEO package offered.

THE INVOLVEMENT OF THE NORTH

Having explained both how and why the South articulated the particular set of demands, making up the call for the

NIEO, it now remains to explain why the North took up the call and became involved in the discussions that were to constitute the NIEO debate.

The first, and most enduring, of the explanations concerns the complex of ties that the North had developed with the South. While it is true that the major trading and financial interests of any one developed country rest with other developed states, the trade and financial interests with the Third World are, nonetheless, substantial. There are considerable direct investments in the South, the South provides a number of key primary products, and it represents an important market for developed countries' manufactured exports. These rather direct economic interests are supplemented by a number of political considerations. On one level, the developed countries have a distinct concern with maintaining friendly relations with developing countries if only to promote and protect their economic interests. On a more general but equally important level, competition among the developed countries themselves creates an interest in the Third World as developed countries pursue special relations in the developing countries in order to maintain themselves in their competition with other developed countries. Thus, the superpowers in particular have conducted a form of political shadow-boxing in the Third World where one of the main objectives is to ensure that the other side does not develop a destabilizing set of special relations. Our first general explanation of why the NIEO demands elicited an involvement from the North is that the political and economic interests of the developed in the developing countries were sufficiently extensive that the costs to these interests of ignoring the demands would have been too great.

A second, and complementary reason why it was difficult for the developed countries to ignore the NIEO demands turns on the politicization and political organization of the Third World. As we have already noted, the Third World proved relatively successful in developing its own permanent organizations and in learning to use its collective pressure to articulate and promote its views within large international organizations. One perfectly simple, but nonetheless extremely important, ramification of these developments was that it was extremely difficult for the North to ignore the South. Furthermore within the context of UNCTAD, with the effective merger of group A and C countries, a precedent of formalized discussion and negotiation between the organized South and the North had been established.

A further ramification of the politicization and political organization of the Third World was that it helped to undermine some of the traditional means of response of the developed to the developing countries and in this respect encouraged, in the NIEO context, a negotiated response from the developed countries through international fora. Traditionally Third World countries, as long as they were organized in terms of the spheres of influence of particular developed countries, were vulnerable to more or less un-fettered overt or covert economic or political intervention by the high-income countries. Although we do not wish to suggest that spheres of influence have completely dis-appeared or have diminished solely under the influence of increasing Third World political organization, it is the case that such political organization has contributed substan-tially to the erosion of spheres of influence, and has in this respect seriously hampered some of the more traditional means of intervention employed by developed countries.

To some extent, therefore, the politicization and political organization of the Third World, though certainly not creat-ing, have reinforced similar tendencies in the North. But in the same way that collective action can be a useful power resource for the South, so it can also be for the North. In-deed there have been a number of attempts, e.g. the Inter-national Energy Agency or the Washington Energy Confer-ence, by the North to split the coherence of the South. In principle this is not a difficult task as the South in many re-spects represents an unholy alliance of widely varying eco-nomic and political systems. Furthermore there is a very obvious point at which Southern power can be split, namely in the isolation of the OPEC countries. Without OPEC's commodity power, the collective power would be seriously reduced. Thus, while collective political organization of the South has certainly been instrumental in extracting atten-tion and a response from the North, it has to be recognized that collective action of the south is a two-edged weapon which runs the risk of being self-defeating.

If the politicization and political organization of the Third World in some respects tended to force a response from the North, there were other factors, and this is our third ex-planation, which more positively had already established some general level of receptivity to the type of issues pro-filed in the NIEO demands. Firstly, development debates were far from novel. At the initiation of the NIEO debate, the Second Development Decade was already well underway. The Development Decades themselves were the product of quite extensive discussion and debate between the developed and developing countries under the auspices of the UN. Furthermore, many of the developed countries had development ministries and well-established aid programmes, overseen and monitored to some extent by the Development Assistance Committee of the OECD. The Yaounde and Arusha Conventions had already established formalized multilateral trade and aid agreements. Or again with the creation of the Generalized System of Preferences the developed countries had accepted the need for multilateral trade concessions which quite clearly contravened a number of important international principles. Finally the World Bank had effectively become a multilateral aid agency for the Third World. Many of the specific issues making up the initial NIEO package were therefore not particularly novel and had already been raised, if not discussed, in several international fora.

A second factor contributing to some degree of receptivity to the NIEO demands was the subject of international interdependence. International interdependence was seen as the product of a growing complexity and reciprocity of the increasing volume of interactions among an increasing number of international or transnational actors across an expanding range of issue areas. The preoccupation with interdependence and its consequences was not, however, confined to academic analysis. More importantly for our purposes there also developed a kind of international rhetoric of interdependence which quickly became common currency in the international pronouncements of many leading national officials. This rhetoric emphasized in the context of a shrinking world the increasing need for cooperative action in confronting a range of problems that were the common responsibility of all mankind. While this rhetoric was not solely directed at development issues, many of its key features were clearly consonant with some of those in the NIEO demands.

A general unwillingness of the North to ignore the South, due partially to Northern political and economic interests in the South and partially to Third World political organization combined with some general receptivity to the NIEO issues can certainly explain why the North may have been predisposed to become involved in the NIEO debate. None of the three explanatory factors discussed thusfar is sufficiently powerful, however, to explain why the North found it well nigh impossible not to respond. It may well have been the case nonetheless that collectively these three predisposing factors alone would have been sufficient to elicit a response from the North. Any speculation on this matter is however made redundant on account of the impact on the North of a series of events which culminated in October 1973.

This train of events began with the demise of the Bretton

Woods system. Under this system, the dollar emerged as
the major medium of exchange. On account of the chronic
gold shortage outside the US. The dollar became not only
a transaction but also a reserve currency. While the dollar
was tied to a particular gold value, other currencies in turn
were tied at relatively fixed rates to the dollar. Since the
dollar took on the role of a reserve currency, foreign
governments were willing to accept dollars without demanding convertability and additionally were unwilling to sell dollars as this would force down the price of the dollar and
therefore the value of their reserves. This system could
work well as long as the real value of the dollar increased.
During the 1960s, however, with increasing balance of payments deficits, due to the Vietnam War and foreign investment, combined with domestic inflation the dollar came to be
very clearly overvalued. At the same time the ability of the
US to convert foreign dollar holdings to gold had completely
gone (by 1971 foreign dollar holdings were five times US
gold stocks) and despite the creation of Special Drawing
Rights (SDRs) in 1969 the ratio of world international
liquidity to world trade had declined dramatically. The
strain of the overvalued dollar on the US and other countries' economies alike proved too great and in December
1971 the Bretton Woods system began to collapse. In the
Smithsonian adjustment the Group of Ten renegotiated their
exchange rates and agreed to expand SDRs. The monetary
crisis, under a series of speculative waves against the
dollar, continued to worsen. In February 1973 the US
government was forced for the second time in fourteen
months to devalue. In March, against renewed selling of
dollars, official exchanges were closed for two weeks. Subsequently major countries decided to abandon fixed exchange
rates and float. The Bretton Woods system was in a state of
collapse.
   On top of these critical strains came the OPEC oil price
rise of November 1973. The high level of demand inelasticity
for oil had placed the developed countries in a position of
vulnerability which they clearly had not fully appreciated.
In the short-term the price rises meant substantial deficits
on the balance of payments with immediate consequences
both for inflation and recession. The transfer of substantially expanded oil payments to the OPEC countries also held
out the prospect of longer term problems. If the OPEC
countries were to use their new revenues to purchase an
expanded volume of exports from the developed countries or
to make long-term investments, then the developed countries
could recoup some of their losses. On the other hand, there

were other rather more dire scenarios. If the OPEC countries did not immediately recycle the new revenues, there
would be an international liquidity problem; if the revenues
were placed in short-demand deposits in the banks of the
developed countries then there would be a substantial
change in bank liabilities with possible serious consequences
for the banking community; or if the OPEC countries so
chose, they could use their new revenues to speculate
against any Western currency. More dire of all was the
spectre of a complete cut-off of oil. Without some rather
dramatic response from the developed countries, such a cut-
off could take the Western economies to the brink of collapse.

Against a background of already serious international
economic strains, the November 1973 OPEC action (and the
threat of future recurrences) was traumatic. As long as
OPEC could not be isolated from the Third World, then the
Third World through OPEC's newly found economic power
could begin to call some tunes. One of these tunes was for
the North to become involved in a debate on a new international economic order - the North concurred.

Notes

1 In much of the present literature on the NIEO the inclusive conceptualization is used, and indeed if you discuss what a New International Economic Order is, this
is a natural starting point. See Karl P. Sauvant and
Hajo Hasenpflug, eds., 'The New International Economic
Order: Confrontation or Cooperation between North and
South?', Boulder, Colorado, Westview Press, 1977.
    Here, however, we are dealing with the NIEO
demands.
2 The first of these three documents is the so-called
'Charter of Algiers' from the Fourth Summit Conference
of Non-Aligned Countries, Algiers, 5-9 September 1973,
reprinted in Alfred George Moss and Harry N.M. Winton,
eds., 'A New International Economic Order', New York,
UNITAR Document Service No. 1, pp. 408-443.
    The second is the 'Manila Declaration and Programme
of Action', adopted by the Third Ministerial Meeting of
the Group of 77 held at Manila from 26 January to 7 February 1976. This was prepared as the Third World platform for UNCTAD IV, Geneva, UNCTAD (TD/195), 1976.
    The third document was prepared as the common
platform for the Group of 77 at UNCTAD V. 'Arusha
Programme for Collective Self-Reliance and Framework

for negotiations', Manila, INCTAD (TD/236), 1979.

3 This goal was presented at UNIDO's Second Conference in Lima, Peru, March 1975.

4 This is evident if we compare the agendas for the Seventh Special Session and UNCTAD IV with those for UNCTAD V and UNIDO III.

5 The demand for a 30 per cent share of world industrial trade was formulated at UNIDO III and repeated in the Arusha Programme.

6 This demand, together with the demand for an Integrated Programme for Commodities, was the central demand in the first years of North-South negotiations after 1973, but demands for regulation of the commodity trade goes back to the beginning of the sixties. See Geoffrey Goodwin and James Mayall, eds., 'A New International Commodity Regime', London, Croom Helm, 1979, p. 19; and I.S. Chada, 'The North-South Negotiation Process in the Field of Commodities', in Arjun Sengupta, ed., 'Commodities, Finance and Trade Issues in North-South Negotiations', London, Frances Pinter, 1980, pp. 7-8.

7 The NIEO demands may be interpreted in different ways. Some see them as attempts to destroy the free international market, see Robert W. Tucker, 'The Inequality of Nations', London, Martin Robertson, 1977, pp. 69-72. Others regard it as a reform proposal that does not challenge existing structures, see Albert Fishlow, A New International Economic Order: What Kind?, in A. Fishlow et al., 'Rich and Poor Nations in the World Economy', New York, McGraw-Hill, 1978, pp. 13-15.
   Part of the background of these different interpretations is the multitude of different demands posed by the Third World. If we take our starting point in the formulated goals of the Third World, it is certainly true that fundamental changes are required.

8 This means that the NIEO demands cover a wide range of economic and political issues. It does not mean that the demands form a coherent whole, on the contrary, many of the demands are contradictory with an unclear differentiation between means and ends.

9 This is clearly brought out in Third World demands for institution building, but is also a fundamental premise in the so-called Brandt Report, see The Report of the Independent Commission on International Development Issues, 'North South: A Programme for Survival', London, Pan Books, 1980, pp. 19-23.

10 United Nations, 'Towards a New Trade Policy for Development', Report by the Secretary-General of the

United Nations Conference on Trade and Development
(Raul Prebisch), E/CONF.46/3, 1964.

11 L.B. Pearson, 'Partners in Development', Report of the
Commission on International Development, Washington,
1969.

PART TWO:
THE COUNTRY STUDIES

AUSTRIA:
ECONOMIC EGOIST, DIPLOMATIC
ACTIVIST AND POLITICAL CONCILIATOR

A. Skuhra

INTRODUCTION

As a member of the developed countries of the North, the
demands from the South for the NIEO were directed just as
much at Austria as at any other developed state. Although
Austria enjoys a very high level of per capita income, even
relative to other developed countries, it is not a very large
contry. As such the Austrian response to the NIEO demands is perhaps on one level not as important as that of
some of the larger and generally more powerful countries,
such as the United States or the Soviet Union.

On the other hand, Austria manifests a number of
characteristics, which, by virtue of demarcating it from
other developed countries, make an analysis of the Austrian
response particularly interesting. Austria has not developed
any substantial ties with the South. Compared with other
OECD countries, Austria has for example pursued a very
modest development assistance programme. While this may
in part be due to the lack of any colonial history, this explanation can only be partial as it is equally true for a number of other countries, especially the Scandinavian ones,
that have pursued a much more active aid programme in the
absence of any former colonial ties. While a general lack of
any special interest in the South would be consistent with
international parochialism, this explanation is scarcely
appropriate in the case of Austria. After the period of
post-war readjustment, Austria has in general been a very
active member of the international diplomatic community.
This activity has been made all the more interesting and
relevant given the adoption by Austria of permanent neutrality. Thus, while in terms of its general economic and political structure Austria is unequivocally aligned with the

capitalist, liberal democracies of the West, its status of permanent neutrality expressly unaligns it with the major OECD countries. In this respect, Austria despite its general lack of involvement in the Third World finds itself enjoying some general similarity or complementarity with some Third World countries. This rather special mix of cross-pressures makes an analysis of the Austrian response to the NIEO demands particularly interesting.

THE NATURE OF THE RESPONSE

The Trade and Commodity Response

Austria's trade relationships with the less developed countries (LDCs) reflects many of the characteristics of the general pattern of North-South trade. Thus a general decline in the relative size of Austria's trade with the LDCs from the mid-fifties through to the early seventies was reversed by the oil crisis. By 1977 the relative size of Austria's Third World trade had returned to the levels of the mid-fifties. (1) The structure of Austria's trade also corresponds quite closely to the typical pattern of North-South trade. Thus, industrial goods constitute 90 per cent of exports, while imports consist primarily of energy, food and other raw materials.

Within this structure there are, however, some features that do not fit with the traditional division of labour. Thus, Austria exports a large amount of raw materials and of semi-finished and finished products of a low degree of processing to the LDCs. For example, Austria exports a considerably higher proportion of machines to the European Community than to the LDCs. This is partly true also for chemicals and transportation and consumer goods. This illustrates a weakness of the Austrian steel industry, which has a low level of diversification of final products. Austria also lacks an efficient distribution system and experienced export merchandising. The export of capital, on the other hand, is increasing rapidly. (2)

Austria has generally followed a policy of trade liberalization and non-protectionism. It joined the General System of Preferences in April 1972. This led to a general reduction in tariffs of 30 per cent. The system was enlarged in January 1975 to include topical agricultural goods and to produce an overall percentage reduction of 50 per cent.

The main exceptions are handicrafts and textiles. Most handicrafts now enter free from tariffs except for those produced from textiles, which remain at the 50 per cent level of reduction. The cancellation of tariffs on handicrafts is based, however, on special agreements with specific countries. Some twenty-two agreements were concluded over the period 1975-7. (3) It is notable, however, that this group of countries contains very few of the so-called 'least developed' of 'most seriously affected countries'. (4)

The government regards these trade liberalization measures as a grant to the developing countries of $80 million. Although this sounds rather impressive, it must be remembered that the government figure could be exaggerated. Without the reduction of trade barriers, the amount of imports to Austria would have been lower anyway. The role of non-tariff barriers is also not to be underestimated. The cancellation of customs for handicrafts is based on special agreements with specific countries in which the origin of the handicraft has to be from one country and has to be proved. (5)

On the commodity question in particular, Austria did initially voice some opposition. Thus, while it abstained in the general vote on the Charter of Economic Rights and Duties of States in the 29th UN General Assembly, Austria did record some reservation on the establishment of producer organizations on the grounds that any protection should also be extended to include consumers. (6) By the UNCTAD IV Meeting, at Nairobi in May 1976, Austria, however, had adopted a relatively sympathetic position. Though opposed to any agreements that would seriously undermine the effective working of the market, Austria, which itself has a relatively low level of natural resources, did express support for an integrated programme of agreements on certain raw materials and for the establishment of a Common Fund. (7) Following this, the Ministry of Foreign Affairs commissioned a detailed study on the consequences and different options of the Integrated Programme of Commodities. This study found that Austria could well profit from such a programme especially in the area of minerals and sugar. As a consequence Austria participated actively in the final UNCTAD agreements that were reached in early 1979. It supported the raw material agreements on tin, coca, coffee, sugar and textiles and also came out in favour of the 'Second Window', to which it pledged a contribution of $2 million.

Thus, while not displaying any marked degree of generosity on the trade and commodity issues, Austria has not, on the other hand, adopted a particularly hard-line stance. Rather it has complied with international economic necessity and has a liberal trade policy with state-supported export promotion.

The Aid Response

Traditionally Austria's aid performance has been relatively
weak compared to other OECD donors. Thus in 1973 and
1974 official development assistance constituted only 0.15
and 0.18 per cent of GNP. Other official flows were rather
larger, so that the combination of the two constituted 0.53
and 0.61 per cent of GNP. At the Seventh Special Session
of the UN in 1975, the Austrian Minister of Foreign Affairs
did however express an intention to strengthen the development assistance efforts with the goal of reaching the target
of 0.7 per cent. Austria also expressed a willingness to
enter international discussions on the debt problem of the
LDCs.
   Austria did indeed enter into the negotiations on a debt
moratorium. By 1978 a compromise was reached between the
donor and recipients. While other countries announced their
reductions, Austria, however, postponed its decision. In
1979 Austria waived some $4.4 million, representing 14.8 per
cent of its outstanding debt. Compared to other donors,
this concession was far from generous. Thus, only New
Zealand waived a smaller amount ($3.6 million), but this, it
is important to note, constituted the whole of its debt.
Other approximately similar OECD donors initiated on the
whole rather more substantial concessions than Austria.
Thus, Finland, Switzerland, Sweden and Denmark waived
respectively $41 million, $69 million, $200 million and $105
million, constituting 100 per cent, 90 per cent, 65 per cent
and 56 per cent of their outstanding debts.
   With reference to the transfer of development assistance,
the so-called other official flows (export credits, private
assistance and private capital) approximately trebled from
1975 to 1978 from $105 to $335 million), though fell back
again in 1979 to $121 million. Official development assist-
ance, the more important component as far as the NIEO demands are concerned, almost trebled from $64.4 million in
1975 to $165.8 million in 1978, but once again fell back to
$126.9 million in 1979. Thus, even by 1979 official develop-
ment assistance constituted only 0.19 per cent of GNP, a
substantial distance from the NIEO aid target. (9)
   Over the period 1975-9 an average of 35 per cent of total
official development assistance was allocated through multilateral agencies. Although Austria contributes, within its
multilateral allocation, quite heavily to the International
Development Agency, the branch of the World Bank that
handles soft loans favouring particularly the 'least developed' and 'most seriously affected' countries, it should be

noted that Austria benefits rather well from the publically advertised projects of the International Bank of Reconstruction and Development. Thus, in 1978 and 1979 Austria had a return flow of some $39.4 million and $27.8 million from World Bank projects. These return flows actually exceeded Austria's concessionary contributions to the World Bank Group in these years. (10) It should also be noted that Austria's multilateral contribution as a percentage of total development assistance, though more favourable than some of the larger donors is rather less favourable than comparable smaller OECD donors. Furthermore, there are no signs that the ratio of multilateral to bilateral contributions is increasing over time. Indeed the average over the period 1975-9 was rather lower than for 1973-4.

The bilateral component of official development does not meet many of the NIEO criteria. In particular the grant or grant-like element is very low, placing Austria among the hardest of all OECD donors. Further, agricultural and infrastructure developments receive relatively low priority. (11) Finally, Austria clearly does not attach any special preference in its bilateral aid programme to the poorest countries. Thus, in 1980 only five out of twenty-three recipients of Austrian aid were among the 'least developed countries'. (12)

It appears therefore that the actual practice of the Austrian aid programme rather belies some of the official statements of support or sympathy for the NIEO aid demands. Traditionally, Austria has been among the harder and least generous of the OECD donors and the practice of the last five years has done little to change this.

The Science and Technology Response

Austria was the host country of the United Nations Conference on Science and Technology for Development (UNCSTD) in Vienna in 1979. As host country Austria was not only actively engaged in the Conference proceedings but also, perhaps naturally, was interested in drawing the Conference to a successful conclusion. There were however some more particular self-interested reasons for Austria's preoccupation with this Conference. In first place, ever since the Conservative majority government of 1966-70, Austria has had a general policy of trying to attract UN organizations (for example UNIDO) to Vienna. Second, it was generally perceived that Austrian security would be enhanced if Vienna could be established internationally as the third UN city.

Even controlling for these rather self-interested motives, Austria played a very active role in the UNCSTD Conference and in general adopted a rather more favourable attitude to the Group of 77 proposals than many other OECD countries. Thus, only Austria and Canada supported the Group of 77 proposal to establish a new inter-state committee. The other developed countries wanted to integrate the agenda of technology transfer into existing UN organizations. Austria also strongly, but unsuccessfully, supported the establishment of an independent coordination administration directly under the UN General Secretariat to be located in Vienna. Austria then supported other institutional ideas such as the establishment of an international centre for patent documentation (INPADOC) in Vienna, which has since been realized (with the largest collection of its kind in the world and free service for the LDCs).

Even if we discount some of the more immediate self-interested motives that underlay the Austrian involvement in UNCSTD and concede that Austria was more favourably disposed than most of the developed countries, it must nonetheless be recognized that Austrian support for Group of 77 proposals was confined to a relatively narrow and innocuous area. Thus, on more fundamental questions, such as free access to Western technology, a new fund and the granting of majority control to the developing countries, Austria expressed its opposition along with the other developed countries.

On the question of industrialization, Austria voted in favour of the industrialization programme constructed at the Second General Conference of UNIDO in Lima in 1975. At the same time, however, Austria did express reservations about the possibility of actually achieving a goal of a 25 per cent share by the developing countries in industrial production by the year 2000. (13)

At the Third General Conference of UNIDO in New Delhi, Chancellor Kreisky again proposed his idea of a Marshall Plan (which he had nurtured for several years). This time the idea was quite well received in spite of the fact that the Conference ended disastrously. Kreisky's plan differs somewhat from the original Marshall Plan because of the different infrastructure requirements of the LDCs. The basic idea is to give long-term credits and/or to invest OPEC money in the declining capacities of the DCs (especially for example Austria's transportation and other industries) to build up the infrastructures of the LDCs. This is obviously not an unselfish proposal and is in fact reflective of the special interests of the Austrian construction and railway industries, but it is nevertheless noteworthy and necessarily based on international, bilateral or tripartite instead of global arrangements.

Although once again Austria appears to be active and displaying a more constructive approach than the hard-line states, it is nonetheless the case that Austrian support is expressed either for very general principles or for designs for which there would be a tangible return for Austria.

THE EXPLANATION OF THE RESPONSE

The Historical Conditions

The Austro-Hungarian Empire had no colonialistic history overseas. In the aftermath of the Second World War Austria was controlled by the four Allied Powers from 1945 to 1955. For a two-year period after the war, Austria received Marshall Plan aid which contributed substantially to the reconstruction and revitalization of its economy. This and other types of assistance led to a lasting sympathy towards the United States. (14) Thus for example when the Swedish government openly criticized American policy towards Vietnam, Austria's parliamentarians remained silent. In 1955 the Government negotiated the *Staatsvertrag* and initiated the policy of permanent neutrality. After the war Austria was ruled by a grand coalition of the Left (SPO) and the Right (OVP) until 1966. After a brief period under majority Conservative government, Austria has been governed by majority Social Democrat governments from 1970 until the present.

The Socio-Economic Conditions

In the reconstruction of the Austrian economy after 1945 one-third of the economy (mainly basic industries such as steel, chemicals and oils) was nationalized. A further third is indirectly controlled by the state by virtue of government ownership of the major banks supplying the capital markets and important industries. The private sector typically consists of smaller industries and businesses, which are represented by the Chamber of Commerce. This structural arrangement of the economy engenders on the one hand a high level of state intervention which is countervailed on the other hand by an equally high level of corporatism under which Chambers of Commerce, Agriculture, Labour and the

Unions have come to enjoy very strong positions. Particularly noteworthy is the system of *Sozialpartnerschaft* whereby a labour-management committee, in which the state only chairs the autonomous bargaining sessions, determines about one-third of all Austrian wages and prices.

These developments have in some respects proved highly successful. The efficiency and growth rates of the Austrian economy are among the best of the OECD countries. Or again the successful pursuit of the policy of *Arbeitsplatzerhaltung* (job security) has enabled Austria to maintain one of the lowest rates of unemployment in the world (around 2 per cent) while still keeping inflation at a low level (around 6 per cent). This relatively highly successful performance of the economy has had a more generalized effect of contributing in large measure to the legitimacy and stability of the political system as a whole. On the other hand, these developments have not been without some disadvantages, for example a low level of democratization, and without some costs. Thus, some argue that the general socialization of production and the privatization of conflict are manifested in the dearth of public conflict and debate and in the very high levels of alcoholism and suicide. (15)

The Foreign Economic Situation

With something over 20 per cent of its GNP coming from exports, Austria relatively is a large trading nation. Almost half of this trade is conducted with the European Community and indeed mainly with the Federal Republic of Germany. Approximately only 10 per cent of Austria's trade is conducted with the Third World. This trade in turn is dominated by the OPEC countries. (16)

Until 1974 Austria generally maintained a surplus on the current account of its balance of payments. Beginning in 1975, however, the balance on the current account has increasingly moved into deficit. There are two rather different explanations for this deficit with their attendant opposed solutions. The majority of economists see the deficit as a phase in a cyclical process in which demand for consumer goods increases. The left-wing explanation, on the other hand, hinges on the view that the deficit reflects a shift to a greater dependence on consumer and investment goods that should be countered by selective import controls. (17) The Government has rejected the options of devaluation, unemployment or neo-mercantilist measures but has chosen to continue its general liberal trade policy combined with

energetic export promotion and as such has been willing to
experience high budget deficits. (18)

   Thus, despite the already noted general success of the
Austrian economy which has given Austria higher growth
rates and lower inflation and unemployment rates than most
of its neighbours, Austria is assuredly not without some
foreign economic problems. What is perhaps particularly
relevant in the context of the NIEO debate is that these
problems have generally increased over the last five or six
years.

The Foreign Policy Situation

The single most important feature of Austria's foreign policy
situation is its policy of permanent neutrality. An analysis
of the voting behaviour at the United Nations over the period
1956-65 reveals an affinity between Austria and other neutral
countries, such as Sweden and Finland. On the other hand,
Austria's voting pattern did not differ substantially from
some core NATO countries. (19)

   Since 1970, however, Austria has shifted to a more active
policy of neutrality. This is in part due to the new government, but also the end of one Cold-War period with the
Nuclear Non-Proliferation Treaty of 1969, and the final shift
of priority to the North-South conflict in which Austria did
not have a definitive position according to its non-colonialist
history. An analysis of voting behaviour in the General
Assembly in 1978 shows Austria to be closest in general to
the smaller OECD countries, in particular Ireland, Denmark,
Australia, Iceland, The Netherlands, Luxembourg, Spain,
Portugal, Sweden and also Japan. To a lesser extent there
is some conformity with many members of the group of non-
aligned states. It is, however, rather more distanced from
the superpowers, particularly from the Soviet Union and its
allies, and on the other hand has no very strong affiliation
as allied countries. (20) The proximity of Austria to a number of smaller Western-European countries is strengthened
in a number of regular multilateral meetings. Thus, within
the Conference on Security and Cooperation in Europe, the
'N+N' (Neutrals and Non-aligned) form a distinct group and
hold regular consultations. Or again Austria has participated since 1977 in the regular meetings of the 'like-minded
countries' where some interest has been shown in developing
an independent position on the North-South dialogue. (21)

   On the other hand, the active neutrality policy should not
be overemphasized. The neutral posture of Austria is based

primarily on the importance attached to mediation and compromise rather than on the search for substantial independent initiatives. This is illustrated well in a number of
official statements. Thus Hertha Firnberg, Minister of
Science and Research, has commented: 'As always in these
matters Austria's attitude is essentially one of conciliation', (22) or again Staatssekretär Nussbaumer, (Under-
secretary of State): 'Austria endeavours internationally
... to reconcile different points of view in the struggle for
new rules of international cooperation, concerning for
example the NIEO, technology transfer or the question of
basic needs'. (23)

The Foreign Policy Decision-Making Situation

According to the Austrian constitution, Parliament is the
arena for formulating and enacting policy. In practice this
does not prove to be the case. The Committee on Foreign
Affairs holds scarcely any substantial discussions and there
is a general consensus among the major political parties on
vital goals such as neutrality and economic and ideological
links to the West. The establishment in 1976 of the larger
parliamentary Council on Foreign Affairs did not substantially alter this situation. (24) The NIEO was never debated
in Parliament, while the debates on development aid, which
since 1974 are required to be held every three years, do not
reveal any new departures.
    During the sixties an inter-ministerial committee of thir-
teen ministries, under the chairmanship of the Chancellery,
was given responsibility for the formulation of development
policy. In 1973 an intra-governmental reorganization then
placed general responsibility on the Chancellery with special areas of responsibility being located in the Ministry of
Foreign Affairs (for foreign policy in general), in the Finance Ministry (for multilateral financial relations), and in
the Ministry of Commerce (for international trade). There
is some conflict of interests and orientation between these
Ministries, in which context it is noteworthy that the Ministry of Foreign Affiars with a generally conservative background is more in accordance with Austria's tradition and
independence. There is also a set of competing interests
within the Chancellery between the big nationalized industry
and the small department of development aid.
    In 1975 the *Beirat für Entwicklungshilfe* (Council on
Development) was established. This was not however a product of the NIEO debate as discussions on such a council

dated from 1971. Its role is to advise the *Staatssekretär* and
the Chancellor on development policy, to comment on the tri-
ennial report to Parliament, and to participate in the three-
year planning programmes for development aid. It is quite
clear, however, that this Council is not an important decision-
decision-making body, because it does not take any independent decisions and serves mainly as a direct link of the
government to the private aid organizations and includes of
course the 'Sozialpartner'. Bilateral financial assistance is
decided in the *Entwicklungshilfe-Export-Komitee*, which consists of representatives from the Chancellery and the Ministries of Finance, Commerce and Foreign Affairs. This Committee has only half a million dollars of credit at its disposal.
Larger amounts are dealt with by a Council consisting of the
same members plus representatives from the Austrian
National Bank and the *Sozialpartnerschaft*. This composition
once again reveals the close association between the government and economic organizations. (25) Multilateral technical
assistance is determined primarily by the Ministry of Foreign
Affairs, while multilateral capital assistance is handled by
the Ministry of Finance.

With reference to the general public it should be noted
that Austria has an active Christan movement which until
1975 provided more bilateral development assistance than the
State. General public discussions of NIEO, however, are
confined more to small groups of leftist Catholics and a critical youth movement. The Chancellery began in 1979 to subsidize an organization for adult education in these matters
under secular direction. (26)

CONCLUSION

At the very outset of the NIEO debate Austria adopted a
somewhat ambivalent position. Thus, in the general vote on
the Charter of Economic Rights and Duties of States at the
29th General Assembly of the United Nations, Austria joined
neither the developed countries that voted in favour nor
those that voted against, but rather abstained. This initial
ambivalence has continued to be a hallmark of the Austrian
response. Thus as we have seen Austria has on occasions
approximated to the stance of the hard-line states, on others
it has appeared to be much more in sympathy with the Group
of 77, while on still others, it has adopted more of an independent initiative.

This ambivalence should not be equated, however, with
equally divided loyalties. In general the independent

initiatives have not taken the form of major substantive contributions. Or again on the question of the relative preference for the Group of 77 as compared with the hardline states, we can say in general that the more important and fundamental the issue the more likely Austria was to approximate to the hard-line position. Furthermore, holding constant the importance of any issue, the greater the political over the economic content of the issue, the more likely Austria was to approximate to the Group of 77 position.

The general ambivalence of the Austrian response was not a consequence of indecision or vacuous vacillation but rather the product of the interplay of three pressures. These pressures while certainly not irreconcilable were equally far from complementary. They do to some extent point in different directions and it is this that explains the variability in the Austrian response across the different issue areas.

The first of these pressures pertains to diplomatic activity. Without doubt in the sphere of international diplomacy, Austria is a very active member of the international community. This has led Austria not only to be a relatively active participant but also to have a predisposition to forestalling confrontation. Closely related to this pressure is a second, namely a strong commitment on the part of Austria to political conciliation. This, as with the case of diplomatic activity, is a product of a number of historical, political and economic developments and particularly the institutionalization of neutrality. This pressure has had the effect of pushing Austria in the direction of seeking to produce at least minimum solutions and compromises. The combined effect of diplomatic activity and political conciliations has been to cast Austria in the role of an international mediator.

While the importance of Austria as an international mediator is beyond dispute, it is subject to three important caveats. In the first instance, the ability of Austria to act as a major mediator is seriously constrained by the position of Austria in the international power hierarchy. Austria quite simply is not one of the major powers. Secondly, though Austria is a neutral state, this neutrality is manifested much more in the areas of international law and security than in economic policy and ideology. In particular, Austria displays a much closer economic and ideological affinity with the West than with the Communist Bloc or the Third World. This factor combined with the relatively low power resources of Austria explains why it has not made any major substantive initiatives. Thirdly, the role of international mediator is not based entirely on altruistic international motives. For a number of rather more self-interested reasons, especially those of status and security, Austria has been very interested in casting itself in the role of international mediator.

While there is a good deal of complementarity in the first two pressures, the third, economic egoism, pulls in a rather different direction. Despite a number of substantial conciliatory gestures and contributions at the political level, Austria's economic concessions to the NIEO demands have been far from generous. This can be partially explained by Austria's lack of economic intercourse, both historically and contemporaneously, with the Third World but also by Austria's satisfaction with the economic status quo. Thus, the Austrian economy, relative to many of its neighbours, is very healthy and those problems it is currently experiencing would not be ameliorated by many of the NIEO demands. It is noticeable that Austria's economic egoism is manifested not only in its opposition to those NIEO demands that required either fundamental change or substantial concessions but also in its support for a smaller number of demands where it perceived that satisfaction of these demands would bring Austria some tangible economic return.

We find therefore that Austria has been pulled in a number of different directions. On the one hand, as a diplomatic activist and political conciliator Austria has been pulled politically in an internationalist direction, while as an economic egoist Austria has been pulled economically in the direction of the national interest. It is the juxtaposition and interplay of political and diplomatic internationalism with economic nationalism that underlies and explains the ambivalence of the Austrian response.

Notes

1 In 1955 12.7 per cent and 9.0 per cent of Austria's exports and imports were conducted with the LDCs. By 1970 these figures had reduced to 6.5 and 6.2 per cent. By 1977 they recovered to 11.1 and 8.5 per cent. See: Stankovsky, J. 'Österreichischer Aussenhandel mit den Entwicklungsländern' (Austrian Foreign Trade with LDCs), Wien, Wiener Institut für Internationale Wirtschaftsvergleiche, Reprint Number 36, September 1978.

2 Klein, E., 'Österreichs Kapitalexport in der Zweiten Republik' (Austria's Capital Export in the Second Republic), 'Österreichische Zeitschrift für Politikwissenschaft', 7, 1978, p. 317.

3 Such agreements were concluded in 1975 with the Republic of Korea, Pakistan, Yugoslavia, Cuba, Uruguay,

Rumania, India and Kenya; in 1976 with Singapore,
Tunisia, Thailand, Malta, Egypt, Spain, Israel, Turkey,
Bangladesh, the Philippines and Ecuador; in 1977 with
Malaysia, Bolivia and Rwanda.

4   For a general discussion, see: Ibrahim, T.E., 'Die öko-
nomische Bedeutung der allgemeinen Zollpräferenzen
für Halb- und Fertigwaren der Entwicklungsländer'
(The Economic Importance of the General Systems of
Preferences for Semiprocessed and Manufactured Goods
of the LDCs), 'Vierteljahresberichte', 1976, pp. 129–142.

5   See also the satisfaction of the Chamber of Commerce
with the enactment: 'Jahresbericht der Bundeskammer für
Handel, Gewerbe und Industrie 1974' (Annual Report),
Wien 1975, p. 106.

6   'Bericht des Bundesministers für Auswärtige Angelegenheiten über die XXIX. Generalversammlung und die VI.
Sondertagung der Vereinten Nationen' (Report of the
Minister of Foreign Affairs on the 29th General Assembly
and the Sixth Special General Assembly of the UN), Wien
1974, pp. 47 and 138.

7   This is especially the opinion of the Chamber of Commerce,
in related issues rather a hardliner, in its Annual Report:
'Jahresbericht der Bundeskammer für Handel, Gewerbe
und Industrie 1976', Wien, 1977, p. 175.

8   'Aussenpolitischer Bericht des Bundesministers für Auswärtige Angelegenheiten 1978' (Annual Report of the
Ministry of Foreign Affairs), Wien, 1979, p. 188.

9   The figures are taken from the annual reports of the
Organization for Economic Cooperation and Development
and its Development Assistance Committee, 'Development
Cooperation', Paris.

10 'Die Presse', 24 September 1979.

11 Kumpfmüller, K.A., 'Austria's development policy in
the 1970's - a contribution towards closing the gap?'
(Ph.D.), Bologna, 1977, p. 184.

12 'Nationalratsprotokolle' (Parliamentary Records), XIV.
GP, 47th Session, 2 February 1977, p. 4546 and XV.
GP, 24th Session, 20 February 1980, p. 2348.

13 'Aussenpolitischer Bericht des Bundesministers für
Auswärtige Angelegenheiten 1975' (Annual Report of the
Ministry of Foreign Affairs), Wien, 1976, p. 96.

14 Ardelt, R. and Haas, H., 'Westintegration Österreichs
nach 1945', Österreichische Zeitschrift für Politikwissenschaft, 4 1975, pp. 279–299.

15 Marin, B., ed., 'Wachstumskrisen in Österreich'
(Growth crises in Austria), vol. 2: Szenarios, Wien,
1979, pp. 1–37.

16 Kernbauer, H., Die Integration Österreichs in die

Weltwirtschaft (The Integration Austria's into the World Economy), 'Österreichische Zeitschrift für Politikwissenshaft', 7, 1978, p. 294.

17 Höll, O. and Kramer, H., 'Kleinstaaten im Internationalen System' (Small States in the International System), Wien, Mimeo, 1977.

18 Katzenstein, P.J., Dependence and Autonomy: Austria in an Interdependent World', 'Österreichische Zeitschrift für Aussenpolitik', 19, 1979, p. 255.

19 Strasser, H., 'Österreich und die Vereinten Nationen' (Austria and the United Nations), Wien, 1967, p. 398.

20 Zemanek, K., Dauernd Neutrale Staaten in den Vereinten Nationen' (Permanent Neutral States in the United Nations), 'Österreichische Zeitschrift für Aussenpolitik', 18, 1978, p. 240, where results of the voting studies of Schindler, N. are referred.

21 Dolman, A.J., 'The Like-Minded Countries and the New International Order, 'Cooperation and Conflict', 14, 1979, p. 57.

22 'Wiener Zeitung', 23 August 1979 (Original quotation: 'Österreich (ist) grundsätzlich ausgleichend wie immer in solchen Fragen').

23 'Entwicklungshilfe-Bericht des Bundeskanzlers', Wien 1980, p. 5 (Original quotation: Österreich bemüht sich international ... um eine Annäherung der Standpunkte beim Ringen um neue Regeln internationaler Zusammenarbeit, ob es sich nun um die NIWO, Fragen des Technologietransfers oder andere Problembereiche, wie etwa die Befriedigung der Grundbedürfnisse, handelt').

24 Derndarsky, M., Die Diskussion um eine 'Doktrin' für die Aussenpolitik Österreichs (The Discussion about a 'Doctrine' for the Austrian Foreign Policy), 'Zeitgeschichte', 7, 1979/80, p. 346-361.

25 Eder, R. and Krobath, H., 'Die Österreichische Entwicklungshilfe: Politik, Organisation, Leistungen' (The Austrian Development Aid:). Wien, 1972, vol. 2, p. 378.

26 See also the new magazine 'EPN' ('Entwicklungspolitische Nachrichten').

BRITAIN:
PRISONER OF PRINCIPLE AND POVERTY OR PAROCHIAL PRAGMATIST

R.D. McKinlay and M.G. Naraine

For Britain the period since the close of the Second World War has been a time of relative economic and political decline. Nonetheless, Britain has remained an active member of the international community. It has continued to be strongly committed to those international organizations in whose establishment it played a very active role; it has remained an important trading, investing and banking power; and despite the loss of the colonial empires, Britain has retained and to some extent expanded many of its political and economic associations with the Third World. Thus, despite some decline, the international position of Britain was still such that it was likely to be not only an interested but also a relatively influential part in the NIEO debate.

THE NATURE OF THE RESPONSE

The Aid Response

By the start of the NIEO debate successive British governments had developed an institutionalized aid programme. This aid programme had not evolved as the result of any explicit or long-term initiative but as a consequence of more immediate and *ad hoc* considerations of foreign policy. Nonetheless the foreign policy basis of the British aid programme was not as explicitly developed as in the case of some of the other major donors, and did contain a humanitarian or welfare component. (1)

In 1975, in its first major statement on aid policy for eight years, the British Government produced a White Paper outlining a very explicit rationale and strategy for aid. (2) Noting the increasingly intractable problems faced by many developing countries, the White Paper asserts '... the present relationship and balance between the rich and poor countries of the world must be remedied.' It then goes on to outline the three 'legs of our new aid strategy':

   (a) to give an increasing emphasis in our bilateral aid towards the poorest countries, especially those in this group most seriously affected by the rise in the price of oil and other commodities;

   (b) to give a special emphasis to programmes oriented towards the poorest groups within these countries, and especially to rural development; and

   (c) to promote situations in which British concessional aid funds can best serve to stimulate matching contributions from other governments ... (3)

Though containing a number of more traditional foreign policy qualifications, the 1975 White Paper does point to a fairly radical change in British development policy. To the extent that the rationale and strategy of the aid programme are clearly structured around welfare or humanitarian criteria, then the new aid policy of 1975 displays a marked consonance with the NIEO demands.

The arrival of the new Conservative Government in May 1979 led to a complete review of aid policy. The results, announced in February 1980, made it clear that the main priority of the aid programme was to be switched from the welfare interests of the recipients to the interests of Britain. Thus, Neil Marten, Minister of Overseas Development, announced to the House of Commons: 'We believe that it is right at the present time to give greater weight in the allocation of our aid to political, industrial and commercial considerations alongside our basic development objectives.' (4) At the same time, in response to a Labour Peer expressing her 'anxiety' that greater weight was being given to political considerations, Lord Carrington, the Secretary of State for Foreign and Commonwealth Affairs, replied:

> There is nothing incompatible with using aid to further foreign policy. Our foreign policy is a thoroughly good one and is in the interests of the peace of the world. To tie our aid to those interests and use it for developing countries in a way beneficial to them and us is not discreditable but sensible. (5)

While this review admittedly contains a number of welfare qualifications, the main emphasis clearly falls on the use of aid to promote British interests. In this respect it deviates substantially from the NIEO demands.

This movement in official statements, from an initially sympathetic to a subsequently unsympathetic position, is not however reflected in the actual practice of the aid programme. An analysis of the practice of the aid programme shows that British governments have never come close to implementing the NIEO aid proposals. On the other hand, there has been a relatively modest, and in general continuous, accommodation to at least some of the main demands. The practice of the aid programme can be examined by looking separately at its structure and performance.

With reference to structural changes in the aid programme, perhaps the most favourable development pertains to the terms of aid. In 1975 the Labour Government decided to supply aid entirely on a grant basis to the poorest countries (defined as those with per capita incomes of less than $200). This led to a general softening of terms so that the grant element rose from 62 per cent in 1973 to 96 per cent in 1975, at which level it has subsequently remained. (6) On the subject of debt rescheduling, the Government in July 1978 proposed to offer relief of repayments of principal and interest on past loans to seventeen of its poorest recipients. The debts in the case of sixteen of those were to be cancelled, while in the case of India local-cost aid was to be provided instead of debt cancellation. On the subject of multilateral aid, Britain has adopted a sympathetic stance towards the 'Third Window' and has contributed, albeit rather modestly, to the subsidy fund on which this 'Window' depends. (7) The percentage of total British aid contributed to multilateral agencies has also increased from a figure of 11 per cent in 1970 to average 33 per cent of total economic aid over the period 1975-8. (8)

There are, on the other hand, some less favourable features of the structure of the aid practice. Untied aid, which increased as a percentage of total aid from 20 per cent in 1973 to 44 per cent in 1975, has subsequently stagnated at the 1975 level. With reference to aid for the 'poorest countries', the percentage of British aid allocated to this category has scarcely changed since 1974, when it was 55 per cent. Since the 'poorest countries' also contain over 60 per cent of the total population of developing countries, then the per capita aid allocation to the 'poorest countries' is slightly lower than to the rest of the developing world. There has also been little change in the geographic distribution of aid. Though the Commonwealth's share of British aid has declined slightly since 1970, it still receives approximately two-thirds of British aid. The most recent new recipients are either Latin American countries, that, to quote the *'Economist'*, have 'juicy trade potential', or countries of particular strategic interest, of which Turkey and Pakistan are the most notable. A final unfavourable structural development is the Aid-Trade Provision. The Aid-Trade Provision was established in 1978 to make available 5 per cent of bilateral aid for projects, which though fulfilling minimum development criteria were primarily of commercial importance to British firms. Not only have almost all the projects funded under the Aid-Trade Provision gone to very large firms dealing with infrastructure projects entailing large requirements for imported capital goods, but also the 5 per cent ceiling has been removed.

As far as the volume of British aid is concerned, the main characteristic is that it has stagnated at a low level. Following a small real increase of a 3.6 per cent over the period 1970-75, the Labour Government in 1975 promised a 4 per cent annual increase. This, however, did not materialize. Before the change of government in 1979 the proposed aid expenditure for 1979/80 was £840 m with a planned real increase of 6 per cent between 1979/80 and 1982/83. The budget of June 1979, however, cut £50 m from the aid programme, while the four-year expenditure figures, published in March 1980, projected a 14 per cent real decrease from 1979/80 to 1983/84. (9) This stagnation is all the more important as it has been imposed on an already low level of aid. With minor fluctuations, British aid as a percentage of GNP has hovered throughout the 1970s at around 0.37 per cent. This is only half the volume proposed by NIEO and only half the IDS target that was rather reluctantly accepted in principle by the British Government in 1974.

From the NIEO perspective, the balance of favourable and unfavourable structural features of the British aid programme does indicate some mild accommodation to the NIEO demands. The performance of the volume component on the other hand, can only be described as dismal. In this respect the un-NIEO like emphasis of the 1979 rather than the 1975 official statement seems to be a more accurate portrayal of the aid practice.

The Trade and Commodities Response

Since Britain is a major trading power, it is not surprising that it should take a keen interest in the NIEO trade and commodity demands. More importantly, Britain has for many years displayed a sympathy towards price stabilization

through international commodity agreements. Indeed this
long concern with and membership of the major commodity
agreements has exposed British governments, more so than
those of many other OECD countries, to the views of the
developing countries. Against this background it might
have been anticipated that Britain would be not only an
interested but also a sympathetic party to the NIEO trade
discussions.

After an admittedly hostile response at the Sixth Special
Session, Britain did indeed adopt quite quickly a relatively
sympathetic and favourable stance. At the Commonwealth
Heads of Government Meeting at Kingston in May 1975,
Prime Minister Wilson was put under great pressure to
address himself to the commodities issues. Rising to the
challenge, Wilson outlined what was later to become a British
policy paper on commodities. (10) The point of departure
for Wilson was that both developed and developing countries
have a mutual interest in stabilizing commodity prices and
establishing a general agreement on commodities. Wilson
then considered a variety of 'commitments' from which such
an agreement could be formed. These included principally
improved access to developed country markets, the diversification and efficient processing of commodities in developing
countries, and price stabilization through buffer stocks and
production controls. Agreements were to be negotiated by
producers and consumers on a commodity by commodity basis.
Except for explicitly rejecting indexation, the financial
details were rather vaguely cast in the format that the financial burden must 'be appropriately financed'.

Superficially, Wilson's statements at Jamaica could be
interpreted as a British endorsement of the NIEO trade demands. This was most certainly not the case. Wilson, in
suggesting that a general commodity agreement be passed on
a loosely related commodity by commodity basis, was propos-
ing a *comprehensive* commodity agreement. Wilson did not
propose an *integrated* programme and never mentioned the
idea of a Common Fund. In this respect, the British Government was endorsing not the NIEO trade demands but the
need for collective action, through commodity agreements, on
Third World trade. As such, Wilson's statements were not a
major policy initiative but rather a fresh impetus to previous
policies.

In the short-run, however, the superficial interpretation
prevailed. Wilson's statements were received with something
approaching euphoria by the Third World and as such they
engendered expectations among the developing countries of a

rapprochement in the commodity negotiations. This is perhaps not too surprising given that the Kingston statements
were the first conciliatory gestures from a major industrial
country on this issue since the antagonistic Sixth Special
Session. Certainly Wilson's proposals were instrumental in
the establishment of a Commonwealth Group of Experts to
examine further details of the NIEO proposals. The interim
report of this Group, produced in August 1975, included an
elaboration of the Integrated Programme for Commodities
(IPC) and a Common Fund. (11) It was endorsed by the
British representative, acting however in a personal capacity.
   Any expectations that the British Government raised at
Kingston in 1975 were dashed at the UNCTAD IV Meeting, at
Nairobi in May 1976, where the British Government expressed
a statement of reservation on the commodity resolution adopted by the conference. (12) In the first place, the British
Government insisted that due to the idiosyncratic nature of
individual commodities, a case-by-case rather than an integrated approach was sounder. Second, since commodity prices
were likely to reach their troughs at more or less the same
time, the economies possible with a Common Fund would be
slight. Furthermore, if contributions to the Fund were to be
mandatory and based on size of commodity imports, then Britain could be involved in contributing disproportionately
large sums. Fourth, the inflexibilities inherent in an IPC
together with a Common Fund could lead to a host of economic inefficiencies, such as production and export quotas or
excessive stock-piling, which in turn could stimulate inflation
or unproductively tie-up limited resources. Fifth, existing
financial institutions, such as the IMF or World Bank, together perhaps with an expanded role for private capital
were the appropriate and adequate means for financing any
commodity agreement. Finally, and not so explicitly voiced,
was a feeling that an IPC together with a substantial Common
Fund could become an OPEC writ large, and as such wield on
a larger scale the political and economic power that OPEC had
already so ably demonstrated. (13)
   While the British position at Nairobi was interpreted by
some as a reversal of its Kingston position, this is, as we
have already argued, essentially a misperception of the Kingston statements. Both Nairobi and Kingston represented a
continuation of more traditional British policies. The reversal came in fact at the European Community Summit of March
1977 and the first round of negotiations on the Fund in April
1977, when the British Government accepted in principle the
idea of a Fund. The reversal, however, was only partial.
While the Government now believed that a Common Fund

could have a role in stabilizing commodity prices, Britain
remained opposed to the idea of direct governmental contributions to the Fund. (14) In the period during the suspension
of the second round of negotiations, the Government continued its reversal and slowly accepted the idea of mandatory
contributions. At a Commonwealth Ministers Meeting in April
1978, Trade Secretary, Edmund Dell, reluctantly conceded
that Britain was willing to contribute to the Fund by way of
paying towards staff and office expenses. It was not until
the UNCTAD V Meeting in Manilla that a qualified promise of
a contribution to the Second Window was made.

When agreement on the Fund and its associated provisions
was finally reached, it was decided that Britain's share of
the mandatory contributions would be $10.5 m out of a total
of $470. Britain, however has as yet to make a contribution
to the Second Window. A recent statement from the Foreign
and Commonwealth Office that '... the Government welcomes
the creation of a Common Fund and continues to support the
work of UNCTAD on the Integrated Programme for Commodities' would seem at best to be something of a distortion. (15)
Britain's traditional conception of an international commodity
agreement has led it throughout the NIEO trade debate to
oppose the IPC and Common Fund. Eventually Britain has
been obliged rather reluctantly to accommodate to the NIEO
demands but this accommodation did not come in 1975, when
Britain erroneously was seen as sympathetic, but after 1977.
This final accommodation, however, has to be set against a
seriously emasculated IPC and Common Fund.

The Science and Technology Response

The British government traditionally has been sympathetic
to many of the key objectives voiced in the science and
technology NIEO demands. Britain has, on the other hand,
diverged quite markedly from developing countries on the
means whereby these objectives are to be pursued.

Thus, the British government has acknowledged the importance of and need for the transfer of technology, the
adaptation of foreign technology to the social and economic
needs of developing countries, the development of indigenous technology, and the training of skilled science personnel. (16) Traditionally, the British have pursued these
needs through the aid programme where technical cooperation
and assistance have constituted 24 and 30 per cent, in 1970
and 1976, of total expenditure. Much of the planning and
administration of this technical assistance has been carried

out by both British and developing country scientists and technical experts. This has led the British government, and the ODM in particular, to the view that the most appropriate means for promoting science and technology is through the apolitical arrangements of scientists, which would be funded through the aid programme.

The first major international meeting of the more specific NIEO demands outlined rather different means for promoting Third World science and technology. The main item on the United Nations Conference on Science and Technology for Development (UNCSTD) agenda in Vienna 1979 was the establishment of a fund to finance science and technology. Through the preparatory meeting and the conference itself, Britain, in contrast to the US and other EC countries, opposed the idea of a fund. Finally under pressure from the other developed countries, Britain did come round to agreeing to the establishment of such a fund. Britain, however, and again in contrast to the other developed countries, has not promised any financial contributions. Against the original demand for mandatory contribution tied to manufacturing surplus with developing countries, the US and the EC have promised voluntary, though as yet unspecified, contributions. The original conference proposals also called for the special committee that would run the fund, to be responsible to the General Assembly. In the negotiations on this topic, Britain played a more positive role. Though opposing the Group of 77 proposal of responsibility to the General Assembly, Britain also opposed responsibility to the Committee for Economic and Social Affairs (ECOSOC), the alternative proposal of the US and most of the EC. Britain did in fact propose a compromise solution whereby an intergovernmental committee, open to all UN members, would report to the General Assembly through ECOSOC.

Britain has also been rather negative on the patents issue and the Code of Conduct for the Transfer of Technology. Together with other western governments, Britain takes the view that private companies have every right to recoup their investments in research and development expenditure, that the flow of technology depends initially on private initiative, and that formal legal intervention would be cumbersome, as well as completely unjustified. Thus, once again reflecting a divergence from the Third World on the question of means, Britain has argued that any codes can only take the form of voluntary guidelines.

THE EXPLANATION OF THE RESPONSE

In this section we outline five sets of explanatory factors
that underlie the British response to the NIEO demands.
After profiling each set of explanatory factors, we indicate
how each has affected each of the three responses outlined
above.

International Liberalism

Although it is impossible to assign precise weights to the
importance of each of the explanatory factors, certainly the
most extensive and deep-rooted is the general ideology that
undermines British foreign economic policy. By ideology we
refer to a set of interrelated predisposing values. These
alone do not specify the details of every foreign policy response, but they do set the basic parameters within which
any specific response is made.

Britain is a strong, though not unwavering, adherent to
the ideology of international economic liberalism. The commitment to a world liberal economic order is supported by a
number of powerful and enduring factors. Britain has been
a long-time supporter of a world liberal economic system and
can indeed claim to be the first major proponent of this position. Furthermore, Britain has attached much significance
to the growth of economic nationalism in the 1930s as a major
contributory factor to World War II. As such a liberal world
economy is seen not only as the means whereby global economic efficiency and welfare can be maximized but also as a
mechanism for promoting peace. Finally, the British willingness to support the US stance on liberalism after 1945 was
based in part on the sadly mistaken belief that Britain could
once again become a major world economic power. On the
other hand, the British commitment to international liberalism
is constrained by a number of factors, chief among which are:
a series of special economic relations with certain countries
(particularly the Commonwealth), a relatively high level of
domestic economic intervention, and concern with the neo-
mercantilist tendencies of other states.

Applied to developing countries, the logic of economic
liberalism with its emphasis on comparative advantage in the
context of unrestricted flows of capital and trade, promises
a number of substantial rewards. Producers in developing
countries will experience an increase in demand allowing them
to reap the rewards of large-scale production; if exports are
of an agricultural origin then an increase will raise rural

income, while if they are of a manufacturing nature then urban unemployment will be reduced; as exports expand, there will be a positive spill-over effect in the stimulation of new associated industries which will in turn further raise incomes and reduce unemployment and in particular help to develop a greater degree of integration in developing countries economies, thereby reducing some of the problems associated with dual economies. Meanwhile developed countries receive cost advantages to consumers from cheaper goods, an export stimulus, and enhanced growth in a scenario of mutual gain to developed and developing countries alike. There is no doubt that this commitment to liberalism in the context of development is strongly held by British governments. Thus, the Labour Government in 1978 declared:

> The Government recognizes the need for its trade, aid and industrial policies to take account of the importance for developing countries of establishing a manufacturing capacity. Indeed, developed countries like Britain as well as the developing countries themselves should benefit from the increased flow of international trade based on specialization. (17)

Or again, in 1980, the Conservative Government declared: 'Trade is of the greatest importance for the developing countries. If the free world were to slide down towards protectionism we would all suffer, but the consequences for developing countries would be particularly serious.' (18)

We can differentiate two general positions within the liberal ideology. According to what may be termed the pure position, very few interventions in the free flow of capital and trade are envisaged, while what may be termed the conpensatory position permits a greater number of temporary restrictions under certain specific conditions if the goals of economic liberalism, greater efficiency and welfare, are enhanced as a consequence.

In the context of economic aid, those holding a pure liberal position are generally opposed to the transfer of economic aid on the grounds that aid introduced biases and distortions that actually hinder development. British governments have generally adopted the compensatory position on grounds not dissimilar to the defence of protection for infant industries. Thus, aid is seen as a temporary expedient enabling low-income countries to compensate for or overcome some of the worst obstacles to development.

The NIEO aid proposals on the other hand envisage a

degree of intervention that goes well beyong even the compensatory liberal position. This in part explains why the NIEO aid proposals have never been fully endorsed by any British Government. On the other hand, the compensatory position has at least ensured a continued supply of aid. It is also the compensatory position which explains some of the favourable (from the NIEO perspective) structural changes that have taken place in recent years. The distinction between pure and compensatory positions can also be used to explain the rather different official positions of 1975 and 1979. In general, right-wing parties approximate more to the pure liberal position and are more prone to spill-over into neo-mercantilism; left-wing parties under the stronger influence of state capitalism and an extensive commitment to social welfare approximate more to the compensatory liberal position and can even spill-over into the interventionist stance urged by the NIEO demands. It is thus now possible to understand why the 1975 White Paper, introduced not only by a Labour Government but by a Minister from the left of the Party, contained a number of echoes of NIEO, and why the harsher statements in 1979 came from a Conservative Government strongly committed to moving back in the direction of a more pure liberal position.

In the context of international trade, any form of dirigist intervention becomes an anathema to the pure liberal position. From the compensatory standpoint, however, while interventions that supercede the market cannot be tolerated, those that enhance the efficient functioning of the market are seen not only as legitimate but also as desirable.

Though strongly committed to liberal trade principles, Britain once again approximates closer to the compensatory than the pure position. In the immediate context of Third World Trade, Britain has argued for some time that widely fluctuating commodity prices have caused serious problems both for developed and developing countries and in the process have hampered the efficient functioning of the international trade system. As such, Britain has been a traditional advocate of international commodity agreements, witness the British support for the Havana Charter, which in its view would restore a more effective market.

From the compensatory position, and even more so from the pure one, the main problem with the NIEO trade demands is that they go well beyond intervening to improve the market to intervening essentially to supercede the market. We, can appreciate therefore that Wilson's position in 1975 was not only consistent with traditional British thinking, but also did not represent any rapprochement to the NIEO demands.

Furthermore, we can appreciate some of the grounds on which the British objections were built. Thus, at the most general level, the British held that it was entirely fanciful to imagine that an IPC and Common Fund could, as the British thought the NIEO protagonists supposed, entirely reorganize a whole section of the international trading system. Furthermore, the British insistence on a commodity-by-commodity approach was based on the idea that separate commodity bodies would better be able to manage the forces of supply and demand that in turn were variable across different commodities. Moreover, a large Common Fund could sustain extended interventions in the market that could promote over-production and stockpiling and a consequent host of disruptions to the economies of both developed and developing countries.

It follows therefore that any necessary financing could well be confined within existing institutions. The type of international commodity agreements, envisaged by the British, would not only be more diversified, and therefore operationally more flexible, but would also be less powerful. Admittedly they would bring some management to the market but the market would still be the single most important regulator.

Britain's adherence to the compensatory liberal positions goes a long way towards explaining the general reticence, or occasionally direct opposition to the IPC and Common Fund. Indeed the major anomaly is not that we can explain the reticence but that this position cannot explain the post 1977 accommodation.

In the context of science and technology, the NIEO demands posit increased government regulation of scientific activity and marked intervention into the private sector to control technology transfer. Once again these dirigiste demands clash directly with the liberal principles held by the British Government and the scientific community. Indeed, in this area the British stance is closer to the pure than the compensatory position. Thus, the Royal Society has declared:

> Scientists and independent scientific bodies are best equipped to determine when to take the initiatve in establishing contacts and activities with their opposite numbers in other countries and central control should be exercised only when the expenditure of public funds is involved in very expensive undertakings. (19)

This has been the basis of practice in Britain, and science policy has always been deregulated and operated on rather pure liberal principles. The idea of establishing an organization under UN control to manage scientific activity alienates both scientists and others who consider that scientific activity ought to be free from political interference.

Most technology transfer in Britain takes place in the private sector with no significant government interference over the generation and transmission of such technologies. In addition, in a country that operates under principles of liberalism, it is expected that firms should be recompensed for their endeavours, whether by way of patents, royalties, licensing fees, or management services, since these are considered to be commodities that fetch a price according to the market. To tamper with this agreement, as is demanded by NIEO, severely threatens the *modus vivendi* of cherished British principles both in theory and in practice.

State of the Economy

A second explanatory factor pertains to the state of the British economy. While many observers have exaggerated both the extent and decline of the British economy and in particular the collapse of the 'social and political fabric' of British society, there is no doubt that the performance of the British economy relative to most other OECD countries has been depressing. On any set of standard economic indicators, such as growth rates of exports or real GNP, unemployment, investment levels, productivity or inflation, Britain consistently comes close to the bottom of the OECD league.

The state of the economy has had two major influences on the British response to the NIEO aid demands. The first relates quite simply to the cost of a NIEO-type programme. This would in the first place require in the case of Britain a substantial expansion in expenditure (approximately a doubling of funds). Aid expenditure clearly involves opportunity costs and must detract from other government programmes. British governments have consistently argued that the economy is in a sufficiently depressed state that no large-scale expansion can take place. In addition to the cost of an expanded volume of aid, the NIEO proposals introduce a further type of cost in the respect that they attempt to remove some of the ways in which the donor can reduce the cost of its programme. Thus the NIEO demands are vigorously opposed to many of the standard ways of reducing the donor's costs, such as tying, maintaining the size of the bilateral component or decreasing the grant element. Again, given the state of

the British economy, it is not surprising that little progress
has been made in these areas since 1975. A further way in
which a donor can reduce its aid costs is to move towards a
neo-mercantilist aid position in which aid is supplied only to
those countries, not necessarily the most needy, which are
thought able to further the donor's foreign policy interests.
The promotion of British foreign policy interests has always
been present in the aid programme. Again it is no coincidence that by 1979 under pressure of continuing stagnation
and recession that greater salience is attached to the foreign
policy returns that Britain could reap from its aid programme.

A second influence of the state of the economy on the
response to the aid proposals is that movement towards a
NIEO-type programme is seen not only as being rather costly
but also as being likely to aggravate a number of the basic
causes of some of Britain's current economic ills. Britain has
a history of balance of payments problems to which the traditional response of a cycle of stop-go deflation-reflation
policies has been applied. An expanded aid programme
contradicts a reflationary phase and undermines the deflation-
ary phase when one of the prime targets of deflation is to
ease balance of payments problems. Labour Governments
have consistently used balance of payments problems as the
reason for not increasing aid. The current Government is
strongly committed to a reduction in the money supply and
in the Public Sector Borrowing Requirement. Other things
being equal this would lead directly to a reduction in real
terms of the aid budget, which is of course exactly what has
happened. The present Government has in fact made it very
explicit that the aid programme is vitally contingent on the
health of the economy: 'It is our policy to cut government
expenditure and if we don't get the economy right, the
whole aid programme will collapse.' (20)

The state of the economy has had a similar two fold influence on the British commodity response. It was in part a
preoccupation with the domestic economy that traditionally
has led Britain to support international commodity agreements.
This was expressed very clearly by Wilson at Kingston in
1975:

The costs for the developed countries as consumers are a
worsening of their inflation, setting up of a ratcheting
mechanism of inflation as wages react up but not down; an
extra burden on their balance of payments; and uncertainty over long-term development of their sources of
supply.' (21)

In short, commodity agreements were seen as one of the
ways in which some problems of the British economy could
be alleviated. On the other hand, exactly the same economic
and operational arguments that the British Government used
against a dirigiste system of international trade in defence
of its milder compensatory position are also relevant in this
context. Thus, the British Government was convinced that
the distortions, induced by an IPC and Common Fund,
would seriously aggravate a series of domestic problems. In
particular Britain could well find itself paying very high
prices for imported raw materials or alternatively facing
restricted supplies. The former problem would immediately
impose balance of payment strains, while either problems,
albeit in different ways, could stimulate inflation and produce
recession.

In addition, the Common Fund could pose a second and
more simple problem in the form of cost. As originally envisaged the Common Fund would have required considerable
subventions. Not only would this be very difficult for an
economy already performing badly, but also Britain, as a
relatively large importer of raw materials, could find itself
faced with a particularly large bill. Not surprisingly therefore the British Government was opposed to mandatory payments. Furthermore, the British Government certainly held
the suspicion that an IPC and large Common Fund, by virtue
of being operationally inept, could either quickly become
bankrupt or worse still could conceivably consume indefinite
sums of money either as ever greater stockpiles were accumulated or as the Common Fund met substantial shortfalls. In
this context, one of the principal objections to indexation
was that it could possibly consume funds indefinitely. The
British resistance to the Common Fund on the grounds of
cost has not only been very consistent but also largely
successful. Thus, it is clear that the Common Fund is grossly
undersubscribed against original targets, while Britain in
particular has promised only a meagre contribution. Furthermore in a manner reminiscent of its comments on the future
size of its aid programme, the British Government, at the
UNCTAD V Meeting, emphasized that a contribution to the
Second Window would be forthcoming only if the British
economy was in 'working order'.

Similarly Britain objected to the science and technology
demands on the grounds of cost. The Group of 77 proposals
of UNCSTD for a special fund of $4 billion, to which contri-
butions would be mandatory and based on a sliding scale
relating to trade surpluses in manufactured goods, would
have entailed a high economic cost for Britain. Neil Marten,

Minister for Overseas Development, stated at UNCSTD ' ...
recent cuts in Briain's public spending meant that there
was no new money left for aid purposes.' (22)

International Power Calculations

The third set of explanatory factors pertains to international
power calculations. It is something of a truism to observe
that the international arena is characterized by a high level
of competition and substantial inequalities in the distribution
of power. Within this environment, states endeavour to
maintain or improve their position in the international power
system. In so doing, states are of course obliged constantly
to monitor the activities of other major international actors.
Consequently, the actions of states are commonly influenced
either by anticipating or reacting to the actions of others.
The NIEO demands were addressed to a relatively large number of international actors and also at least portended some
important changes in the international power system. It is
not surprising, therefore, to discover that the British response was relatively strongly influenced by calculations of
the likely effect on the British position in the international
power system not only of the NIEO demands themselves but
also of the responses of other states to these demands.
    At the most general level, any full-scale implementation
of the NIEO demands would clearly bring a number of substantial economic and political changes which in turn would
alter the distribution of international power. In the first
place, the changes engendered in the NIEO demands could
entail a reallocation of economic capabilities. Since Britain,
despite its relative decline, is still comfortably located as a
major power in the international status quo, any substantial reallocations of economic power would clearly be of no
benefit to Britain. A second way in which some general
change in the distribution of international power could be
affected by the NIEO demands was in the expansion of
international intergovernmental organizations (IGOs). The
NIEO demands as a whole envisaged power changes in existing IGOs in favour of the Third World, the expansion of
existing IGOs, and the creation of a number of new IGOs.
While Britain traditionally has accepted the view that IGOs
are necessary in order to foster and monitor a minimum
level of international cooperation, Britain, like many other
developed states, has been opposed to any supra-national
development on the part of IGOs. This is partially because
Britain has been unwilling to surrender what it perceives

to be national decision-making autonomy to international
bodies, and partially because the current range of IGOs has
been relatively beneficial to developed country interests.
Not surprisingly, therefore, throughout the NIEO debate
Britain has consistently opposed the establishment of new
IGOs or the substantial expansion of existing ones. These
two general ways in which the NIEO demands could alter
the current distribution of power contribute quite substantially to the rather negative general British response.

In the context of economic aid, the main influence of
international power calculations has been to inhibit Britain
from moving too far in a concessionary, and NIEO-like, direction. More precisely, Britain has been well aware of the
potential costs of making concessions when other high-
income country competitors are not doing the same. For
example, the 1975 White Paper states explicitly that the best
way of allocating aid would be ' ... for some international
agreement on appropriate criteria for determining the country
distribution of aid ... and then joint action for achieving
that pattern.' It goes on immediately, however, to note that
no individual donor could 'counteract all the biases,' and as
such 'the role of the "residual donor" is understandably
sought by no one.' (23) Or again, a Select Committee Report
of 1977 notes, with concern, the use of credit mixte, to which
it refers as a 'judicious mixture of aid finance and commercial
finance'. This judicious mixture is seen as 'a powerful tool
by which some of our competitors, most notably the French
and the Japanese, have penetrated traditional British markets
and in some cases have built up a dominant commercial position.' (24) It goes on to suggest that although the use of
credit mixte is to be deplored, the Government may well be
obliged 'to fight the opposition with its own weapon'. (25)
The British Government is, in other words, very well aware
of the foreign policy utilities of bilateral economic aid and is
clearly unwilling to surrender these unless it is convinced
that other donors are doing likewise. Thus, while other
factors certainly influenced the rather negative form of the
aid response, the thrust of the international power calculations indicated that any substantial accommodation to the
NIEO demands would be irrational.

The influence of international power calculations on the
commodity response is more complex but also more important.
Indeed, these calculations are primarily responsible for the
British reversal on commodities from 1977. At the outset of
the NIEO debate, due to fear of new raw material cartels or
of further use of OPEC power, it might have been expected
that some accommodation to the NIEO commodity demands

would have been forthcoming. However, the commodity proposals met with combined opposition from all the major industrialized states at the same time that the threat of cartel action was receding. Rather curiously, once the major coercive threat of the Third World had to some extent been defused, the developed countries began to 'convert' to the Third World commodity position. The developed countries had to admit that the poor economic performance, if not stagnation, of many developing countries was in part due to falling commodity prices. Furthermore, given that some Third World countries did supply important raw materials, then there clearly must be a limit beyond which any deterioration could not be allowed to go. Against a background of economic deterioration and western intransigence, there was a possibility that Third World countries may look towards the Communist Bloc. This suspicion was sharpened by the crises in Angola, Zaire and Namibia. The 'conversion' in early 1977 of the major western industralized states was primarily due to the calculation that it would be politically expedient to exhibit some interest in and accommodation to the commodity demands. Thus once a commitment in principle was made to the Common Fund, the major remaining objective of the negotiations was to minimize the economic costs of this concession. These calculations have proved to be extremely successful. The political gesture of acceding to the Common Fund has indeed placated the Third World; meanwhile, the economic costs have been minimized - the Fund is relatively small and existing international economic institutions have not been disturbed.

The Group of 77 science and technology proposals presented two main threats as far as international power considerations were concerned. First, the demands entailed a new and relatively powerful intergovernmental organization, to which Britain was in principle opposed. Secondly, the proposals would have resulted in a change in the balance of research and development and a shift in policy-making control in favour of the Third World, thereby reducing the ability of western states to exercise control over technical know-how. Since other northern states were also opposed to the more radical science and technology demands, the international power threats inherent in these demands were not very real. Nonetheless, once the more radical demands had been defused, there was some advantage for Britain in concurring with the severely emasculated alternative package that appeared from UNCSTD. On the one hand, this enabled Britain, along with the other developed countries, to avoid a position of outright rejection and to give the appearance of

meeting the substance of the demands without in any way
compromising the status quo. Furthermore, the low cost
agreement ensured that Britain did not alienate itself from
its other, slightly more favourably inclined, EC partners.

Extra-Governmental Pressures

Thusfar our explanation of the British response has focused
almost entirely on the British government. This is, in fact
largely appropriate as it has been the government that has
been responsible for formulating the British response. On
the other hand, it is of course the case that government
policy is in some measure a reflection of extra-governmental
pressure. In the case of the NIEO demands, British extra-
governmental pressure has been either passive or more
actively negative, and as such has been generally consonant
with the British government's own position.

In the populace as a whole, there is very little interest in
or support for development issues. Thus a 1979 survey
found that two-thirds of the British people had '... parochial and introverted attitudes, unsympathetic to a world perspective, clinging to the past and untutored to approach the
future constructively.' (26) This is hardly the basis from
which support for a large-scale concessionary development
programme could be constructed. More specifically on the
subject of aid, only 46 per cent were in favour of British aid
as compared with 62 per cent in 1969. (27) This decline was
attributed by the 1979 survey to the deterioration of the economy and a preoccupation by the populace with inflation and
unemployment. The Confederation of British Industry, the
main employers' group, which has never been a strong advocate of aid programmes, has recently been more vocal in
complaining that it is not consulted sufficiently about the aid
programme, that the programme is not sufficiently geared to
trade benefits, and that the Government does not supply
enough information sufficiently efficient for British firms to
achieve maximum benefit from bilateral or multilateral aid.
The Trade Union Congress, traditionally a strong supporter
of increased aid, has recently displayed a distinct lack of
sympathy for aid in general and has called for close links to
be established between aid and trade and between aid and
domestic employment.

While, with the possible exception of some complaints from
the Confederation of British Industry, extra-governmental
pressures in the aid area have been passive, such pressures
in the commodity area have been more actively negative. The

original proposals for the IPC and a large Common Fund
raised the possibility that the Common Fund may intervene
directly in the market. The subsequent reduction in the
role of the market would automatically entail a reduction in
the role of major commodity interests, such as the London
Commodity Exchange (sugar, cocoa, coffee, rubber etc.),
the Metal Exchange (copper, tin, lead, zinc) and the Baltic
Exchange (grains, oils, fats) and their supporting financial
institutions. Not surprisingly the City of London became a
vociferous opponent of the Common Fund. (28)

The main extra-governmental pressure in the area of
science demands has been the Royal Society. This group has
been a staunch advocate of the view that science policy is
best left to the scientist, and as such was opposed to the
Group of 77 proposal that the Advisory Committee on the
Application of Science and Technology should be abolished.
In the field of technology the main opposition has come from
the Confederation of British Industry, which has been primarily concerned with the Paris Convention on Industrial
Property and has been insistent that firms be recompensed
for their innovations.

Intra-Governmental Organization

In addition to noting that the British response is in part a
function of the influence of groups outside the government,
it is of course something of a misnomer to pretend that the
British government itself is a homogeneous entity. The final
set of explanatory factors relates to the plurality of key
government departments responsible for the formulation of
foreign policy. The particular array of government departments together with their interactions influence not only the
content but also the general form of foreign policy outputs.

Although there is a general coherence in each of the
British responses, there is also some diversity and inconsis-
tency. This is in part due to the variety of interests of the
different ministries engaged in formulating the response. In
the case of aid, these different interests constitute an amal-
gam of not entirely consistent elements. Thus, the Ministry
of Overseas Development, the Ministry that produced the
1975 White Paper, has been in favour of an expanded programme, greater concessionary elements and a stronger orientation to humanitarian or welfare considerations. The Treasury on the other has been strongly committed to a low volume of aid. The Department of Trade has been concerned to
ensure some economic return for British commercial interests,

while the Foreign Office has been primarily preoccupied with trying to tie aid allocation to British foreign policy interests.

There has been a similar, though rather more complementary, diversity in the commodity response. The Treasury has consistently opposed the Common Fund partly on grounds of cost and partly on grounds of the estimated loss of earnings on invisibles from the futures market. The Ministry of Overseas Development, has been opposed to the IPC and Common Fund on the grounds that the poorest countries would receive little benefit, though it has been rather more favourably disposed to the other measures, which it held could help development in the poorest countries. The Department of Trade has produced a host of technical arguments against the commodity scheme and has shown special concern about the intervention of a Common Fund in the market. The Foreign Office, on the other hand, has cautioned against a response dictated purely by technical economic considerations, and has argued successfully that more general political considerations should also be taken into account.

In the area of the science and technology demands, government departments have been more united in their opposition. The Ministry of Overseas Development has been opposed to the establishment of a separate organization to manage science and technology activities; the Treasury has been concerned about the estimated costs of the proposals; and the Department of Trade has been worried about the ramifications for British industry of the intended revision of patents and other technology transfer costs.

While the plurality of interests has contributed some variation or diversity in the British response, it is noticeable that most of the key ministries, albeit for different reasons, are generally opposed to the NIEO demands. The major exception is the Ministry for Overseas Development. This Ministry was founded under Fabian influence in 1964 and was designed to initiate, coordinate and implement British development policy. As such it is not surprising that it has proved to be the Ministry most favourably disposed to the NIEO proposals. On the other hand, the Ministry for Overseas Development has never been allowed to fulfil the original proposals. Its status and autonomy have been continuously eroded so that it is now essentially an administrative department for aid. Consequently its ability to influence the general thrust of the other key departments has been relatively slight.

A final point of importance concerning the plurality of government department is their influence on the general form of British foreign policy. The 1977 Select Committee Report comments ' ... nowhere is foreign economic policy conceived of as a whole ...' (29) It suggests that there is no long-term strategic inter-departmental liaison, and whenever coordination does take place it is '... in response to a perceived conflict of interests over a particular issue. In short, it is *ad hoc* and short-term.' (30) Wallace makes much the same point when he characterizes British foreign economic policy as '... the pursuit of a collection of separate departmental policies, only loosely coordinated within the pragmatic context of overall foreign policy.' (31) The British responses to the NIEO demands, particular in the areas of aid and commodities, seem to bear very clearly the imprint of a rather *ad hoc*, defensive, pragmatic but nonetheless generally coherent approach to decision-making.

CONCLUSION

Few would disagree with Lord Carrington when he asserted that:

> Successive governments have been opposed to the NIEO as advocated by the Group of 77, on the grounds that its implementation would do damage to the world economic system, and hence to both developed and developing countries. That remains the position of Her Majesty's Government. (32)

With the exception of a number of relatively minor accommodations, the British response to the NIEO demands has been overwhelmingly negative.

There is greater scope for disagreement, however, on what accounts for the negative response. The British government has consistently used both its commitment to liberal economic principles and the sorry state of the economy to explain its opposition. In this respect, the government has cast itself as a prisoner of principle and poverty. On the other hand, some Third World opinion has depicted Britain, rather less favourably, in terms of parochial pragmatism. Thus, for example, the Indian Ambassador to the UN, Brajesh Mishra, clearly had Britain in mind when he charged that a few of the developed countries '... continued to be influenced by short-term gains and they still consider international co-operation as a zero-sum game'. The focus of these countries is '... not global but parochial'. (33)

There can be little doubt that any large-scale acceptance of the NIEO demands would impose a substantial financial burden. Equally there can be little doubt that the NIEO demands are quite antithetical to the conception of a world liberal economic system. Since many important pressure groups and key government departments are both concerned with the poor performance of the British economy and are strongly motivated by liberal interests, there can also be little doubt that both principle and poverty have had an important influence on the British response.

On the other hand, quite apart from the fact that Britain has grossly exaggerated its financial constraints, it is quite clear that poverty is relative. Thus, even Prime Minister Callaghan could comment: 'We cannot be an island of relative wealth in a world of poverty.' (34) Furthermore, quite apart from the fact that Britain is not an unwavering adherent of liberal economic principles, its general foreign policy position is not of course solely premised on these principles. Britain has a variety of both more specific and more general political interests and the NIEO package was certainly sufficiently extensive to have ramifications for them. Like many other states, Britain is concerned to maintain its position in the international status quo and its foreign policy is as a consequence strongly conditioned by realist calculations. Since once again there are many important pressure groups and government departments that are motivated by these considerations, it is not surprising to find that the British response has been strongly influenced by a number of pragmatic international power calculations.

Neither the British government's nor Ambassador Mishra's explanations are entirely satisfactory. The rather negative response from Britain is a function of a mixture of power pragmatism, principle and poverty.

Notes

1 See, for example: McKinlay, R.D. and Little, R., A Foreign-Policy Model of the Distribution of British Bilateral Aid, 1960-70, 'British Journal of Political Science, 8, 3, 1978 and Wallace, W., 'The Foreign Policy Process in Britain', London, Royal Institute of International Affairs, 1975.
2 Ministry of Overseas Development, 'The Changing Emphasis in British Aid Policies', London, Command 6270, 1975.
3 Ibid., p. 50.
4 Hansard, 'House of Commons', London, vol. 978/979, 1980, p. 464.
5 Quoted in 'The Times', 21 February 1980.

6   The figures used in this and related paragraphs are taken from the annual reviews of the Organization for Economic Cooperation and Development, 'Development Cooperation', Paris.

7   The 'Third Window' is a lending facilities established by the IBRD by which loans are made at an interest rate intermediate between its normal one and those for IDA credits. Since the resources for this facility are borrowed in the usual way, the Bank requires a subsidy to underwrite the difference between its borrowing and lending rates.

8   Multilateral aid as a percentage of total aid rose in 1979 and may remain relatively high for some time. This is simply because when the Government cut the real size of the aid programme it could not as quickly reduce earlier and long-standing commitments to multilateral agencies. The new Minister of Overseas Development as pointed out, however: 'As we need more room for manoeuvre in bilateral aid, we shall need to look more critically at our expenditure on multilateral aid programmes.' Lord Carrington has been rather more explicit. He has stated that the government is seeking to redress the balance (i.e. to cut multilateral aid) because it is bilateral aid that is 'most useful to this country'.

9   See: Hewitt, A. and Sutton, M., British Aid: A Change of Direction, 'Overseas Development Institute Review', 1, 1980.

10 'World Interdependence and Trade in Commodities', London, HMSO, Command 6061, May 1975.

11 Commonwealth Secretariat, 'Towards a New International Economic Order: Report by a Commonwealth Group of Experts', Commonwealth Secretariat, August, 1975.

12 'UNCTAD: Report of the Conference on its Fourth Session', London, HMSO, Command 6708, 1977.

13 House of Lords Select Committee on Commodity Prices, 'House of Lords Bulletin', 165, vol. 1, 1977, p. lxxvii.

14 Select Committee on Overseas Development, 'The Forthcoming UNCTAD Negotiations', House of Commons Paper, 222, 1977.

15 Foreign and Commonwealth Office, 'The Brandt Commission Report', London, 1980, p. 19.

16 Ministry of Overseas Development, 'Science and Technology for Development: the British National Paper for UNCSTD', 1979.

17 Secretary of State for Foreign and Commonwealth Affairs, 'Trade and Aid', London, Command 7213, 1978, p. 1.

18 Hansard, 'House of Commons', London, vol. 978/979, 1980, p. 464.

19   Ministry of Overseas Development, 'Science and Techno-
     logy for Development', London, 1979.
20   Mr. N. Marten, the current Minister of Overseas
     Development, in an interview in 'Spur', the newspaper
     of the World Development Movement, September 1979,
     p. 2.
21   'World Interdependence and Trade in Commodities', op.
     cit., p. 3.
22   Neil Marten's address to UNCSTD, 24 August 1979.
23   Ministry of Overseas Development, 'The Changing
     Emphasis in British Aid Policies', op. cit., p. 10.
24   Select Committee on Overseas Development, 'Trade and
     Aid', London, House of Commons Paper, 125, 1977,
     p. xxii. Under the British Parliamentary system, the
     primary responsibility of Select Committees, often on
     Government initiative, is to investigate and comment
     upon policy areas. The Reports from Select Committees
     are usually very interesting documents. Not only are
     they commonly very candid and wide-ranging in their
     criticisms and evaluations of Government policy, but they
     also have access to personnel and information which are
     not readily available to outside researchers. Select Com-
     mittee Reports are as such not government statements
     but they are statements from within the government in
     that members of the Committee are appointed from the
     House and report to it.
25   Ibid., p. xxiii.
26   T.S. Bowles, 'Survey of Attitudes towards Overseas
     Development', London HMSO, 1979. (This survey was
     commissioned by the Ministry of Overseas Development).
27   The earlier survey was also commissioned by the Ministry
     of Overseas Development: Rauta, I., 'Aid and Overseas
     Development', London, HMSO, 1971.
28   In response to increasing protectionist pressure, the
     Foreign Office published a report showing that the
     major causes of unemployment were changes in demand,
     higher productivity, and imports from developed coun-
     tries. Indeed the UK has a net trade surplus with the
     newly industrializing countries. See: Foreign Office:
     'The Newly Industrializing Countries and the Adjustment
     Problem', London, 1979.
29   Select Committee on Overseas Development, 'Trade and
     Aid', op. cit., p. xv.
30   Ibid., p. viii.
31   W. Wallace, The Management of Foreign Economic Policy
     in Britain, 'International Affairs', 50, 2, 1974, p. 261.
32   Hansard, 'House of Lords Debates', vol. 401, 1979,
     p. 1498.

33 These comments were made in the setting of the Eleventh Session and were quoted in the 'Guardian', 24 September 1980.
34 Hansard, 'House of Commons', vol. 899, 1975, p. 939.

DENMARK:

BRIDGE-BUILDING OVER WIDENING GULFS

H.H. Holm

A major goal of Danish foreign policy has always been to avoid too many cross-currents and the turbulence that follows, by trying to bridge the gulfs between the different fora where Denmark is involved. Denmark is part of Europe, part of Scandinavia and part of the West and an active supporter of global cooperation.

Even though Danish foreign policy goals have shifted over the years from a very careful neutrality to a policy of alignment, the policy has always been conditioned by the wish to avoid turbulence, that could endanger the sovereignty of the small kingdom. The division of the world into blocs was not a Danish preference, and Denmark only reluctantly entered NATO in 1949 when it was clear that there was no alternative. The market division of Europe into the EEC on the one hand and EFTA on the other was in economic terms a major problem for Denmark, since this placed two of the major markets, Germany and the UK, in different market groups. The expansion of the EEC in 1973 solved this problem, but at the same time accentuated the problem of Danish cooperation with the Nordic countries.

Compatibility and compromise-building are major concerns of Danish foreign policy. The East-West tensions, the growing economic divisions among the Western countries, the relationship between the EC and the Nordic countries and the North-South confrontations are cross-currents over which Denmark would like to build bridges. Danish Third World policy is an example of such a bridge-building attempt, but bridge-building over widening gulfs is a difficult undertaking.

63

THE NATURE OF THE RESPONSE

The Danish response to the demands for a New International
Economic Order has been presented at the major North-South
Conferences from 1974 and onwards. The Danish statements
at these conferences express the desire to help the developing countries and the obligation that all developed countries
have to do something about the inequality problem. The
Danish arguments are usually couched in an analogy to the
internal Danish development experience. It is stressed that
Denmark has solved the development problem through a combination of solidarity and governmental control. Denmark
advocates that these principles be made the basis of the
development of the international system. At UNCTAD V the
Danish development minister expressed this in the following
way:

> A basic aim of the North-South dialogue should be
> increased international division of labour, coupled with a
> more extensive and genuine solidarity between industrial-
> ized countries and developing countries. Division of
> labour and solidarity have been driving forces behind the
> prosperity of my own country. Economic and social pro-
> gress was furthered by measures adapted to individual
> groups and circumstances. In the international economic
> cooperation the different stages of development of coun-
> tries call for a similar approach. (1)

In relation to specific proposals at the conferences Denmark
expresses a positive attitude. She supports 'the legitimate
and logical demands' of the developing world, but this
general positive attitude is conditioned.

First of all, it is stated that specific proposals must be
further negotiated in the future, and preferably in the
'relevant' forum (e.g. GATT instead of UNCTAD).

Secondly, Danish support both in terms of pledges and
in terms of political support is only given if the idea is also
supported by most other countries. This was clearly illustrated by UNCTAD V. Even though Denmark had decided on
on a voluntary contribution to the Common Fund prior to the
conference, this was not announced until at the very end of
the conference when all the Nordic countries, The Netherlands, Belgium and others had made their pledges. (2)

This principle of accepting what other states can agree
on was clearly expressed in an instruction to the Danish
delegation to the 11th Special Session of the UN:

If the majority of the other donor countries should wish
not to stand on this principle (of refusing further debt
relief), it is the position of the Ministry of Foreign Affairs
that Denmark should not stand isolated, or practically
isolated, in opposition to the phrasing of the document.(3)

In overall terms, the Danish policy statements are positive,
but reluctant. The support is conditional on support from
other states and on an understanding that binding commitments should be avoided.

On specific issues, however, differences may exist from
this overall pattern, and in what follows we shall look more
closely at Danish policy on aid issues, trade and industrialization and financial issues.

Aid Policy

Danish aid policy is based on a number of central principles:
— the adherence to internationally accepted aid targets like
   the present 0.7 per cent of GNP and a willingness to
   accept even a 1 per cent target;
— the distribution of aid between bilateral and multilateral
   assistance on a fifty-fifty basis. And an equal split of
   the bilateral aid between loans that are tied to Danish
   procurement and gifts that are untied;
— assistance is given without imposing any political conditions, and on the basis of the priorities of the recipients
   as established in their developing planning. Danish
   assistance is concentrated on the poorest of the developing countries and with a strong basic needs focus. (4)
These basic principles are overall guidelines, but actual aid
policy differs in several respects from these principles.

During the 1970s, Denmark has made a major effort to expand the volume of aid, and attaches great importance to fulfilling the 0.7 per cent target. Aid is viewed as one of the
most important expressions of solidarity with the Third World
and its struggle to achieve development. (5) Denmark
reached the target temporarily in 1978 and used this as a
basis for scolding other donors who had not fulfilled the
target.

Denmark belongs to the much too small group of countries
that have reached the 0.7 per cent target. For a number
of years our rolling 5 year plans have built on a steady
yearly increase in ODA in recognition of the need for a
high ODA performance. Such targets should therefore be

maintained in the new international development strategy.
The targets should aim at a substantial increase in ODA.
The industrialized countries should recognize that without
a high rate of implementation they will have to face a
credibility gap *vis-à-vis* the developing countries. (6)

Despite the importance Denmark attaches to the aid target,
the government decided to cut development aid in 1980 to
0.66 per cent of GNP. Due to internal economic difficulties,
Denmark had to face its own credibility gap.

This, however, is used to press even harder for some
sort of burden-sharing between the donor countries on the
basis of the comparative standing of the individual country's
economy.

In a situation where Denmark is experiencing severe economic difficulties it is becoming increasingly difficult to
justify to the public that small countries like ours have
to continue to carry such a great share of the burden
while other industrialized countries in comparatively
better economic situations continue to lag behind. (7)

In 1980 Danish bilateral assistance amounted to 57 per
cent of the Danish official development assistance (ODA).
This bilateral assistance serves two purposes. It is spurred
by economic self-interest, it is ideologically motivated and it
should help to create a greater understanding for the need
to give tax money to the developing world. The latter is one
of the official motivations for bilateral aid. This type of aid
is easier to identify for the public, it is claimed, since they
can be told that Denmark financed this hospital in Zaire, for
example, or that experimental farm in India. Looking at the
public debate, one could, however, be led to the opposite
impression: that bilateral aid is dangerous because it is much
easier to criticize. But bilateral aid undoubtedly has other
advantages. It creates a set of special relationships between
Denmark and the 'adopted' countries (at present Bangladesh,
India, Tanzania and Kenya). Hereby Denmark's influence,
reputation and standing are improved.

The bilateral aid is divided between tied state loans and
gifts, and even though Denmark supports the demand that
all development assistance should be untied, this support is
conditioned by the argument that Denmark cannot change
policy before a general agreement on 'untying' is reached
among donor countries. The Danish acceptance of this Third
World demand is, however, only a general principle and is
not followed by policy action. (8)

The size of the bilateral aid programme is still relatively small when compared with other countries. Multilateral aid is an important element in Danish aid policy, since support for multilateral institutions is considered to be a support of the idea of peaceful settlement of disputes, international governing, negotiation and internationalism. This is further underlined when we look at the distribution of Danish multilateral aid where the largest receiver is the UNDP, which is a universal organization within the UN system, whereas IBRD, which is part of the World Bank group, gets a much smaller share (13 per cent and 5 per cent respectively in 1980). In this way Danish development policy even in budget terms is on line with the general foreign policy orientation typical for a minor power: international organizations and institutions are seen as potential small state allies.

Officially, it is claimed that development assistance is neutral. Danish development assistance is given without strings attached. It is the recipient country that decides where to use the assistance, and assistance is not an official support to the government, but support to the people.

This neutrality is something of a misnomer. Denmark has reacted by cutting off development assistance because of internal developments which she did not approve of, and the choice of countries is by no means neutral (9) (e.g. Denmark does not support Kampuchea or Chile).

Furthermore, the principle of the neutrality of the Danish aid programme conflicts with the principle of basic needs and the effort to reach the poorest in the poor countries. The strict implementation of the basic needs policy would soon bring the Danish government into conflict with recipient Third World nations eager to preserve their sovereignty.

Trade Policy

In relation to the trade issue the Danish position is clearly anti-protectionistic. At the UNCTAD conferences this position is used for scolding the other industrialized countries. They should consider giving better access to products from the developing countries and should realise that the erection of trade barriers is a major threat to stability. The Danish support in this area to the developing countries' demands is only natural, considering that Denmark with her high foreign trade ratio may encounter severe problems if protectionism should increase.

The industrialized countries must continue to improve

access for the export goods of developing countries to
their markets. They must expand their systems of preference and improve the utilization and functioning of
these systems for the benefit of the industrialization of
the developing countries. The industrialized countries
should realize that this would not only be advantageous
for the developing countries but also for themselves. (10)

Due to the membership of the EC, trade policy is an EC
matter, and the EC has been very reluctant to accept free-
trade provisions in relation to the Third World. During the
debate on the International Development Strategy for the
1980s, the Group of 77 proposed an international trade conference to revise existing rules and principles governing
international trade in order to increase the Third World
share of world trade. This proposal together with a proposal on the dismantling of existing import restrictions
against Third World imports before 1985 was countered by
the EC with vague statements endorsing free trade and with
flat refusal to discuss particulars. (11)

The current trade policy of the EC has drawn heavy criticism from a number of places, including the World Bank, and
the critics have pointed to the advent of 'organized free
trade', 'orderly market arrangements' etc. as examples of
the growth of protectionist tendencies in the EC trade
policy. (12) Some of the affected groups in Denmark support
this EC policy, and in relation to areas like textiles and steel
Denmark is enjoying the 'benefits' of protection while at the
same time arguing against it internationally. (13) In this
respect the Danish criticism of protectionism is an example of
a free-rider policy.

The trade and industralization issues have strong linkages,
because one of the ways the developing countries hope to
achieve industrialization in the Third World is through industrial redeployment combined with international free trade.

Danish policy here is that a new international division of
labour is supported if developed on the basis of real comparative advantage, but Denmark joins the EC in pointing to the
internal social and political consequences and difficulties in
pressing redeployment through.

Redeployment leads in many cases to serious social problems in our countries. We are ready to face the consequences through positive adjustment policies. But we
cannot subscribe to the idea that the termination of our
lines of production be one of the objectives of the establishment of the New International Economic Order or the
achievement of the Lima objective. (14)

International negotiations on the question of Third World industrialization has as a consequence of these attitudes ground to a halt as was clearly seen at UNIDO III in 1979.

Danish trade policy is a typical example of a policy designed to meet the needs of an economic structure where trade and especially export is the prime motor in economic growth. Due to the heavy concentration of both export and import on a few countries (more than 50 per cent of the export goes to West Germany, Great Britain, Sweden and Norway) and the constant problem of a large balance of trade deficit, the promotion of exports has been a dominant feature in Danish trade policy for a number of years. (15)

Despite the minor importance of the developing countries as export markets for Danish products, the contraction of demand in the traditional Danish markets in the 1970s have spurred new initiatives to try to expand the export to the developing countries. Export guarantees, industrialization funds and expansion of trade promotion activities of the Danish foreign service are some of the measures the Danish government has employed to increase exports to the Third World.

The lack of indigenous resources means that the growth in Danish exports is dependent on increased imports of raw materials and semi-manufactured goods, and consequently Danish trade policy has contained few import restrictions. Today Danish import restrictions are, however, an EC matter, and as a consequence a number of EC restrictions today apply to Danish imports. The import has become increasingly concentrated on the EC partners to the point where over half of all Danish imports come from the other EC countries.

The recession, unemployment and growing balance of payments deficit has made these common import restrictions more acceptable to Denmark, and due to the growing internal problems created by unemployment, state support for ailing industries have increased in magnitude, even though Denmark comparatively speaking still is relatively restrictive in giving out direct support for ailing industries.

The Danish attempt to use the developing countries as a reserve market for increased exports have until now not been very successful, and if we look at the exports to the Third World, it is the OPEC countries that have absorbed the major share of Danish Third World exports. The Danish aid budget has therefore attracted considerable attention from groups in Danish society interested in the promotion of exports. One of the consequences of this is that the tying of aid both directly and indirectly is maintained as official policy, and

the Ministry of Foreign Affairs has greatly expanded its
services to the industrial sector. (16) It has been calculated by the Ministry of Foreign Affairs that 70 per cent of
the bilateral aid returns to Denmark as orders for Danish
products or services. Denmark has also been trying to
squeeze more out of the Danish contribution to multilateral
organizations in the form of orders to Danish industry.
Safeguarding industry interests is furthermore clearly
evident in the Danish position on the demands for transfer
of technology to the Third World and the demands for cargo-
sharing in international shipping (17)
     These trends are in opposition to the declared free-trade
philosophy and the positive attitude to structural adjustment,
but are related to the pressure exerted by the interested
groups.
     The Federation of Danish Industry has been pressing for
increased bilateral aid to the Third World because this type
of aid is more beneficial to Danish industry. (18) Furthermore, various labour unions have reluctantly supported the
employers' demands for orderly market arrangements in the
field of clothing and textiles. Denmark supported free trade
and the demands from the Third World for increased access
for their goods, but ... there are also other interests and
demands to consider!
     Danish policy on trade and industrialization is, despite its
liberal overtones, almost exclusively based on Danish needs
and interests. Policy actions in this field concentrate on the
promotion of Danish industry, and anticipatory structural
adjustment policies are considered impossible and impractical.

Monetary and Financial Matters

The demands from the Third World for increased share in
international decision-making on monetary issues, for a link
between SDR-allocation and financial needs of developing
countries and for revision of present IMF loan conditions are
resisted by almost all of the countries in the North.
     Danish policy here is in total accordance with the overall
policy of the North. It is not perceived to be in the Danish
interest to support any demands that will endanger the
autonomy of the IMF, nor to support links between international liquidity and development finance. (19)
     Danish policy on these issues is torn between two differ-
ent sets of considerations. On the one hand, the persistent
deficit in the Danish balance of payments leads Denmark to
support the idea of expansion of international liquidity

through a strengthening of the IMF's lending capacity and resources. On the other hand, the difficulty in securing continuing financing of the balance of payments deficit also means that Denmark sees a great danger in changing the international monetary system, because 'the alternative, it seems to us ... (is a) fragmented monetary system which is not viable ...'. Behind these remarks lurks the realization, that Denmark is very vulnerable in international monetary matters and therefore clinging on to the status quo in order not to expose this vulnerability to unforeseen changes. (20)

Consequently, Denmark has supported a policy of moderate internal reform in both the IMF and the World Bank in order to accommodate demands and thereby secure the working of the present system. The universality of these organizations is regarded as a sacrosanct principle, and Denmark supports a better international coordination and surveillance of balance of payments adjustment policies and a higher degree of exchange rate stability. Danish participation in and active support for the European Monetary System is a concrete example of this policy.

If we compare the Danish Third World policy to the demands of the developing countries for a New International Economic Order, we find that on the aid issue Denmark attaches some importance to fulfilling internationally agreed targets, gives large contributions to multilateral institutions and at least officially rejects the use of development aid as a foreign policy instrument.

On trade and industrialization issues, Denmark follows a policy of rhetorical support for the Third World demands, but in terms of policy actions she follows the EC policy line. In financial and monetary matters Denmark 'understands the aspirations of the Third World', but defends the status quo. Why is that?

THE EXPLANATION OF THE RESPONSE

The Foreign Policy Tradition

Overall categorization of the foreign policy of states is a popular but hazardous undertaking, but in order to shed some light on some of the background factors in the shaping of Danish Third World policy a short description of the Danish foreign policy tradition shall be attempted here.

In the comparison between the foreign policy of different states stress sensitivity and influence capability have been used as distinguishing variables, and Danish foreign policy

accordingly placed as an example of a policy determined by
low influence capability and high stress sensitivity. (21)
If we look at Danish foreign policy in a broad historical
perspective, it is, however, difficult to subsume Danish
foreign policy under one heading.

At least since 1864 Danish foreign policy has been a 'low
key' foreign policy typical of a minor power. In terms of
material power, military power, motivational power, potential
power and achievement record Denmark is a minor power
with low influence capability. (22) Consequently, Danish
Foreign policy has had to adapt to changes in the environment, and has had little possibility of changing the environment to further its own goals. This 'adaptation' was done
in the interwar period through a policy of neutrality
described as a 'stay put' policy, and in the period after the
Second World War through a policy of alignment with the
dominant world power. Even this policy of alignment has,
however, been a 'low key' alignment, and the different
Danish 'alignments' have been used as a basis for perceiving
Denmark as fulfilling a bridge-building role.

The traditional descriptions of Danish foreign policy
stress the different alignments by explaining Danish foreign
policy through its institutional affiliations. (23)

In official statements Danish foreign policy is said to
build on four pillars: NATO, the UN, the EC, and Nordic
cooperation. According to official logic, it is exactly because
of this foundation of Danish policy and the multiple member-
ships that Denmark is in a bridge-building position. In order
to be accepted by other states as the bridge-builder' - and
there are certainly many states that would like to see themselves in this mediator role - Denmark has to have a very
flexible foreign policy, and it is essential that none of the
four institutional corner-stones of Danish foreign policy have
overlapping jurisdiction since this would put Denmark in a
cross-pressure situation and make it very difficult to keep
the issues apart from each other.

The low-key foreign policy tradition combined with the
attempt to play a bridge-building role means that Danish
foreign policy has been one of passive adjustment to external changes.

A major shift in Danish foreign policy has, however, come
with the membership of the EC. Through the EC membership
Danish influence capability has been perceived to increase,
and increased participation and involvement in major power
politics has been the result. Naturally, this has meant that
Danish foreign policy in many aspects is directed towards
the internal discussions within the EC, since the prerequisite

for international influence through the EC is the coordination
of foreign policy among the EC member countries.

In the last couple of years Danish foreign policy has also
shown examples of a more independent foreign policy stance
in security and in economic matters, due in part to internal
political discussion within the Danish political system, but
probably also to the overall reassertion of European foreign
policy independence.

The Welfare Ideology

Both internally and externally ideological arguments are
important elements in Danish policy statements on Third
World issues. The development of Danish society is seen as
a result of solidarity, state control and intervention to prevent too large differences to develop within the Danish
society. In relation to the Third World, the same type of
intervention and solidarity is advocated by Danish governments. (24)

The importance Denmark attaches to fulfilling the 0.7 per
cent ODA target, the Danish readiness to accept the concept
of a New International Economic Order and the basic needs
focus of aid policy shows that the ideological argument is
important also in terms of actual policy.

Since Third World policy is seen in ideological terms, Denmark stresses the moral obligation of all states, whether they
are former colonial powers or not, to make a major effort to
help the Third World. But the welfare ideology of solidarity
and steered change is primarily influential in terms of the
aid policy, and there is an ensuing tendency in Danish perceptions of the NIEO demands to focus on the aid issues.
The welfare ideology has also been one of the foundations of
the Nordic cooperation within aid policy, and it is today especially seen in Nordic cooperation on social development
issues. The role of women in the development process is
thus made into a Nordic theme presented at the North-South
conferences whenever possible.

On ideological grounds, Denmark accepts the NIEO demands as morally justified and legitimate, and even though
disagreement may exist on individual issues, Denmark recognized the need for international regulation and the unaccept-
ability of the inequality in the present system. Accordingly,
Denmark argues that it is the common interest of all countries
that a new and more equitable economic order is developed.

Denmark's Role in the International System

The debate on a New International Economic Order has been
a debate going on in the global system, and this system is
perceived to be changing. Danish sensitivity to major
changes in the global system was clearly evident during the
so-called oil crisis in 1973-4. Denmark reacted very strongly
to this crisis: internally by imposing severe limitations on oil
consumption and externally by reacting reluctantly or even
negatively to the demands from the Third World. (25) On
the other hand, traditional Danish support for the UN system and the strong welfare ideology among decision-makers
soon made Denmark respond positively albeit passively to
the Third World demands.

Denmark expresses great interest in achieving global
solutions to the problems of the Third World countries, and
consequently confrontation at international conferences between North and South is avoided. Denmark usually takes a
middle position on issues that divide North and South. This
middle position is necessitated by the simultaneous Danish
reliance on economic cooperation within the EC, security
assurance within NATO, support for international cooperation within the UN and ideological and cultural affinity to the
Nordic countries.

The traditional strong Danish support for the UN system
is also evident in relation to Third World policy, and Denmark has in her UN policy tried to reduce confrontation
within the UN over Third World demands. On the other
hand, Denmark attaches importance to the effective functioning of the UN system, and has only reluctantly accepted the
proliferation of studies and new institutions created by the
demands for a NIEO. It is in line with this policy that Denmark has been very reluctant to grant the Third World special favours in relation to the UN, such as the convening of
special meetings or providing of secretariat support for
Third World preparations.

The Third World's use of their majority in the UN is regarded with some scepticism by Denmark, since the UN is
regarded as a forum for international conciliation and not a
forum for majority decisions. Despite general support for
the UN system on the grounds of small state interest in
international norms and regulations, Denmark joins the other
industrialized countries in support for the rationalization of
the UN system.

In relation to Third World policy, the Nordic countries
have had an important role as a forum for coordination of
policy. Despite obvious differences, the tradition for inter-

Nordic cooperation in this field is strong. The Danish entry into the EC has changed the nature of Nordic cooperation in this area. First and foremost because all aspects of trade policy is an EC prerogative, but also because the area of development cooperation is an area where the EC has been very active. Consequently, inter-Nordic policy coordination has declined in importance, and the differences in, for example, the actual trade policy of the Nordic countries have become greater over time.

The combination of economic integration and foreign policy coordination in the EC has made the EC the single most important affiliation for Denmark. (26) On the one hand, it has meant increased involvement, e.g. through the Lome negotiations, where Denmark now has to take part in negotiations with all the former French and British colonies, and on the other hand, it has meant reduced freedom of action, e.g. in trade, where strong interest groups in other EC countries have made the EC conclude a number of 'fair' trade agreements with the developing countries. These orderly market arrangements are at least in principle contrary to the traditional Danish policy of free trade.

Security policy is only marginally important in shaping Third World policy, but instances may be found where security considerations have been important. It has been argued that the start of the Danish bilateral aid programme in 1960 was due to the US policy or burden sharing within the NATO alliance. (27) This has been strongly disputed, and whatever the fact of the matter is, it seems likely that the Danish relations to the superpowers exert only a marginal influence in shaping Third World policy. An example of this marginal influence may be seen in the recent Danish loan to Turkey. This gesture was a result of outside pressure and obviously a result of security rather than development considerations. Nevertheless, the loan was financed out of the funds allocated for development assistance.

The attempt to balance security considerations, economic motivations and support for global norms of cooperation finds expression in the Danish policy in relation to the different fora where Denmark participates. The overall politicization of Third World issues has increased the cross-pressure put on Denmark in these different fora for Danish policy. The Danish attempt to avoid conflicting demands has meant that Third World policy has varied according to the fora through which it was enacted. The general support for the Third World is still maintained in the UN, whereas actual policy actions have to accommodate both the requirements of a common EC policy, the security considerations of NATO and the importance attached to Nordic cooperation.

A balance between Nordic, global and EC adjustment is a major and indeed unrealistic goal. The very different nature and importance of these fora and the overriding importance of short-term economic considerations have, however, made it natural for Denmark to lean on EC cooperation and common stance whenever possible. Consequently, Danish policy towards the NIEO demands is increasingly expressed through the EC with the exception of Danish policy on the volume of aid and on social development issues. (28)

The Internal Constraints

The Third World policy of a weak state has some special characteristics. For a country with a reduced number of policy alternatives adjustment is a must, but with conflicting demands it is not evident what to adjust to. The internal consequences of the demands put forward by the Group of 77 mean that Third World policy becomes a politically sensitive issue internally, and accommodating the demands put forward is not easy. On the other hand, it is important for a weak state like Denmark to be on good terms with the Third World. Denmark is in no position to be a 'hardliner' in relation to the demands for changes in the international system. The problem is one of gaining international status without creating internal opposition. One way to by-pass this problem is to keep the different fora apart. If internal debate in Denmark on the question of, for example, structural adjustment and protectionism can be reduced to a minimum, the decision-makers will have an increased freedom of action internationally. (29) Another possibility is to attempt to strike a balance between the external demands for an active and accommodating policy and the internal demands for safeguarding of specific group interests in terms of employment, profit, economic security etc.

The internal stimuli have gained increasing prominence in shaping Third World policy due to the politicization of the international economic issues and the severe economic recession.

This is noticeable in the assessment of the economic capability. Despite the lack of indigenous resources, Denmark is perceived to be only mildly affected by a form of regulation of the international trade in commodities, and consequently Denmark reluctantly supported the proposal for a Common Fund. (30)

Both externally and internally Denmark pursues a policy

of balance and bridge-building. (31) This may be done in two ways: active and reactive. An active policy of balance is geared towards altering the confronting demands, whereas a reactive policy of balance merely adjusts to the posed demands and tries to interpret the demands in such a way that tension between the demands is reduced. When confronted with demands, a reactive policy will seek to find the most accommodating response. This naturally leads to different policy statements depending upon the forum in which they are presented, and it also leads to a very cautious policy influenced heavily by the actions of other states.

One main objective is to avoid any kind of obligation that will upset the balance between the internal and the external demands. The policy pursued in relation to the demands for structural adjustment is a prime example. From the very beginning, these demands have been accepted, and Denmark has underlined that structural changes are necessary and should be carried through despite difficulties due to the confrontation with existing interests. The international economic development has to be guided and planned, it is claimed. (32) Despite this being official Danish policy, Denmark has done nothing to further this process of structural adjustment. On the contrary, various forms of subsidies and protectionism have been employed to secure employment in Denmark and to lessen the balance of payments problem. (33) This problem is now so prominent that it was the starting point for the Danish policy statement at UNCTAD V:

> It is a sad fact that the global economic situation in many respects is no less serious today than it was at the time of UNCTAD IV. Despite some improvement in 1978 the international economic situation is still very fragile. In many countries - like my own - growth rates are still low, but as the balance of payments deficit remains high our possibilities of implementing a more expansive economic policy are very limited. (34)

The fact that internal problems are mentioned in policy statements at international conferences supposed to be dealing with the problems of the Third World is a clear example of the importance of the internal constraints on the Danish NIEO attitude.

A positive attitude towards the demands from the Third World will create internal opposition in Denmark from groups that feel their interests threatened, but on the other hand a large discrepancy between policy statements on these

issues in international fora and actual policy will create a
credibility problem for Danish Third World policy. Consequently, some sort of balance is attempted.

One way is to stress internal difficulties in Denmark as
an explanation for the Danish inability to do something active
in relation to the Third World, and hereby dampen expectations from the Third World. Another way is to ensure the
preservation of group interests by including internal groups
in policy-making as was done when a representative of the
Danish Shipowner Association took part in UNCTAD V as a
member of the Danish delegation. At UNCSTD, the Danish
delegation included representatives from the Federation of
Danish Industries, and at UNIDO III also representatives
from the Federation of Labour. Despite the attempts to
strike some sort of balance between the internal and the external demands, it is still useful to keep these fora apart.
Consequently, the resolutions from international conferences
like UNCTAD are not considered in the light of their internal
consequences.

The broad nature of the demands from the Third World
has drawn interest groups into policy-making, and consequently it has become increasingly difficult to conduct Third
World policy independently of economic and trade policy.
Since Third World policy no longer is the sole responsibility
of the Ministry of Foreign Affairs, but also of the Ministry
of Trade, the National Bank etc., coordination of policy has
become a very important and difficult task. All of this
reduces the number of alternatives that policy-makers may
choose from and a passive, reactive policy seems the least
'risky' one. The Danish policy on international monetary
issues may be understood in this light. The Ministry of
Finance and the National Bank are responsible for outlining
Danish policy in this field, and foreign policy considerations
are here second to the goal of monetary stability. The Danish support for moderate reform of the IMF and the IBRD
shows the importance attached to securing the status quo in
this field.

The strong importance of interest groups in relation to
Third World policy is no new feature in Danish assistance
policy, where all the major interest groups have exerted
influence through the Council for Development Assistance.
This is an advisory body to the Minister where interest
groups make their views heard.

What is new is that interest groups are delegated responsibility in terms of policy-making in this area as has been
done in the Danish preparations for several North-South
conferences.

Parliamentary opposition to the ruling Third World policy is virtually non-existent. Most discussions on Third World policy have focussed on minor issues (e.g. the Dkr. 22 million given to support the liberation movements in Southern Africa) and even though dissent is expressed from both the left- and the right-wing in the Danish parliament, there are only shades of difference between the reformism of the Social Democratic Party and the liberalism of the center-right parties. Except for the right-wing Progress Party,(35) most of the parliamentary parties share the welfare ideology outlined above. (36) Parliamentary opposition has, however, been important in introducing further limits on the freedom of action of the government in this field, both through the control over the money spent and through the control over further funding. (37) These attempts to reduce government expenditure set further limits to the Danish Third World activity.

The balance of payments problem, the activity of the interest organizations and the parliamentary opposition have all reduced the possibilities of an active Danish Third World policy.

CONCLUSION

Danish policy is shaped by the 'low key' tradition of Danish foreign policy and the welfare ideology of decision-makers, creating difference between the international policy statements and policy implementation. Even though Denmark is very much in favour of global solutions, the EC has very naturally become a focus for attention, and consequently initiatives are taken in the internal EC negotiations and not in relation to the Third World.

Despite ideological willingness to accommodate external demands, the limits of the internal system both in terms of economics, politics and group interests are so narrow that there is very little room for manoeuvre.

The conflicting demands from the external and the internal surroundings create the Danish policy of reactive balance. Denmark attempts to be supportive of the Third World demands without entering into any binding commitments. There is a Danish foreign policy tradition for a passive stance, but at the same time the welfare ideology of the decision-makers dictates an active role in solving world problems.

Aid policy is the area where ideology seems to be a major factor in shaping policy, but even in aid policy it is clearly

seen that economic interests have become important. In
trade and industrialization, both economic problems and
interest expressed by interest groups and political parties
severely limit the possibility for Denmark to maintain the
principles of free trade. On monetary issues, Denmark does
not even support the Third World in principle.

Danish Third World policy has to adjust itself to many different demands. In the international system there are demands for global solutions, for regional and for bilateral
ones. Denmark has here steered a middle course. Internally
the economic situation, the interest groups and parliament
create constraints on Danish Third World policy. In other
words, there is little freedom of action for Danish policy-
makers: balancing seems necessary; the global demands versus the demands for an increased number of orders to Danish
industry, foreign policy tradition versus welfare ideology,
and value-promotive Third World policy versus economic
Third World policy.

Like all balancing, the Danish reactive balance is a goal
more than it is reality: Danish Third World policy contains
all the above-mentioned elements together, but with widening
gulfs bridge-building becomes very difficult. (38)

Danish support for Third World demands serves to
increase Danish standing and status in the Third World, but
at the same time these policy statements give rise to reactions
from the internal environment. Opposition to conducted
policy is created and may create further limitations to the
decision-makers' freedom of action in the future.

On the other hand, the lack of implementation of the
policy principles adhered to internationally may lead to a
loss of credibility. With the debate on a New International
Economic Order entering the phase of operational decisions
it may prove hard to remain one of the 'like-minded', or one
of the 'Scandinavian' countries.

Notes

1 See statement by Lise Østergaard, Minister without
   Portfolio with special responsibility for Foreign Affairs
   at UNCTAD V, Manila, 10 May 1979.
2 See Hans-Henrik Holm, A Dialogue between Deafs:
   UNCTAD V and the North-South Negotiations', in
   Christian Thune, ed., 'Dansk Udenrigspolitik Årbog
   1979', Copenhagen, Samfundvidenskabeligt Forlag,
   1980, pp. 129-151.
3 See Uffe Torm, Danish Third World Policy in the IN, in

'Kristeligt Dagblad', 25 September 1980.
4   See 'Denmark's Development Assistance 1979', Annual
    Report submitted to the Development Assistance Com-
    mittee of the OECD, Copenhagen, Ministry of Foreign
    Affairs, 1980, pp. 5-6.
5   'It is my impression that the developing countries -
    and rightly so - regard the willingness of the indus-
    trialized countries to render development assistance as
    one of the most important expressions of solidarity with
    the Third World and its struggle to achieve develop-
    ment', Statment by Mr. Kjeld Olesen, Minister of
    Foreign Affairs of Denmark, at the Eleventh Special
    Session of the United Nations General Assembly, 25
    August 1980.
6   Statement by the Danish minister at UNCTAD V, op.
    cit.
7   Danish statement in the UN General Assembly, 2.
    Committee on agenda item 59, see 'De Forende Nationers
    34. Generalforsamling', Copenhagen, Ministry of Foreign
    Affairs, 1980, p. 34.
8   See 'Folketingstidende', 22 April 1979, cols. 8709 and
    8713.
9   See Klaus Jørgensen, 'Hjaelp fra Danmark' (Aid from
    Denmark), Odense, Universitetsforlaget, 1977, p. 272.
    The decision to terminate aid to Pakistan in August 1971
    is an example.
10 Danish statement at UNCTAD V, op. cit.
11 See 'Synoptic table on the policy measures of the new
    international development strategy', New York, United
    Nations, 24 April 1980, pp. 6-8.
12 See Robert S. McNamara, 'Address to UNCTAD V',
    10 May 1979.
13 It has been estimated that Denmark would lose 3,000
    jobs a year if existing import restrictions were dis-
    mantled. See Max Kruse, 'Danmark og den ny økono-
    miske verdensorden', Aarhus, 1980, pp. 89-91.
14 See 'Beretning fra den danske delegation til UNIDO
    III', New Delhi, 21 January - 9 February 1980, EEC
    statement on agenda item 5d.
15 See 'Danmarks eksportmarkeder', Copenhagen, Ministry
    of Foreign Affairs, 1980, pp. 17-18.
16 The Ministry of Foreign Affairs received an extra 20
    million Dkr. to expand its services to the export sector.
    In the Ministry of Foreign Affairs' magazine in March
    1979 this is described in detail under the heading:
    'The Ministry of Foreign Affairs is the extra member of
    your company's export-division'. The Ministry has

has also established new trade assistance in several
Third World countries and tries to secure more orders
to Danish industry from the international organizations.

17   The Danish preparations for UNCSTD have been subject to harsh criticism for concentrating on the need of
Danish industry more than on the need of the developing countries for science and technology. The Danish
position paper was characterized as a catalogue of what
Danish firms have to offer, not a list of what Denmark
can do for the developing countries. See Uffe Torm,
Træk den danske rapport til teknologi-konferencen til-
bage', 'Kontakt', 1978-79, No. 5, p. 40.

18   See Industrirådet, 'Industrien og u-landene', Copenhagen, 1977.

19   See De Forenede Nationers 34. generalforsamling, op.
cit., p. 274.

20   See 'Statement by Ivar Nørgaard', Minister of Economic
Affairs and Governor of the Fund for Denmark, at the
Joint Annual Discussion of the IMF, Washington D.C.,
1 October 1980.

21   See Nikolaj Petersen, Adaptation as a Framework for
the Analysis of Foreign Policy Behaviour', in 'Cooperation and Conflict', Vol. XII, pp. 221-250.

22   See Steven L. Spiegel, 'Dominance and Diversity',
Boston, Little, Brown and Co., 1972, pp. 93-96.

23   The classical statement is found in Per Hækkerup,
Minister for Foreign Affairs, 'Danish Foreign Policy',
Copenhagen, Fremad, 1965, pp. 45-46.

24   For a detailed analysis of the content of this ideology,
see Asbjørn Løvbræk, Arve Ofstad, The Role of Like-
Minded Countries in the North-South Contradictions:
The Cast of Norway's Policy towards a NIEO', in
'Cooperation and Conflict', Vol. XIV, pp. 121-132.

25   This was clearly evidenced at the debate in the UN on
the Charter on Economic Rights and Duties of States
in 1974. Six countries voted against the Charter: USA,
UK, Fed. Rep. of Germany, Belgium, Luxembourg and
Denmark.

26   In the report from the Ministry of Foreign Affairs on
'Danish Participation in International Development Cooperation', Copenhagen, 1979, p. 150, this is stated
as follows:

Within the EEC cooperation before and during international conferences on development issues have become closer and closer. This holds true for CIEC,
the UN North-South committee, UNCTAD V and in

the preparation for the third development decade.
Increasingly the EEC speaks with one voice through
the country occupying the post of chairman.

27 This is argued by Klaus Jørgensen, 'Hjælp fra
    Danmark', op. cit.
28 On these issues Denmark has tried to press the other
    EEC countries into a more forthcoming attitude towards
    the Third World demands and succeeded in doing so at
    the Eleventh Special Session of the UN General
    Assembly in 1980.
29 This is supported by Bernard C. Cohen, 'The Public's
    Impact on Foreign Policy', Boston, Little, Brown and
    Co., 1973, pp. 160-161. A discussion on the nature of
    of the Danish debate of Third World issues is found in
    Gunnar Adler-Karlsson, Den modvillige almisse (The
    Reluctant Alms), 'Udvikling', Ministry of Foreign
    Affairs, 1978, No. 4, pp. 10-12.
30 This was the conclusion of an internal report made by
    the Ministry of Foreign Affairs on international raw-
    material problems in relation to the Danish economy
    in April 1975.
31 See Hans-Henrik Holm, Reaktiv Balance: Dansk uden-
    rigspolitik og kravene til en ny økonomisk verdensor-
    den, in N. Amstrup and I. Faurby, eds., 'Studier i
    dansk udenrigspolitik' (Studies in Danish Foreign
    Policy), Aarhus, Politica, 1978, pp. 337-373.
32 See Statement made by Ivar Nørgaard, Minister for
    External Economic Affairs, at UNCTAD IV, Nairobi,
    May 1976.
33 This is evidenced in a recent GATT study: 'Adjust-
    ment Trade and Growth in Developed and Developing
    Countries', Geneva, GATT, 1978. Here the Danish
    public subsidies to enterprises in 1976 are calculated
    at 2.8 per cent of GDP. The EC average is 2.4 per
    cent. See p. 89.
34 Lise Østergaard at UNCTAD V, op. cit.
35 The Progress Party argues that development assistance
    'introduces the glittering plastic world of Marilyn
    Monroe to people on the development level of the Vik-
    ings - they are better off left alone'. This party
    receives around 14 per cent of the Danish vote. See
    Mogens Glistrup, Vi gør dem rodløse ..., in 'Aarhus
    Stiftstidende', 31 August 1975.
36 For a detailed analysis of the content of this ideology,
    see Asbjørn Løvbræk and Arve Ofstad, The Role of
    Like-Minded Countries in the North-South Contradiction:

The Cast of Norway's Policy towards a NIEO, 'Cooperation and Conflict', Vol. XIV, op. cit., pp. 121-132.

37   The yearly reports from the accounting agency for
     budgetary overview contains very hard criticism of
     ineffectiveness in Danish aid administration.   See
     'Beretning til statsrevisorerne om revisionen af udgif-
     terne til Danmarks statslige bistand til udviklingslan-
     dene i finansåret 1978-79', Copenhagen, Rigsrevisionen,
     1980.

38   The widening gulfs refer to the changes in the inter-
     national system whereby the demands in the various
     fora where Denmark is participating conflict increas-
     ingly.   For a more detailed outline of these changes,
     see the introductory and the concluding chapter.

EUROPEAN COMMUNITY:

THE ATTRITION OF NEGOTIATION AND THE NEGOTIATION OF ATTRITION

U. Steffens

Editors' Note

This chapter must of necessity deviate somewhat from the others primarily because the European Community (EC) is not a single state actor. EC policies for the most part are a synthesis of the different policies of the member states, which continue to exercise primary control over their decision-making capabilities. As such it is impossible to follow the format of the single country study chapters and examine the response of the EC. Rather, as a consequence of the particular structure and organization of the EC, it is necessary to focus on the role of the EC in modifying the response of the constituent member states. Since the role of the EC in the NIEO debate is qualitatively different from the response of individual Northern states, the following paper does not encompass the whole gamut of the NIEO demands but focuses primarily on the critical issue of the Integrated Programme for Commodities and particularly on the Common Fund.

INTRODUCTION

A number of factors have contributed to the involvement of the European Community (EC) in the NIEO negotiations. In the first place, the EC is expressly endowed with some formal-legal authority in the field of international trade policy. This authority resides in Articles 113 and 238 of the EEC treaty. Additionally Article 116 stipulates that member states ' ... shall, in respect of all matters of particular interest to the common market, proceed within the framework of international organization of an economic character only by common action.' Although the interpretation of these Treaty provisions has been a continuing source of conflict among the member states and the major Community institutions, these provisions do on one level very clearly prescribe the need for EC coordination and the search for a common standpoint.

Apart from Treaty provisions, the member states have obligations to coordinate and harmonize their development policies. (1) In this context also under the system of European Political Coopration (EPC) the Community countries consult, and frequently act together, in areas not covered by the Community Treaties.

The EC also has a history of involvement in multilateral trade negotiations with developing countries. The EC took a lead among the developed countries by joining the Generalized System of Preferences (GSP) in June 1971. (2) Furthermore the EC has instituted a series of Conventions (Yaounde, Arusha and Lome) with a group of African, Caribbean and Pacific countries (ACPs). The significance of the EC involvement in the GSP and particularly in the Yaounde, Arusha and Lome Conventions for the NIEO debate was twofold. In the first place, it indicated that the EC member states could engage in concerted action. Second, the EC displayed at least some willingness to show some special preference to Third World countries. While such EC involvement could be seen as having some positive predisposing influence on EC participation in the NIEO debate, some qualifications must nonetheless be noted. The GSP is not under the influence of the developing countries and does not include a number of sensitive products, especially these falling under the Common Agricultural Policy (CAP). (3) The Yaounde, Arusha and Lome Conventions furthermore do not include all the Group of 77 countries but a selected number of Third World countries, essentially former colonies. As such they represent a type of 'closed-shop', which excludes a number of important countries, especially the newly industrializing ones. Furthermore, the System of Stabilization of Export Earnings (STABEX), established under Lome, provided a system of export stabilization that was very different in form from that planned by the Integrated Programme for Commodities (IPC). In particular STABEX does not influence commodity prices and as such does not contravene the liberal commitment to free trade.

THE NATURE OF THE RESPONSE

Resolution 93, adopted at the UNCTAD IV Meeting in 1976, stated that a Common Fund was to be the key element in the

design for an IPC. The same resolution invited those states
that wished to participate in the negotiations on a Common
Fund and the overall question of the IPC to submit their
proposals to the Secretary-General by the end of September
1976.

In response to this request the Commission outlined and
circulated internally a proposal. This proposal accepted in
principle the idea of a Common Fund and suggested that such
a fund should take the general form of a 'clearing-house'.
The financial structure was to be designed in such a way as
to restrict the money to be spent to an absolute minimum. At
the same time precautions were to be taken not to intrude into
the financial activities of other international organizations.
A number of possible means for financing the fund were suggested. These included individual contributions of the funds
of those International Commodity Agreements (ICAs) becoming
members of the Common Fund, loans from the international
financial market, and direct government contributions. (4)

In some respects the Commission proposal could be considered to be a constructive response to Resolution 93. On the
other hand, it has to be recognized that the substance of
this proposal had little in common with the aspirations of the
UNCTAD Secretariat. The proposal reflected the Commission's assessment that only a limited number of ICAs would
be established, which in turn would restrict the role of a
Common Fund. The Commission envisaged that the Common
Fund would only play a compensatory role, and consequently
it considered the fears of global interventionism to be exaggerated. Furthermore, as long as a conciliatory response
was made, then the discord that existed among the developing countries would help to push matters in the 'right direction'. (5)

This initial proposal, despite its only mild accommodation
to the UNCTAD position, met with a mixed response. The
Federal Republic of Germany expressed severe reservations
about the Common Fund project as a whole and decided not
to take part in the deliberations of the respective Working
Group of the Council of Ministers. The other delegations
were able to go along with the Commission's proposal in
general terms. Britain and Ireland did, however, voice substantial opposition against a proposal, suggested by The
Netherlands and Denmark, for direct government contributions. Some days later the Federal Republic submitted a
counter proposal suggesting in essence that the EC should
deliberate as to whether a Common Fund should be established at all. This proposal, however, was rejected by the
other member states on the grounds that the EC had already

committed itself to the establishment of a Common Fund by
virtue of agreeing with the consensus at UNCTAD IV. (6)

Neither the Working Group nor the Committee of Permanent Representatives (COREPER) managed to foster an agreement. At this stage the German Minister of Foreign Affairs
requested an adjournment of the EC's deliberations until the
meeting of the European Council on 29/30 November 1976.
The consequence was that the EC was not able to come to any
agreement prior to the opening conference on the Common
Fund that was to be convened in Geneva at the end of November. The lack of a common position was one of the main reasons for the failure of the first preparatory meeting. (7)

At this stage in the discussions the conflicting views of
the EC member states had resolved into three rather different
positions. The 'restrictive position' did not even accept in
principle the creation of a Common Fund. If it proved impossible to prevent the establishment of a Common Fund, then
this position suggested that the Fund should work as a clearing-house without proper capital and within strict accordance
with the commodity agreements. This position was advocated
by the Federal Republic (and by the USA and Japan). The
'middle position' accepted in principle the establishment of
some form of Common Fund. The Fund should work with proper resources, become active in the financial markets and
could provide certain back-up facilities for the members of
the ICAs. This position was adopted by France, Belgium,
Ireland and to a much lesser extent by Britain. The 'progressive position' argued that the Fund should take a form
somewhat intermediate between that of the middle position
and the general form advocated by the Group of 77. This
position was adopted by The Netherlands and to a lesser
extent by Denmark.

On account of these differences of opinion the EC was unable to define a common position and indeed could not even
reach agreement as to whether the EC as such should take
part in the negotiations. As a consequence the EC was
unable to negotiate constructively throughout the three Preparatory Conferences that ran from late 1976 to early 1977.

As the first Negotiating Conference was to convene in
March 1977, the EC came under pressure to resolve its internal conflicts. Parallel to the UNCTAD negotiations on the
Common Fund, the EC countries were involved in the Conference of International Economic Cooperation (CIEC), that had
been running since December 1975. (8) Originally devised
as a conference dealing with energy questions, it had been
generalized as the oil-exporting countries had succeeded in
putting on the agenda issues of economic development,

including commodities. On the very day that negotiations on
the Common Fund started in Geneva, the Council of Ministers met in Brussels to attempt to resolve some of the initial
conflicts. The first signs of some consensus, albeit of a
very general nature, began to appear. As a consequence of
this meeting it was accepted that the EC should participate
in negotiations. Furthermore, it was agreed that the general
principle of a Common Fund would not be opposed. It was
clear, however, that any Common Fund would be seriously
emasculated as compared against the Group of 77's demands.
Thus, neither the Common Fund nor any International Commodity Agreements should have any power to raise prices
above those set by the market. Additionally the financial
assistance of the Common Fund should be constrained within
any International Commodity Agreements. Finally, while the
EC was prepared to discuss a 'Second Window', conceding
that measures to diversify and raise LDC productivity may be
necessary, the EC emphasized that it would not accept any
provisions of the Common Fund that overlapped with the policies of the World Bank. (9)

Although this emergent consensus was still very general
and indeed belied a number of serious disagreements, it is
interesting to note at this stage that the EC had progressed
slightly beyond the Group B countries of UNCTAD (essentially the OECD countries). Thus at the close of the First
Negotiation Conference, in April 1977, the Group B countries
would only concede 'that there *could* be a Common Fund'.
(10) Meanwhile the European Council, at its meeting in
Rome on 28 March 1977, had declared: 'The Conference
agrees that there should be a Common Fund. Such a Common
Fund should contribute to the attainment of the objectives
of the Integrated Programme of Commodities as embodied in
Resolution 93 (UNCTAD IV), and should be satisfactorily
worked out and accepted by a wide range of developed
countries.' (11) The more favourable EC formulation was
not however made official policy as the EC was obliged to
maintain the overall solidarity of Group B.

In the intensive discussions in the run-up to the second
round of negotiations, scheduled to begin in November 1977,
at least one question, that of whether a Common Fund should
be established, seemed to be resolved. Thus, the final document from the meetings of the Conference on International
Economic Cooperation declared: '...that a Common Fund
should be established as a new Organization and should serve
as the main instrument in reaching the goals agreed on in the
IPC according to Resolution 93 of UNCTAD IV. The countries taking part in the CIEC pledged to bring the forthcoming

second round of the UN negotiating conference for the CF to a successful end'. (12) Since the EC, along with a number of major OECD countries, had participated in the CIEC discussions, it now felt politically committed to a Common Fund.

The resolution of this question only served to intensify conflict over other issues. Three issues in particular became the focus of dispute. (13) First, there was the question of whether the Fund should have proper resources at its own disposal that would exceed the deposits coming from the ICAs. This question was of paramount importance since it would provide an ICA with back-up facilities, i.e. it could draw on additional financial resources surpassing its normal drawing rights. Second, there was the question of how the proper resources should be raised to guarantee the back-up facility, and to whom it should be assigned, i.e. either directly to the Common Fund or to the Individual ICAs. (The first option would mean that governments would provide resources to meet the requirements of any ICA, irrespective of whether they would be part of it.) Finally, there was disagreement on the principles and financing of the 'Second Window'. (14)

Once again the initial onus of finding some compromise solution fell on the Commission. (15) As usual the Commission suggested a mixed set of solutions, corresponding roughly to the spectrum of viewpoints taken by the member states. Since the Committee of Permanent Representatives could not reach any agreement on the basis of the Commission's suggestions, the matter was again passed to the Council of Ministers. The Council itself, meeting in October 1977, could not however produce any common position. The strenuous and time-consuming attempts at coordination only led to arguments on minor technical points. The consequences of the internal dissent of the EC were very serious for the second round of negotiations which broke down at the start of December. The Dutch and the Danes, however, did not hesitate to state that their positions differed from that of Group B (and therefore also from the EC). (16)

During the recess of nearly one year, contacts between the groups were maintained through an inter-governmental committee. The search for a compromise that could be negotiable in the eyes of the Group of 77 took place in the Commission of the EC, in the Council of Ministers, and within the OECD. (17) The industrial nations of the West had to make concessions if they did not want to jeopardize the North-South dialogue on a global scale. Finally, the Group B countries, including the EC, agreed to a series of stipulations under which they would be willing to resume negotiations. (18)

These included acceptance in principle of a 'Second Window',
subject to the caveat that it should be separated from the
'First Window'. The 'First Window' should be subsidized
through voluntary governmental contributions and should act
only on the basis of conjoint understanding between consumers and producers of raw materials. It was supposed to
act in close cooperation with other international organizations
active in this area. Furthermore, there was some general
willingness to negotiate on the deposit/credit ratio of the
'First Window', i.e. the relative size of any ICA's resources
that it would deposit with the Common Fund in order to obtain the desired credit from the Fund.

The second round of negotiations resumed in November
1978 and for the first time real progress towards some agreed
position between the North and South was achieved.
Although the EC group of countries did manage to maintain
their external cohesion throughout these discussions, internal differences of opinion, both on the content as well as the
strategy of negotiations, continued. Thus, France, Britain
and the Federal Republic of Germany clearly favoured coordination at the OECD level and attached only subordinate
importance to EC coordination. France in particular was concerned to display its foreign policy independence from the EC.
Or again, despite some, albeit rather mild, accommodation to
the Group of 77 position, both the Federal Republic and Britain continued to stand by their restrictive viewpoints. Meanwhile, those countries more closely connected with the progressive viewpoint, The Netherlands, Denmark and to a lesser extent Belgium, were compelled to adapt under 'solidarity
of the Community' to the more restrictive position held by the
larger member states.

The final agreements were reached in the third round of
negotiations and the closing conference held respectively in
March 1979 and June 1980. (19) These agreements, however,
had little in common with the original project of the Group of
77.

As far as the second part of the Integrated Programme of
Commodities is concerned, namely the ICAs, only one Agreement has been concluded. The International Rubber Agreement, concluded in 1979, did not produce any important dispute concerning its contents. (20) On the other hand, its
legal implementation highlighted one of the more general
problems of the EC constitution. The conflict between the
Commission and the Council of Ministers centred on the problem of formal membership in the Rubber Agreement. The
Council argued in favour of joint membership of both the EC
and the member states. On the grounds that the Rubber

Agreement fell under the provisions of Article 113 of the EEC Treaty, the Commission argued that only the EC should become a member. The Commission's position has been confirmed by the European Court. (21)

With another vital commodity, sugar, the EC was unable to join an existing international agreement. (22) The case of sugar does not reveal an instance of internal conflict but one in which the whole EC policy came under attack from the developing countries. The EC had developed from a former net importer to the world's largest sugar exporter in a very short period of time. This position was enhanced by the guaranteed import of 1.2 million metric tons per annum from those developing countries that are members of the Lome Convention. The EC could not accept the system of price restrictions and export limitations set by the International Sugar Agreement. Contingent, however, on the recovery of the world sugar market, the EC is now prepared to negotiate its entry into the Sugar Agreement. (23)

Our analysis of the role of the EC in the negotiations on the IPC yields two major conclusions. The first, and perhaps least surprising, is that the EC has not contributed any major substantive independent initiatives. The second, and rather more surprising one, is that the EC has not played a major negotiating role.

THE EXPLANATION OF THE ROLE

The role of the EC and its ability to modify the original response of the member states is deeply influenced by the nature of the EC itself. The main factor explaining the absence of major EC initiatives and the low profile of the EC, especially in the Common Fund negotiations, is the continuing economic and political heterogeneity of the EC member states. This heterogeneity is further enhanced by the institutional structure of the EC itself.

On the one hand, it cannot be denied that the EC has fostered a considerable degree of integration among the member states. All the member states have experienced a substantial growth in intra-Community trade, there is an impressive array of Community-wide organizations, both at the governmental and non-governmental levels, and a number of common policies have been produced. On the other hand, it is equally clear that the EC has not engendered convergence in economic and social structures or even political orientations. The former colonial powers still today are strongly involved in the economies and even politics of their former colonies and therefore are eager to maintain a special relationship with them. This policy is reflected in the preferential agreements the EC has established with specific countries of the Third World. It runs counter to the declared interest of the developing world in so far as it contains a discriminatory element. At the same time a country, like the Federal Republic, lacking strong colonial ties would prefer a more global approach which would better suit its own interests. Though this special conflict has been resolved in the formulation of the EEC Treaty, the limited jurisdiction of the Community Treaties in foreign relations in general reflects that the individual European countries have little in common in this domain. The EC's jurisdiction only covers those aspects of foreign economic policies which accrue from the internal regime of the customs union, i.e. a common foreign trade policy.

This implies that the EC, as an international organization, only had to respond when the NIEO negotiations entailed trade policies. On the other hand the ability to define a common European position is strongly determined by the internal development of the Community. Especially in the 1970s the inter-governmental element of European cooperation have been strengthened. The Commission, originally established to provide an explicitly European impetus and dynamics for the Community independent of national governments, has been effectively countervailed, if not actually subordinated, first by the Council of Ministers and COREPER and more recently by the European Council. At the same time the extension of European cooperation to other areas such as foreign policy has produced bodies of a strictly inter-governmental nature.

Given that the Community has developed much more along the lines of an inter-governmental organization in which the national interests of individual states have not been subordinated to supra-national considerations, it is not surprising that the EC has not played any major role in the NIEO negotiations.

The simultaneous existence of a system known as European Political Cooperation gives some insights into the difficulties Europeans face in meeting a challenge by common action if this challenge contains a mixture of political and economic aspects. Within the EC the difficulties are further enhanced through the distinction made by Article 113 and 116 of the EEC Treaty. The NIEO demands very often entail aspects of both provisions. Whereas in the case of Article 113 the EC 'as such' has the sole competence to act, Article 116 deals with economic aspects not covered by the Treaty but which are of 'particular interest to the common market' and where

only *member states* should act commonly. Article 116 estab-
lishes in no way a competence of the EC 'as such'.

In this situation it is not surprising that in a case like
the Common Fund, which represents a mixture of political
and economic elements only partly covered by the EEC Treaty,
the Commission could not play its initiating or even mediating
role. It has met considerable opposition in the COREPER and
in the Council of Ministers, In these bodies the use of the
unanimity principle has made it relatively easy for any state
to produce a stalemate. The general stagnation has only been
resolved, when indeed it has actually been resolved, by the
European Council. In this context however, it is important
to note that the European Council is pre-empting a role that
should be carried out by the Commission. On the other hand
the case of the International Rubber Agreement shows some
successful cooperation of EC member states under the guidance of the Commission. The Rubber Agreement falls under
the provisions of Article 113 of the EEC Treaty and there was
thus little chance for member states to deviate from the position defined by the Commission. Other areas of successful
cooperation include a common position in the Helsinki conference and a more or less united Community voice in the United
Nations. Furthermore the EC has succeeded in producing
joint action in the GATT trade talks (Tokyo round) and the
CIEC. But it is noteworthy that for instance in the case of
GATT a Community delegation and nine member states delegation participated in the talks, and the issues negotiated in
Helsinki fell under the sole umbrella of the EPC which provides only a loose framework of coordination. Thus the special mixture of content in the Common Fund negotiations is
one major explanation of the very low-key negotiating role of
the EC in this issue. In general the Council of Ministers have
only been willing to concede any substantial degree of autonomy to the EC when the subject matters at hand either involved little controversy or was of a primarily technical
nature.

In the context of the Common Fund, some of the member
states argued that the subject matter went well beyond detailed or technical questions concerning specific trade agreements. On the contrary the issue of the Common Fund raised
a question about a radically new international commodity
regime. This explains why an argument was made that the
EC 'as such' had little competence to negotiate in this area.
Even after this issue was resolved, it was still clear that
some member states held the view that the NIEO demands, at
least as originally cast, had extensive detrimental ramifications for their vital interests. Again in general, we can note

that the more important an issue area is for the vital interests of a member state, the more unwilling it is to transfer
any substantial latitude in decision-making to the EC. This
is why the EC has made so few inroads in the area of what
might be called 'high politics'.

One related factor accounts for the low-key negotiating
role. The conflict of views among the members, which in itself is not at all unusual, has led to a division between the
hardliners and progressives which corresponds to some extent with that between the large and the small states. While
it would be an exaggeration to claim that the Federal Republic of Germany and Britain have manipulated the smaller countries against their will into a much less compromising position,
something of this process has definitely been at work.
Although both the Federal Republic and Britain have made
some accommodation, this accommodation has to be set against
a range of initially inflexible and hostile positions on nearly
all the NIEO demands. While the hardliners and progressives
have both moved towards each other, the distance that has
been covered by the latter is much greater.

We know that substantial discussions did not take place
among the developed countries. What is of particular relevance for our problem is that the hardline EC states were
much more favourably disposed to coordination within the
OECD than within the EC. This is explained in the first
place by the fact that the OECD offered a wider and looser
framework which would not produce legally binding decisions
and which would not seriously compromise the national sovereignty or autonomy of any state. Second, discussion within the OECD offered the Federal Republic and Britain the
opportunity of allying with other major hardline states, notably the USA and Japan. The combined effect of a general
unwillingness on the part of the hardline states to concede
any decision-making latitude together with a general preference for an OECD rather than EC forum, superimposed on a
more extensive and enduring set of obstacles to joint EC
action, explain the very low-key contribution of the EC to
the NIEO negotiations.

CONCLUSION

The EC has most certainly not made any major positive or constructive contribution to the NIEO debate, at least in issues
where this debate had to deal with overall challenges like the
Common Fund. This fact corresponds more or less with the
general condition of the EC where a muddling-through in the

already integrated sectors and an overall stalemate to further integration in traditional supra-national terms can easily be observed. Additionally there seemed to be no question that the EC is not the adequate forum for the member states to deal with the overall design of relations among the industrial and the developing world. This adequate forum is provided by the OECD which also fits better with the general imperative of bloc-bargaining in the case of NIEO.

On ther other hand, it would be erroneous to dismiss the EC as having been entirely unimportant. While we are perhaps accustomed to assessing importance in terms of positive effects, or what is done, it is also the case that importance can be derived from negative effects, or what is not done. It is in this latter context that rather paradoxically the relatively insignificant contribution of the EC has in some respects been rather important. The stalemate and procrastination of the coordination in the EC induced by the negotiation of attrition and inducing the attrition of negotiation has contributed, admittedly along with a number of other factors, to the general emasculation of the NIEO demands - an outcome which is of course consonant with the perceived interests of the hardline states.

Notes

1   See the decisions taken by the Council of Ministers in July 1974 and December 1976, published in: Bundesministerium für Wirtschaftliche Zusammenarbeit, 'Bericht zur Entwicklungs politik der Bundesregierung' (Zweiter Bericht), Bonn, November 1977, pp. 76-77.

2   A comrehensive analysis of the GSP can be found in: A. Borrman, C. Borrman, M. Steger, 'Das Allgemeine Zollpraferenzsystem der EG', Hamburg, Verlag Weltarchiv, 1979.

3   Concerning the problems of the CAP and EC's politics of development, see: O. Matzke, Die Gemeinsame Agrarpolitik - Belastung für den Nord-Süd Dialog in 'Aus Politik und Zeitgeschichte - Beilage zur Wahenzeitung Das Parlament', B 5/80, pp. 15-31.

4   See Commission of the EC, Doc. COM (76) 359.

5   Interviews held in the Commission.

6   See UNCTAD, Doc. TD/RES/93 (IV).

7   See UNCTAD, Doc. TD/B/IPC/CF/2.

8   See W. Wessels, ed., 'Europa und der Nord-Süd Dialog', Bonn, Europa Union Verlag, 1977; and S. Taylor, EEC Coordination to the North South Conference, 'World

Today', November, 1977.

9   European Communities, The Council, Doc. T/217/77.

10 Interview held in the Commission.

11 Deutsche Gesellschaft für Auswärtige Politik, 'Europa Archiv', Bonn, 32/1977, p. D.236.

12 Commission of the EC, Doc. COM (77) 365 final, p. 2.

13 Interview held in the Commission.

14 On the subject of the 'Second Window', the Commission commented: 'It is difficult to see what the advantages would be for international cooperation from the establishment of a new, unexperienced, and relatively small agency', Doc. COM (77) 365, p. 4.

15 Ibid.

16 Interview held in the Commission.

17 Commission of the EC, Doc. COM (78) 22 final, and COM (78) 496 final.

18 UNCTAD, 'Fundamental Elements of a Common Fund' Proposals by the Group B', Doc. TD/IPC/CF/CONF/CRP.1.

19 The first fundamental agreement on a Common Fund reached in Spril 1979 is published in 'Trade and Development - An UNCTAD Review', Spril, 1979, pp. 95-97.

20 See Commission of the EC, Doc. COM (79) 145 final.

21 See Gutachen des Europäischen Gerichtshofes 1/78, 'Amtsblatt der Europäischen Gemeinschaften', C799, 1979.

22 Concerning the general problem of the EC sugar policy, see: C. Webb, Mr Cube versus Monsieur Beet, in H. Wallace, W. Wallace and C. Webb, eds., 'Policy-Making in the European Communities', London, Wiley, 1979.

23 Commission of the EC, Doc. COM (80) 475 final.

FEDERAL REPUBLIC OF GERMANY:
THE KNIGHTS OF THE HOLY GRAIL

J. Betz and M. Kreile

INTRODUCTION

In negotiations on international economic reform, the Federal
Republic of Germany has often acted as an outspoken hardliner and staunch defender of the principles of economic
liberalism. The New International Economic Order advocated
by the Group of 77 has been widely perceived as a fundamental threat to Germany's economic interests. The demands put
forward by the LDCs seemed to collide with the system of
rules that governed the world economy in the post-war era.
The spread of state interventionism in international economic
relations has become the nightmare that haunts the archi-
tects of German foreign economic policy. These perceptions
are rooted in the post-war experience of the German economy,
the level of internationalization it has reached, and in the
ideology of economic liberalism which has shaped West
Germany's domestic and foreign economic policies. These
structural and ideological factors which determined the
German strategy towards NIEO in general, will be outlined
briefly in the first two sections of this article. We will then
present the positions taken by the German government during the negotiations in various international bodies with regard to the following issues.
— debt relief for developing countries;
— transfer of technology;
— the Integrated Programme for Commodities.
It can be demonstrated that the attitude of rigidity which
characterized the German response did not in fact preclude
accommodation on specific LDC demands. We will finally
address the question whether the German approach to different issues areas follows a common pattern and provide
a tentative explanation for the differences between the German position and that of other industrial countries.

STRUCTURE AND INTERESTS

West Germany's 'economic miracle' is associated with the
'old' international economic order. Rising from wartime
defeat and destruction, West Germany, within barely three
decades, became the world's second largest trading nation.
The establishment of a liberal capitalist system after the fall
of Fascism took place under the auspices of American hegemony. The Pax Americana provided a congenial environment
for the German strategy of export-oriented growth, as world
trade flourished under the rules set by GATT and the Bretton Woods system. Export-oriented growth created full
employment and prosperity which, in turn, guaranteed popular support for the market economy and the system of democratic institutions. This experience accounts significantly
for the German commitment to a liberal regime of international
trade, payments and investment. It also accounts for the
tendency to prescribe to the world at large the recipes that
have proven successful at home.

The extent of international involvement of the German
economy - and hence the importance attributed to the rule
governing international trade and investment - is illustrated
by the following figures. In 1977, the FRG accounted for
10.5 per cent of world exports (US: 10.8 per cent). The
share of exports in GNP was 27.6 per cent, one out of five
jobs depending on exports. The export dependence of key
industrial sectors (e.g. machine-building, automobiles,
chemicals) amounts to more than 50 per cent. The LDC share
in German exports came to 13.3 per cent in 1978 (imports:
13.7), and OPEC countries accounted for another 8.6 per
cent (imports: 8). German direct investment abroad came to
48.5 billion DM at the end of 1976, the IDC share being 22
per cent (10.8 billion DM; OPEC excluded). (1) The German
economy is also highly dependent on imported raw materials.
The Federal Republic imports about 100 per cent of its tin,
manganese, nickel, and copper requirements, 95 per cent of
its oil and iron ore, etc. However, the import share of LDCs
exceeds 50 per cent only for agricultural products like tea,
coffee, and natural fibres and for oil and tin. (2)

The preservation of an open and liberal world economy,
i.e. the securing of trade and investment opportunities is considered a vital requirement for the future success of Germany's international economic strategy. The dominant conception of economic policy holds that the German economy has
to adjust to changes in the international division of labour by
speeding up technological innovation and structural change.
This means that German industry has to specialize in

technology-intensive branches in order to maintain its international competitiveness. Research and technology policy is assigned the task of stimulating the development of new products and technologies. Labour-intensive production lines and traditional consumer goods industries will have to be abandoned to newly industrializing countries or to be redeployed via foreign investment. This strategy of 'technological flight ahead' serves also the interests of the LDCs, it is claimed, because it facilitates the development strategy of export-oriented industrialization. This 'institutional wisdom' which unites government and opposition, the leading industrial groups and the majority of academic economists, is challenged by protectionist alliances of employers and labour unions in the declining sectors and by a number of economists and social scientists from the Left. The critics of the official strategy emphasize the risks of large-scale unemployment in the FRG and question the development prospects export-oriented industrialization offers to LDCs. (3)

Defending the 'Free Market' :
The Knights of the Holy Grail vs. the Group of 77

It would be difficult to explain adequately the German position on NIEO without taking into account the power of free market ideology. Free market ideology provides the prism through which German interests are perceived. According to former State Secretary (Foreign Office) Hermes, the market 'has up to now been demonstrated to constitute the best method of providing prosperity and freedom for the greatest possible number of individuals. The market tends to balance interests and is consequently conducive to peace and order.' (4) According to this view, social equity requires that the market mechanism be supervised and corrected, if necessary, in order to help the economically weak. This model is not only valid in a national context, but applies also internationally:

> The theoretical response therefore also applies in practice that a liberal market system can make possible to achieve balanced economic interests on an international scale. In addition, and this is particularly important for us, the market represents an objectifying force which reflects concrete facts and can completely ignore political disputes. The free market thus constitutes an excellent means of preserving peace. This fact alone makes the preservation of free world trade a foreign policy goal of the first order. (5)

Development assistance is considered the social element in the international market economy and corresponds to an imperative of solidarity. The policy of development cooperation is intended to serve global peace and stability and to further the long-term interests of the German economy.

Free market orthodoxy having turned into a secular religion, rhetoric often prevails over analysis. Not surprisingly, it was the Integrated Commodity Programme in particular which came under heavy fire from government officials and economic experts. No arguments and no paper were spared to repel the pagans' attack on the holy grail. According to Wolfgang Hager, the initial German position on commodity price stabilization was due to an abstract and idealistic conception of international trade.

> As in no other country, in Germany the proposals for buffer stocks and the like were seen as make-or-break issues that would decide the future of the entire world trading system. Even the most elementary knowledge of world commodity markets would have dispelled the notion that there was a market system to be destroyed here, at least a system that was relevant to the textbook advantages of markets: efficient allocation of factors, prices that provide useful signals to users, and such. A look at real commodity markets would have found a chaotic coexistence of very strong private oligopolies and monopolies, widespread state trading (including stock piling, price setting, and such), concerted manipulation by big producers and traders of the big exchanges (London and Chicago, for example), and the existence of economic mechanisms that worked toward imbalance between supply and demand in the medium term. (6)

Ironically enough, free-market dogmatists often present themselves as non-ideological pragmatists. Third World élites are accused of being emotional, inspired by 'post-colonial resentment' and bent on political-psychological confrontation. Their ill-advised demands are based on a misunderstanding of their genuine interests, do not make economic sense and are detrimental to a climate of confidence. (7) When the German delegation at Nairobi finally accepted the principle of a Common Fund, this concession was stigmatized by the CDU/CSU parliamentary opposition as a betrayal of the market economy. For the opposition, the battle ' freedom vs. socialism' (CDU election slogan of 1976) had to be fought not only at home but also on a world scale.

Orthodox liberalism is strongest in the CDU/CSU and in

the Federation of German Industry (BDI). Within the admin-
instration, the Ministry of Economics is a traditional strong-
hold of free-market philosophy. However, the liberal coalition
which perceives German interests as being best served by
the existing international economic order also includes the
SPD and FDP leadership, the labour unions, the overwhelm-
ing part of public opinion and the majority of academic economists. Disagreement within the liberal coalition centres on
the extent of the reforms needed to improve the working of
the system and the nature of the concessions to be offered to
the LDCs. The most active proponents of corrective intervention are to be found in the SPD, the German Federation of
Labour Unions (DGB) and the Ministry for Economic Cooperation. The domestic constituency for NIEO does not carry
much political weight. The groups most sympathetic to Third
World demands are the youth organizations of the SPD and
FDP, Third World activists in the churches and radical stu-
dents and academics. (8)

A liberal alternative to NIEO was submitted by the Academic Advisory Council to the Federal Ministry of Economics
in its report of November 1976. The Council stipulates that
a reforming of the international economic order will have to
satisfy three basic tenets: the 'respect for individual interests', the 'principle of effectiveness', and the 'principle of
a separation of objectives'. Under the third principle a
'series of rules and measures should be devised together
with appropriate institutional facilities in order to:
— aspire to a statically and dynamically efficient international
  allocation of the scarce resources available;
— implement the provision of international funds and where
  appropriate a coordination of national economic policies in
  such a way as to ensure a smooth functioning of the allocation mechanism and a lessening of the risk of international recession or inflation (stabilization);
— achieve a partial evening out of the differences in the
  levels of international prosperity and in a case of emer-
  gency to furnish assistance (distribution).' (9)
The authors criticize the demands made by the developing
countries on the grounds that they infringe the three principles mentioned in various ways and then advocate a series
of measures they deem consistent with principles of market
economy, such as:
— 'fundamental changes ... in raising the funds available
  for redistribution';
— 'the long overdue removal of tariff and non-tariff barriers
  in the way of products from DCs';
— the establishment of 'investment guarantee zones' in the

form of 'open clubs', open to countries ready to promote
and to protect international private investment.
Compensatory financing and case-by-case commodity agreements with buffer stocks are proposed as instruments of
international stabilization.

These proposals were to a large extent part of the Federal
Government's strategy in the NIEO negotiations. The
government tried to soften its rigid position with regard to
some of the LDC's core demands by offering a certain number of side payments and by stressing its commitment to a
liberal import policy. An opening of markets to LDC exports
combined with an increase in official development assistance
(ODA) is still held to be the most promising offer and a constructive response to legitimate grievances. (10)

Debt Relief for Developing Countries

In accordance with most of the other developed countries,
the Federal Government rejected from the beginning of the
negotiations demands for generalized debt relief and advocated instead the maintenance of solutions on a case-by-case
basis. Regarding the modalities of future debt renegotiations, however, it demonstrated some flexibility. The reasons put forward for the refusal of generalized debt relief
were:

(a) the 'real interests' of the developing countries themselves whose creditworthiness in international capital
markets would be affected by the writing off of past
debt, 'whereas thanks to the hitherto usual stabilization
programmes within the framework of case-by-case negotiations the confidence of the private lenders too ... is
strengthened...' (11) This explains also why the
Federal Government remains very much attached to the
maintenance of the respective roles of the IMF and the
IBRD in the debt consolidated process.

(b) an indiscriminate debt relief operation would punish
those countries 'which pay decently for their debts.' (12)

(c) The Finance Ministry and the Bundesbank in particular
rejected the idea of a general debt crisis as did international banks and the US Government. According to
Dr. Emminger, President of the Bundesbank, the prospect of widespread and imminent debt default was but
one of the many fairytales circulating. Only a small
group of countries was in a disastrous debt situation.
For the rest of the Third World, debt services payments
as proportion of export income had not increased over

the last 10 years. Moreover, the proportion of debt owed
by LDCs was negligible. (13)

Consequently, the Federal Government offered at UNCTAD
IV only debt relief for individual countries which were confronted with particular difficulties, while opposing a general
debt renegotiation conference whose mandate would have been
wider than the setting of general criteria for future debt
moratoria. (14) In compensation, however, the Federal
Government contributed a heavy proportion (31 per cent of
the European Community share) to the one-shot operation of
the Special Action Programme set up by the Conference on
International Economic Cooperation.

When we try to identify the underlying motives for the
rigid position taken by the Federal Government up to March
1978, we have first to realize that the financial costs of
generalized debt relief - no matter if only for LDCs or also
for MSACs - would have been higher for the FRG than for
all other developed countries except the United States. This
becomes especially significant, if we compare only the lost
debt service payments.

Countries like Sweden, Canada, The Netherlands, and
Switzerland which have first converted their past ODA loans
into grants did not have to pay much for their generosity.
Yet, budgetary reasons in a narrow sense were not decisive
for the German position. The conversion of past ODA loans
to LDCs into grants would have meant a net loss of only
DM 80 million p.a., which would have been covered - according to the Chancellor and the competent ministers - primarily
through reductions in normal project assistance. (15) The
drawback of indiscriminate debt relief to LDCs was that it
would benefit also those countries which, for a variety of
reasons, did not receive new loans (e.g. Uganda, the
People's Republic of Yemen and the Central African Empire).
(16) The government was also afraid that debt relief for
LDCs would lead directly to demands from less poor countries,
since the British government had already signalled its preference for the inclusion of the MSACs (i.e. the former British
colonies) into generalized debt relief operations. (17) It was
the consensus-building process in the European Community
which allowed the Federal Government to hide behind its even
more rigid partners (France). In addition, the German
government was concerned that the planned general debt conference would generate enough political pressure from the
'77' to bring about debt relief for all developing countries
and to set a precedent for future debt renegotiations under
primarily political criteria (perhaps even under UNCTAD
auspices). (18)

The preparations of the decisive ministerial meeting of the Trade and Development Board of UNCTAD (March 1978) which produced the two resolutions on the adjustment of the terms of past ODA loans and on the criteria for future debt renegotiations, saw intense internal discussions in the Federal Government about the official line in the debt question. The Ministry of Finance, which demonstrated particular reluctance, was put under joint pressure from the Foreign Office, the Ministry of Economic Cooperation and even the Ministry of Economics to agree to generous debt relief measures for the LDCs. (19)   The merely recommending character of the resolutions adopted in March 1978 relieved the Federal Government from further decisions until it came under heavy international attack as a result of its poor financial assistance to developing countries.   At the joint annual meeting of the IMF and the IBRD (September 1978), the German Minister of Economic Cooperation, reacting to McNamara's criticism of German ODA performance, announced a more or less generalized debt relief for the LDCs. (20) Later, the Federal Government was prepared to be more generous by its own initiative.   In the question of debt relief for borderline cases, which came up at the session of the Trade and Development Board in November 1979, it was ready to include Pakistan (and possibly even India) into the group profiting from the conversion of past ODA loans into grants.   However, some other members of the European Community, France above all, did not want to join. (21)

More cooperation-mindedness than in the question of debt relief was displayed by the Federal Government regarding the establishment of an international framework destined to provide guidance for future debt renegotiations.   Here, the debate focused on the role of a future debt commission which the developing countries wanted as a partial replacement of the Paris Club.   One can safely assume that this proposal aimed at reducing the roles of the IMF and the World Bank in favour of UNCTAD.   It also tended to emphasize development goals at the expense of pure balance of payments considerations.

The US Government above all, but also the British and Japanese governments resisted any proposal which they feared could impair the traditional procedures of the Paris Club, whereas the Federal Government would have accepted a broader mandate for the new coordinating agency (to be administered jointly by the IMF and the World Bank) and an enhanced role of UNCTAD in reviewing the implementations of the guidelines. (22)   It is worth mentioning that in the question of the framework for future debt renegotiations,

the positions of *all* industrialized countries were very close
to one another - even the Swedish government stressed the
merits of the case-by-case approach (23) - and that Paris
Club proceedings were at no time affected by the more or
less progressive stance some developed country took at the
more politicized UNCTAD meetings. (24)

Transfer of Technology

The Federal Government has in general acknowledged the
necessity to further the transfer of technology to developing
contries and to reduce the technological gap between industrial countries and the Third World. For this purpose, it
has already developed in the public domain a series of initiatives, such as technological cooperation treaties, the free
transfer of publicly owned intermediate technologies and the
step-up of publicly financed research in areas of interest to
developing countries. (25) At the same time, the government has stated that technological progress represents by no
means a 'common heritage of mankind' free of charge, but
has been achieved with high costs and is therefore rightly
protected by law. (26) Technological knowledge being primarily owned by private companies, the operational possibilities of governments are considerably reduced. (27)
    It follows from the principle of non-intervention into the
domain of private property that the government identifies as
possible areas for concessions above all official assistance for
the creation of technological infrastructures in developing
countries which should enable them to evaluate, to choose,
to adapt and to utilize foreign technologies. (28) Sometimes
the premise of non-interference into private affairs is presented as higher wisdom, e.g. when the ongoing negotiations
on the reform of the international legal order (WIPO revision,
Code on the Transfer of Technology) are treated as second-
ary relative to the establishment of adequate technological
infrastructures. (29) Let us now consider in more detail the
German position regarding the reform of the international
legal order and in the UNCSTD negotiations which dealt with
the financing of infrastructural prerequisites for the transfer of technologies to developing countries.
    *(a) Negotiations on a Code of Conduct for the Transfer
        of Technology (TOT-code)*
The main concern of the Federal Government with the TOT-
code in the version of the '77' was its legally binding character. This legally binding force could only be achieved by an
international treaty whose provisions could be transformed

into national law. This transformation, however, would
imply directive interferences in the domestic civil law and
was to be rejected because it violated the liberal principles
of economic organization prevailing in the FRG. (30) The
government could not compel corporations to transfer pro-
prietary technologies to LDCs under preferential conditions.
(31)

The Ministry of Economics objected strongly to the whole-
sale incorporation of export restrictions into the catalogue
of restrictive practices, as it considered legitimate the desire
of the transferring enterprises to protect themselves against
the inroads of technology recipients into their own markets.
(32) As for other relevant items of the TOT-code, the
government was in fact prepared to make concessions. It
accepted in principle the incorporation of transfers between
transnational corporations and their affiliates into the TOT-
code and backed the proposal of the socialist countries in
the difficult question of dispute settlement. Here the Group
of 77 voted for the dominance of the law of the receiving
countries, the socialist countries favoured the institution of
an arbitration commission and Group B wanted the choice of
the law applied being left to the contracting parties. (33)
The Federal Government went as far as to concede an international institutional machinery to review the implementation
of the TOT-code. This machinery was thought of as a compensation for the non-binding character of the code and was
also intended to lead to a review of all aspects of the code
itself, including the final decision on its legal character. (34)

Certainly, these concessions are not too far reaching.
Without binding force of the code even an effective implementation machinery would lead to nothing more than annual reports on infringements of the code. Likewise, the set-up of
an international arbitration commission will practically be
meaningless for it is impossible to come to grips with the con-
tested questions at the level of the contracting parties themselves, the decisions of the arbitration process will have only
symbolic importance. (35) Although the FRG offered only
modest concessions, it did not figure among the extreme hard-
liners which can be identified as the United States, Switzerland and Great Britain. This ranking can be explained by
the different positions of these countries in the international
technology business. The FRG has always had a negative
balance of payments in the domain of patents, licences, and
production processes. True, this considerable deficit has
diminished relatively in the last five years as the flow of
direct investment abroad has accelerated. The reason for
the permanent negative patent and license balance is to be

sought in the relative undervaluation of the German Mark
and the comparatively low wage level up to the end of the
sixties, which led to the prevalence of exports over direct
investment and license production arrangements. Furthermore, the deficit is due above all to the transfers between
foreign corporations and their German affiliates, concentrated to a high degree in technology intensive sectors. (36)
It goes without saying that the balance of payments with
developing countries relating to patent etc. is positive for
the Federal Republic. But the amount of this surplus is
negligible if compared to the total export surplus of the last
years.

A closer look at the patent balance of other industrial
countries shows a negative correlation between transfer surplus and concession mindedness in the negotiations on the
reform of the international legal order for the transfer of
technology. Countries with high volumes of patent and
license transfers relative to their export receipts and with a
positive balance are also those resisting most any change in
the legal provisions.

  (b) *The United Nations Conference on Science and Techno-
      logy for Development (UNCSTD)*

The main substantive outcomes of UNCSTD were:
1 concrete provisions for the institutional follow-up of the
   conference;
2 the establishment of an Interim Fund for the financing of
   science- and technology-related activities.

The debate on institutional innovation ended with a relative
success of the developing countries, namely the establishment of a new Inter-governmental Committee open to all
states which shall report through ECOSOC to the General
Assembly and which shall replace ACAST whose mandate was
more limited. All industrialized countries, above all the
United States and the Soviet Union, would have preferred
the institutional status quo, as their influence is better safe-
guarded in ECOSOC and the former ACAST. The countries
of the European Community, and the Federal Republic in
particular, were more prone to concessions and succeeded in
contributing to the final compromise. (37)

A second institutional innovation is the new Centre for
Science and Technology headed by an Under- or Assistant
Secretary. It will be removed from the Department of International Economic and Social Affairs and placed under the
guidance of the Director-General for Development and International Economic Cooperation. This means increasing the
influence of the developing countries on science and technology policy formulation within the United Nations. The

developed countries, especially France and to a lesser extent
Great Britain, would have preferred to maintain the mandate
of the Department of International Economic and Social Affairs as it is dominated by Western (especially French) bureau-
crats. The Federal Republic was less engaged in this question and would have backed the proposal of the ' 77' at an
early stage. In the final vote, the countries of the European
Community abstained.

Concerning the establishment of the Interim Fund, the
developing countries made their most spectacular concession.
Neither its financial volume nor its modalities (voluntary contributions vs. automaticity) came very close to the original
conception of the ' 77'. The initiative for the revised Interim
Fund came from the United States and was thoroughly prepared in cooperation with UNDP which shall also administrate
the new fund. The countries of the European Community
were less enthusiastic about a new sectoral fund. Great
Britain was very much opposed and made reservations during
the final resolution of UNCSTD, whereas the French government planned to raise the necessary contributions simply by
budgetary shifts. The Federal Government was also skepti-
cal towards a new fund, as it is generally opposed to the proliferation of financing agencies. It wanted to place the
Interim Fund under the strict auspices of UNDP, to guarantee the application of the traditional financial control procedures of that organization, but was more prepared than
other developed countries to leave the formulation of guidelines for project selection to the new Intergovernmental Committee.

On the other subjects dealt with at UNCSTD (the scope of
scientific and technological information systems, the conditions and terms of technology transfer) the German position
was rigid. Like most other Western countries - the unity of
the developed countries in those issues was considerable -
the FRG insisted on the exclusion of topics that might prejudice the outcome of the negotiations on a TOT-code and on
the revision of the Paris Convention. Moreover, the Federal
Government opposed anything that might be regarded as
potential encroachment on private property rights. (38)

The Integrated Programme for Commodities

From the beginning of the negotiations up to 1978, the
Federal Government considered the Integrated Programme for
Commodities (IPC), and especially its key element, the Com-
mon Fund (CF) as being highly detrimental to the prosperity

of the world economy. The IPC was seen as a step towards
the suspension of the market mechanism in commodity trade
and its replacement by a complicated system of controls and
instructions managed by a huge and expensive bureaucratic
apparatus. The German authorities believed further that
diversification in developing countries would be obstructed
by guaranteed prices for commodities leading not only to
global misallocation of resources, but also to surplus production which would have to be stockpiled according to the pattern of the subsidized agricultural products in the Common
Market.

Their main reservation was that the IPC might lead to inflationary pressures on a world level (given the natural tendency of producing countries to fix prices above the market
trend) which would discriminate unduly among countries,
favouring most commodity-rich industrialized countries like
the United States, the Soviet Union and South Africa, while
penalizing stability-minded countries with no substantial raw
material production such as the Federal Republic and most of
the least developed countries. (39)

Consequently, the strategic goal of the Federal Government was to prevent the adoption of the IPC or at least to
retard decisions on the Common Fund as long as intensive
negotiations on new international commodity agreements had
not taken place. Beginning with spring 1975, parts of the
Federal Government, especially the Ministry for Economic Cooperation, began to think about the necessity to offer the
developing countries an attractive alternative to their IPC
proposal in the form of a globalized STABEX model for export
earnings stabilization. After difficult internal discussions -
the Economics Ministry first voted against a global stabilization scheme for export receipts and favoured later (as did
the Foreign Office) the less generous IMF compensatory facility as a model - the Federal Government presented the outline of its stabilization scheme at the Seventh Special Session
of the United Nations in 1975. This facility was to stabilize
the commodity exports of the poorer developing countries by
providing them with credits (on IMF or softer terms) for export shortfalls, shortfalls being calculated according to a formula taking into account the export performance of the last
two years and hypothetical growth rates for the next two
years. (40)

This proposal was intended to offer attractive, though
market-oriented measures, which would not favour inflationary tendencies and would avoid bureaucratic interference
(e.g. supply management) in the world commodity trade.
The fact that only poorer developing countries would qualify

for credit assistance was also considered an important advantage.   The federal Government, like the US Administration, was pleased with the idea of putting the facility under IMF tutelage.   Finally, necessary capital requirements were believed to be considerably lower (by about 50 per cent) (41) than those for the Common Fund.   This was partly due to the fantastic financial estimates for the CF, the German government operating at a time with the figure of DM 40 billion. (42)

However, it was a tough job to win supporters for the export stabilization scheme even among the developed countries.   The French government favoured new commodity agreements, while the Nordic countries and The Netherlands at that stage backed more or less unconditionally the proposals of the Group of 77 and would have accepted an export stabilization facility only as a supplement to the CF.   The Group of 77 never left any doubt that they would not accept the proposed facility as an alternative to the CF, thus alarming the other developed countries (and soon the United States, too) that in the end they would have to pay both. Nevertheless, the German government presented its export stabilization scheme untiringly during the years to come and tried to win support for it even as late as during the session of the Joint Development Committee in Washington in September 1978.

It is important to note, however, that the German proposal as well as the corresponding American one, both put forward in a hurry, were neither conceived nor calculated thoroughly.   The German proposals which in fact were only very preliminary ideas (even the paper of September 1978 figuring officially only as rough draft (Skizze) (43)) spoke at different times of different numbers of beneficiaries, commodities included, financial requirements and credit terms. As the German government continued to put forward its proposal at a time when its chances of realization were practically zero, we can safely assume that its function was primarily that of an alibi. (44)

In preparing their strategy for UNCTAD IV, the EC countries reached an agreement on the French proposal, conceiving the CF as a clearing house for settled commodity agreements, the latter being financed in part by government contributions.   The CF would not have management functions and finance of its own. (45)   The British and the German governments had strong reservations even to this modest concept and tried to gain support for a negotiating calendar. This would have meant that negotiations for a CF would have started a year later than those for the individual commodity agreements, the number of which was to be reduced to three (tea, jute, and hard fibres) according to the German conception. Yet, even within the EEC, there was no chance to maintain this position. (46)

Between UNCTAD IV and the Negotiating Conference for the CF (November 1977) the Federal Republic made a series of minor concessions concerning the modalities of the CF. This resulted above all from the concerted pressure exerted by the French and the Dutch governments within the European Community in favour of a more flexible attitude towards the CF proposal. Simultaneously, the Federal Government, in bilateral talks, sought the backing of the US Administration for its narrower conceptions and again for its export stabilization scheme. (47) But it turned out that the US Administration had already developed a relatively far-reaching proposal for a CF, which came very close to the French pool concept, so leaving the German government alone in its stubborn refusal of an integrated commodity programme. This experience, following the traumatic one at Nairobi, prepared the ground for accepting a CF as a pool of commodity agreements, financed by government contributions but with no capital and management functions of its own. (48)

Parallel to international pressure, the domestic consensus was shifting as well. Since October 1975, the Ministry of Economic Cooperation favoured a more flexible attitude towards IPC. The Foreign Office joined in November 1976 for political reasons. It feared that the German position would antagonize the LDCs excessively at a moment when other industrial countries became more accommodating. To appear as an isolated hardliner would also undermine the diplomatic efforts aimed at the development of a credible new Africa policy. The Chancellor and the Ministry of Finance were left alone with their invariable preference for export stabilization measures, (49) but finally, they too gave in at the eve of the second session of the Negotiating Conference (March 1979).

The change in the German position and the relative satisfaction of the Government with the agreement reached at that session (which was more or less only confirmed by the final agreement in June 1980) was motivated by:
— the above mentioned foreign policy considerations;
— fears of being accused at UNCTAD V because of its poor ODA record;
— a more realistic calculation of German financial contributions to the future CF and the ICAs (especially since only very few of the latter would be forthcoming)
— the fact that the final consensus came very close to what

the developed countries had offered at the Negotiating
Conference in November 1977 and contained the German
policy essentials, namely no market intervention of the
Common Fund itself, equal participation of producers and
consumers in financing the agreements, the requirement
of qualified majorities in voting on important questions
(granting a veto power to Group B) and the financial and
operational autonomy of ICAs.
The autonomy of the ICAs *vis-à-vis* the CF was of paramount
importance to the German government. To this effect the CF
would have to be designed as a resource pool having at best
symbolic financial means of its own. (50) A CF with manager-
ial functions and a large amount of capital paid in advance
(i.e. before the conclusion of new ICAs) was considered to:
— lead to the fixing of high intervention prices, as those
   ICAs acting in this manner would gather the largest share
   of the Fund's resources;
— favour a more liberal spending of money in general;
— occasion the interference of government dependent managers with the autonomy of ICAs, thus imposing itself as a
   global commodities agency;
— lead to the conclusion of ICAs which were technically and
   economically not viable, whereas the individual financing
   of agreements would reduce their number to the technically sound ones (reducing thereby total capital requirements as well);
— necessitate a higher percentage share to be borne by the
   developed countries in the financing of the whole undertaking. (51)
Consequently, the government expressed its satisfaction with
the agreement of March 1979 which accepts the CF on principle while safeguarding the autonomy of ICAs. (52)
    Concerning the financing of the 'other measures,' the so-
called 'second window', the Federal Government showed a
less pronounced opposition to the demands of the '77'. At
an early stage of the negotiations, the Ministry of Economics
sought to gain support inside the government and within the
EC for a system of diversification, market improvement and
short-term stocking measures. With a generously financed
programme of this kind it hoped to reduce the demands of
the '77' regarding the first window. This initiative did not
even succeed at home. At the EC summits in Rome and London, the proposal was kindly recommended for further studies. (53) Later, the Federal Government joined the other
EC countries. They were more favourable to the financing
of the other measures than the US Administration, as those
measures would benefit above all the commodity poor ACP

countries which therefore manifested a vivid interest in their institutionalization.

It is easy to see that Germany counted among the hard-liners in the IPC negotiations, being surpassed only by the United States. The reasons for the German resistance to ICP may not only be found in the tirelessly repeated preference for the market mechanism but also - and perhaps more convincingly - in structural characteristics of the German commodity-based industry.

— Among Group B countries, the Federal Republic is the country with the second largest trade deficit in commodities, (54) whereas countries like the US, Canada, Australia, Norway, and Sweden show a sometimes substantial trade surplus. This would, however, not explain the opposition of the US and Canada to IPC, nor the more positive attitude of equally commodity-dependent countries like The Netherlands, France and Japan.

— If we exclude, however, agricultural raw materials and include also the processing of minerals into the trade balance, the picture looks somewhat different: the US becomes a heavy net importer, while France and Japan export more refined commodities than they import, whereas the figures for The Netherlands are fairly balanced. Again, the situation of the Federal Republic is disadvantageous. Countries with large processing facilities could have passed on IPC-induced price increases to other consumer countries.

— Officially- and privately-owned commodity stocks in the federal Republic are modest in volume compared to some other developed countries, not to speak of the United States. Recent discussions about the financing of larger stocks through parts of the huge currency reserves accumulated by the Bundesbank have met with strong Bundesbank opposition.

— The capital basis of the German mining industry is relatively small. The participation of German enterprises in foreign mining ventures has been rather modest until recently. Only in the last four to five years, due to special tax treatment of exploration and investment activities in the commodity sector and to concentration processes in the industry itself, a significant diversification of sources of supplies has taken place.

CONCLUSION

Although the German strategy on the whole appears as a

defence of the existing international economic order and as
an exercise in 'damage control', the Federal Government
sometimes proved less uncompromising than its affirmation
of principles suggested. Looking for regularities in the
German position across the issue areas examined, we find
that the government proved conciliatory with regard to:
— new institutional arrangements which reorganized or coordinated existing activities;
— institutions for implementation deprived of sanction
  mechanisms;
— one-shot financial actions or concessions involving limited
  financial costs in the foreseeable future and no long-term
  obligations.
— new funds, provided that they were placed under the
  authority or supervision of traditional institutions (UNDP,
  World Bank) and financed through voluntary contributions.
The German position was uncompromising when free market
essentials were threatened by:
— encroachments on the operating autonomy and property
  rights of private firms;
— the establishment of international political agencies disposed to limit the realms of private initiative;
— arrangements likely to give priority to political considerations over economic criteria (e.g. debt commission, IPC).
  It should be noted that the German position has become
more flexible over time. This indicates a certain learning
process which was conditioned by the experience of isolation
at Nairobi (1976). Subsequently, the Federal Government
intensified its efforts to reach a consensus at Brussels before
confronting the developing countries. Foreign policy considerations advanced by the Foreign Office began to figure
more prominently in the decision-making process. The
Foreign Office felt that a too rigid posture would negatively
affect Germany's relations with the Third World in general
and jeopardize the overtures to the African countries. Not
surprisingly, the readiness to make concessions increased
as the losses the Federal Republic was likely to incur diminished. Partly, the losses feared were a product of unrealistic cost estimates (originally the CF requirements were put at
40 billion DM). With a more sober evaluation of costs and a
more realistic assessment of LDC bargaining power, the fears
decreased. Moreover, the approval of new institutions at the
expense of existing ones is not costly, as the FRG does not
have many posts to lose in the UN bureaucracy. The acceptance of new funds was made easier by the fact that the Federal Republic has some leeway to increase its multilateral
aid given the low level of ODA. An eventual reduction of

bilateral assistance would not hurt traditional client states as in the case of Britain and France.

A critical evaluation of the German position must take into account the fact that there has been a remarkable degree of unity among the industrialized countries with respect to the hard core choices. Even the Scandinavian countries opposed interventions of the CF outside the ICAs (not interventions in general), general debt renegotiations including private debt, and the financial structure of the Interim Fund as proposed by the Group of 77. This does not mean that there were no principal differences at all between the hardliners and the 'like-minded countries'. But the unity in the hard core choices demonstrates that the 'like-minded countries' are sometimes free-riders of the intransigence of the hard-liners. It should also be asked what the record of the Federal Republic is with respect to the market-oriented alternatives (increase in ODA, liberalization of imports from LDCs, technology transfer through private investment) it has proposed. In other words: Does the Federal Government practice what it preaches?

As far as ODA is concerned, the government takes pride in the fact that 'in the past two years ..., the Federal Republic of Germany, in spite of its unfavourably bugetary situation, has doubled its official development assistance from 3.2 to 6.1 billion DM.' (55) The GNP share of 0.44 per cent in 1979 compares favourably with the 0.27 per cent of 1977, but is still a far cry from the 0.7 per cent goal whose continuing validity is periodically reaffirmed by successive German development ministers. The multilateral share of German ODA (35.3 per cent in 1979) compares favourably with the DAC average of 28.9 per cent or the multilateral share of other donor countries: Australia 26.1, Belgium 31.3, Canada 45.1, France 17.3, Japan 27.2, The Netherlands 31.4, Sweden 35.1, UK 43.7 and USA 13 per cent. As far as the tying of aid is concerned, there is a general tendency re-cently for an increase in the tied portion of development assistance. The FRG performs rather well in this respect with US $3.2 billion of untied ODA out of a total of $4 billion in 1979. The biggest 'sinners' in this area are France, the US, the United Kingdom and Japan among the large donor countries. However, with regard to the terms performance, German ODA comes out as somewhat stingy. In 1978, the grant element of total ODA commitments was 86.6 per cent as compared to 96.6 for Canada, 92.3 for France, 99.9 for Sweden, 93.9 for the UK and 89.4 for the United States. Among the large donors only Japan did worse with 75 per cent. The Federal Government supports a substantial increase in official aid for the least developed countries in the framework of an extensive international programme of action. The more advanced developing countries are reminded that the transfer of private resources will be of crucial importance for them. Their efforts to attract direct investment 'would be greatly facilitated if it were possible to re-establish at last general recognition of protection of private investment by international law.' (56)

In the field of trade, Germany has been firmly committed to the opening of markets to developing countries, but it had also to reckon with the protectionist interests of its European partners. The available data indicate that LDC exporters have been relatively successful in the German market. Between 1974 and 1979 German imports from non-oil exporting developing countries rose from 16 billion to more than 27 billion DM, the proportion of manufactures and semi-manufactures growing from 42 to 52 per cent. The trade surplus of the non-oil exporting LDCs in trade with the FRG amounted to 2.6 billion DM in the first half of 1980. (57) The imports of manufactures from non-oil exporting LDCs have a higher market share in the FRG than in the European Community as a whole (FRG market share for extra-European LDCs in 1978, 16 per cent; for European LDCs, 10.7 per cent; EC market share, 15 per cent and 8.8 per cent respectively).(58) Under the General System of Preferences the Federal Republic accounts for 40 per cent of preferential imports, Britain for 22 per cent and the Benelux countries for 14.6 per cent. (59) In 1979, 345 applications were filed with the EC Commission to implement the safeguard provisions of the EC treaty, 268 concerning the textile sector. Out of these 345 applications, 145 were initiated by France, only 6 by the Federal Republic. (60) It was the Federal Government which opposed the restrictive quota provisions of the textile agreement. (61) These examples seem to confirm the conclusion of a recent study by the Deutsche Institut fur Wirtschaftsforschung (DIW) according to which the Federal Republic ranks third behind Sweden and The Netherlands for the most liberal import policy. (62)

On the other hand, it should be pointed out that the barriers to imports from LDCs that exist at the EC level are still significant. The concessions made to the developing countries in the Tokyo Round remain within narrow limits or represent only vague declarations of intention. (63) Liberalization in the area of tariffs has been undermined by the imposition of new quotas, voluntary export restraints agreements and the introduction of non-tariff barriers. The sectors most affected by the new protectionism are textiles and

clothing, shows, machine-building, iron and steel products
and the electronics industry. These are precisely the sectors in which the most advanced developing countries (Brazil, Taiwan, South Korea etc.) are the most competitive. (63)
The protectionist pressures at the European Community
level are linked to the fact that the burden of adjustment to
increased LDC imports is distributed unequally among member countries as are the benefits from the expansion of export markets. (64) If protectionist measures become more
and more an integral part of sectoral crisis management in
the European Community, the credibility of the German commitment to free trade is bound to suffer. The proposal of
an 'international liberalization plan' made by Foreign Minister Genscher at the Eleventh Special Session of the General
Assembly in August 1980 seems to reflect these conflicting
pressures:

> Such a plan would take account of the export opportuni-
> ties of developing countries and provide for the gradual
> elimination of customs barriers, of quantitative restric-
> tions on imports, non-tariff trade barriers, and subsi-
> dies. The plan would thus reduce the need for selective
> protection measures since companies in industrialized coun-
> tries would be enabled to adjust themselves in time to the
> lowering of trade barriers. (65)

Yet, as things stand now, the prospects for an international
liberalization plan are rather bleak. The champions of free
trade are condemned to fight rearguard actions.

Notes

1   Deutsche Bundesbank, 'Monatsberichte', April 1979,
    p. 33.
2   'Entwicklungspolitik', Materialien Nr. 65 (Bundesminis-
    terium fuer wirtschaftliche Zusammenarbeit), Bonn
    April 1980, pp. 32, 35.
3   Cf. Gerd Junne, Internationalisierung und Arbeitslosig-
    keit, in: 'Leviathan' 1979, Nr. 1, pp. 57-58' Folker
    Froebel et al., 'Die neue internationale Arbeitsteilung',
    Reinbek 1977; Alfred Pfaller (ed.), Industrialization for
    export - better prospects for LDCs?, Special issue of
    'Vierteljahresberichte Probleme der Entwicklungslaender',
    Nr. 75, March 1979.
4   Peter Hermes, Foreign Policy and Economic Interests,
    'Aussenpolitik' (English Edition), Vol. 29, No. 3 (1978),
    pp. 243-256, p. 244.

5 ibid., p. 245.
6 Wolfgang Hager, Germany: An Extraordinary Trader, in: W. Kohl and G. Basevi (eds.), 'West Germany: A European and Global Power', Lexington/Mass. 1980, pp. 3-19, p. 13.
7 Cf. Bremer Gesellschaft fuer Wirtschaftsforschung e.V. (ed.), 'Auswertung der Dokumentation der vierten Welthandels-und Entwicklungskonferenz Nairobi 1976', Baden-Baden, 1978.
8 A part of the last mentioned group argues that NIEO is a reformist impasse and propose to LDCs a strategy of dissociation from the capitalist world economy combined with collective self-reliance. See Dieter Senghaas, 'Weltwirtschaftsordnung und Entwicklungspolitik', Frankfurt 1977.
9 Problems of a New International Economic Order. The Report of the Academic Advisory Council to the Federal Ministry of Economics (Summary), in: 'The German Economic Review', Vol. 15, No. 1 (1977), pp. 72 ff.
10 See 'Jahresgutachten des Sachverstaendigenrats zur Begutachtung der gesamtwirtschaftlichen Entwicklund 1979/80', Bundestagsdrucksache 8/3420, p. 190.
11 'Frankfurter Rundschau', 4/8/1976; see also Dritter Bericht zur Entwicklungspolitik der Bunesregierung, in: 'Deutscher Bundestag', 8 Wahlperiode, Drucksache 8/1185, p. 41.
12 'Frankfurter Rundschau', 5/24/1976.
13 Cf. 'Entwicklungspolitik', Spiegel der Presse 37/1978, p. 1151 f. The arguments of international bankers in: D.O. Beim, Rescuing the LDCs, 'Foreign Affairs', July 1977, and H. van B Cleveland/W.H. Bruce Brittain, 'Are the LDCs in over their heads?, 'Foreign Affairs' July 1977; for the position of the US and other Western governments see the UNCTAD documents: TAD/INF/944; TD/B/690; TD/B/685/Add.1; TD/AC.2/10.
14 Cf. 'Frankfurther Rundschau', 5/28/1976.
15 'Die Welt', 3/23/1978.
16 Interview (J.B.) at the Ministry of Economic Cooperation.
17 See 'Nachrichten fuer Aussenhandel', 3/16/1978.
18 Interview (J.B.) at the Ministry of Economics; for the French position see J. François-Poncet in: 'Economica', 7/25/2976.
19 'Die Zeit', 8/3/1978.
20 'Wirtschaftswoche', 41/1978.
21 Interviews (J.B.) at the Ministries of Economics and Economic Cooperation.
22 ibid.

23 Cf. TD/B/690, p. 12.

24 Cf. note 21.

25 Cf. Per Fischer, Technologie als Mittel der Entwicklung, 'Europa-Archiv', 20/1979, pp. 633 ff.; Rainer Offergeld, Anmerkungen zum Thema Neue Weltwirtschaftsordnung, 'Die Neue Gesellschaft', 9/1978.

26 See Offergeld op. cit.

27 Cf. Fischer, op. cit. (note 25).

28 Cf. Volker Hauff, Forschung und Technologie im Dienste der Entwicklung, 'Bulletin', 99/1979.

29 Cf. Fischer op. cit. (note 25) and Wolfgang Hillebrand et al., 'Nord-Sued-Dialog-Eine Zwischenbilanz', DIE Berlin 1980.

30 Cf. Vermerk ueber den Stand der Arbeiten an einem internationalen Verhaltenskodex fuer den Technologie-transfer, BMZ, Bonn, February 14, 1979; 'Handelsblatt' 10/20/1978.

31 'Handelsblatt', 3/12/1979.

32 Interview at the Ministry of Economics (J.B.).

33 Interviews (J.B.) at the Ministries of Economics and Economic Cooperation; for the different proposals concerning dispute settlement cf. TD/CODE/TOT/20.

34 Cf. Vermerk...)note 30).

35 See Hildebrand et al., op. cit. (note 29).

36 Cf. Siegfried Greif, Die deutsche Patent-und Lizenz-bilanz, 'Gewerblicher Rechtsschutz und Urheberrecht', Int. 10/1979, pp. 450 ff.

37 Cf. Volker Rittberger, Weltwissenschaftskonferenz fuer Entwicklung, 'Wirtschaft und Wissenschaft', 3/1979, pp. 17 ff.; id., United Nations Conference Politics and the New International Economic Order in the Field of Science and Technology', 'Journal of International Affairs', 1/1979, pp. 63 ff.

38 For this information we are indebted to Volker Rittberger.

39 The arguments are extracted from a multitude of official German statements.

40 Cf. Rede des Bundesaussenministers vor den Vereinten Nationen, 'Entwicklungspolitik', Materialien Nr. 51, Bonn Bonn, November 1975; EMZ, 'Skizze von Vorstellungen fuer ein weltweites Rohstoffstabilisierungsprogramm', Bonn, August 17, 1978.

41 See 'Sueddeutsche Zeitung;, 9/14/1976; 'Handelsblatt', 5/3/1977.

42 Cf. Protokoll der Debatten des Deutschen Bundestags, 'Entwicklungspolitik', Materilien Nr. 53, June 1976.

43 EMZ, Skizze..(note 40).

44 These conclusions were drawn from various interviews
    conducted by Joachim Betz at the Ministry of Economic
    Cooperation and at the Foreign Office.

45 Cf.'Die Welt', 8/27/1975; 'Suedeutsche Zeitung',
    8/27/1975.

46 Cf. 'Handelsblatt', 5/21/1976; 'Entwicklungspolitik',
    Materialien Nr. 53, p. 113, 115.

47 Cf. 'Suedeutsche Zeitung', 3/9/1977.

48 'Neue Zuericher Zeitung', 10/26/1977; 'Welt der Arbeit',
    11/24/1977.

49 'Frankfurter Rundschau', 11/14/1978; 'Handelsblatt',
    10/27/1978.

50 H.D. Genscher, Freier Welthandel als Bedingung fuer
    Fortschritt und Entwicklung, 'Bulletin', 11/3/1978;
    'Die Welt', 8/14/1978.

51 See R. Offergeld, op. cit. (note 25); Hans-Juergen
    Stryk, Verhandlungsstand und Alternativkonzepte in
    der Diskussion um den Gemeinsamen Fonds, in: Th.
    Dams/G. Grohs (eds.), 'Kontroversen in der inter-
    nationalen Rohstoffpolitik', Muenchen 1977.

52 Cf. Bonner Stimmen zum Gemeinsamen Fonds, 'Entwick-
    lung und Zusammenarbeit', 5/1979, p. 12 f.

53 Interview (J.B.) at the Ministry of Economics.

54 Cf. Manfred Tietzel, 'Internationale Rohstoffpolitik',
    Bonn-Bad Godesberg 1977, p. 22.

55 Speech by Herr Hans-Dietrich Genscher, Minister of
    Foreign Affairs of the Federal Republic of Germany,
    at the 11th Special Session of the General Assembly of
    the United Nations on August 27, 1980, in: 'Statements
    and Speeches', Vol. III/No. 13, 27 August 1980, German
    Information Center, New York, p. 6. The following
    figures are from OECD, 'Development Cooperation:
    1980 Review', Paris 1980.

56 Speech by Minister Genscher, loc. cit., p. 6.

57 ibid. p. 8.

58 'DIW-Wochenbericht', 38/79, p. 398.

59 Cf. Axel-Borrmann et al., 'Das Allgemeine Praeferenz-
    system der EG', Hamburg 1979.

60 'Handelsblatt', 12/21/1979.

61 'Bundestagsdrucksache', 7/3986.

62 Cf. 'BMZ-Aktuell', 22 July, 1980.

63 Cf. 'Entwicklungspolitik', Materialien Nr. 65, Bonn
    April 1980 (Rueckwirkungen der Entwicklungszusammen-
    arbeit), p. 17.

64 Cf. Wolfgang Hager, op. cit., p. 15.

65 Genscher (note 55), p. 7 f.

FRANCE:
EGOISM BIEN TEMPERÉ

M.C. Smouts

INTRODUCTION

Unlike her major western partners France has shown little
reluctance to adopt the expression 'New International Economic Order' in her vocabulary. Whereas American delegations
for a while received instructions to oppose any resolution
mentioning the NIEO, and German representatives did not
hide their mistrust toward a 'misleading term' bringing no
progress but futile discussions, the decision-makers in
France did not hesitate to adopt rather early this terminology which sums up in four words all the demands of the
Third World countries.

Addressing himself to the heads of State of French-
speaking Africa (March 1975), and later during official
visits to Algeria (April 1975), Morocco (May 1975) and Zaire
(August 1975), Valéry Giscard d'Estaing stressed the necessity to remedy the 'international economic disorder' and to
replace the 'old which is sinking into the past' with a new
international order. At the beginning of his presidency the
'new order' as a motto on the international scene echoed the
notion of 'change' put forward at home. It is supposed to
'express the will for renovation and concerted management
of change which inspires the French government and must
push the international community forwards.' (1)

Both a historical tradition and a new consciousness explain this conciliatory and positive attitude. Support for a
'new international economic order' would seem to be the logical outcome of the policy which France had pursued for more
than ten years in her relations with developing countries.
From the UNCTAD I on, France has put forward proposals
which met the requirements of the Third World.

An economic doctrine between planned economy and free

market led her to hold a specific stand within the group of industrialized countries. While both the United States and West Germany were firmly attached to the free play of the marked forces, France was in favour of a commodity policy with price stabilization and market organization. She also insisted on the importance of aid and accepted the UN objective of one per cent of GNP as net transfer of resources to developing countries (an objective reduced to 0.7 per cent, which France has never been able to reach), though she proclaimed her intention to replace the broadly disparaged system of 'aid' by a 'cooperation in equality'. At the same time, diplomacy directed toward the Third World in general, West Africa and the Arab countries in particular, has been a constant preoccupation of French foreign policy since the sixties. Valéry d'Estaing pursued that policy by extending it toward East Africa and by trying to strengthen it in the Mediterranean basin.

Relations with the 'South' give France's foreign policy a framework in which the country can exercise her influence and have an international role which she has never given up. The image of France as a 'friend of the Third World' is a part of the Gaullist heritage and has a historical value that is appreciated by all the components of the French body politics.

The 'worldwide' relevance of the NIEO fitted almost perfectly the worldwide ('*mondialiste*') approach of the former French president for whom the major problems 'exist from now on a world level' and 'foreign policy aims at trying to find out the rules permitting to deal with the problems of mankind'. (2) In the economic field, in particular, French officials are guided by a two-fold belief. Firstly, the monetary crisis of 1970-71 and the oil crisis of 1973 have disturbed the world economy, and the monetary and commercial mechanisms set up after World War II no longer meet the challenge of the new international economic deal. An increasing interdependence between internal growth and the external environment makes France particularly vulnerable to this situation of imbalance and confusion which 'is not compatible with a firm and steady management of economy'. The creation of a new international 'order', i.e. 'an organization able to prevent the dramatic upheavals which occurred in recent years' is a necessity for France. (3) Secondly, in a world which is becoming more and more multipolar, the creation of an order capable of 'regulating' interdependence will be possible not through confrontation, but through concerted effort:

'I am convinced', Valéry Giscard d'Estaing stated, 'that
there will be only a world economic order if a world consensus on this system exists ... a world order must not
be the victory of some countries taking advantage of a
temporary power pattern, but it must be a victory, I
would say, of mankind over itself, because the question
is a question of worldwide economic organization of mankind.'

The year 1973 brought about an important change: OPEC
proved that no lasting international order could be set up if
the Third World countries did not help define the rules of the
game. France understood this quite early and, contrary to
the United States, she adopted an attitude of dialogue and
conciliation from the very beginning of the oil crisis: Michel
Jobert suggested a Euro-Arab conference to convene in
November 1973 and then a UN conference on energy in January 1974, while refusing to be part of a coalition including
the largest oil consumers within an international energy
agency which was discussed in Washington in February 1974.
Especially between October 1974 and June 1977, France under-
took a very intensive diplomatic activity and made every possible effort to initiate negotiations which were to allow a true
North-South dialogue. Significantly enough, in the agreements reached during the Conference on International Economic Cooperation (CIEC), French officials particularly point
out the last part of the communique calling for the pursuing of
of the North-South dialogue.
    Thus, during the first years following the adoption of the
Declaration on a New International Economic Order by the UN,
France could claim, with evidence, to have understood the
necessity of, and the stakes involved in the negotiations between developing and industrialized countries. She has proposed a framework and procedures for the definition of a new
world order.
    As far as the content of the new order to be set up is con-
cerned, France's contribution is a lot more nebulous. There
is an evident gap between the worldwide humanitarian points
of view which her diplomats express in international forums
and the quite pragmatic approach of her experts and economic agents on three important items on the NIEO agenda:
Commodity Trade, Industrialization and Transfer of Technology, Aid and Development Finance.

THE NATURE OF THE RESPONSE

The Restructuring of the Commodity Markets

Well before the expression of 'NIEO' appeared and even
before the representatives of the Third World demanded an
'integrated programme' within the UNCTAD after vain
attempts to reach commodity agreements, France favoured
negotiations between producers and consumers to regulate
commodity trade. French politicians and economists agree on
the need for a multilateral stabilization scheme. As one top
official says: 'This is neither a tactical position nor a position required by circumstances, we know that it is in our
interest as consumers to strive for agreement and for regulation of the commodity markets.' (4)
      Highly dependent on raw material imports (5), the French
economy is very much affected by world price fluctuations,
in oil, of course, but also in industrially processed agricultural products (cotton, wool, wood), and in agricultural raw
materials (for example France must import 85 per cent of her
needs for protein for animal consumption). Any disruption of
supplies affecting the price or the amount of key industrial
raw materials (in particular copper, phosphates, chrome,
cobalt, titanium, zirconium, platinum for which France is
totally dependent on her imports) would have far-reaching
consequences for strategic sectors (arms) as well as for all
the channels of production in important branches such as
electronics, aeronautics, automobiles, etc. (6)
      The security of supply and price stabilization are thus
major concerns for France since erratic price fluctuations
counteract any internal policy of stabilization of consumer
prices and thwart the efforts made to reduce inflation.
Besides, in international conferences and in bilateral summits
with African leaders, France declares to be concerned with
'prices - it has to be said - imposed by consumers on producers below net cost, thus impeding the normal development
of the latter'. (7) Finally, we must remember that developing countries are not the major producers of many commodities. Industrialized countries account for a large fraction of
the total world supply of some raw materials including metals,
minerals and food crops. Therefore, negotiations on commodity agreements do not always reflect the usual cleavage
between developing countries and rich nations.
      Thus, theoretically, France did not consider that de-
mands of the Third World producers for 'stable' and 'beneficial' prices unreasonable. Unlike the United States and
Germany, she agreed that the prices of commodities should

not be solely governed by the law of supply and demand.
On the diplomatic level, the question of price stabilization of
primary commodities was a subject on which France could
show some flexibility and thereby demonstrate her willingness to search for a new economic order. At UNCTAD IV in
Nairobi 1976, all the discussions focused on the 'Integrated
Programme' and the 'Common Fund' which would finance it.
Between the 'Group of 77' which was anxious to see the
problem of commodities discussed in a global framework
including prices stabilization, buffer stocks and the creation
of 6 billions dollar Fund on the one hand and, on the other,
the large industrialized countries which firmly opposed any
planned market organization and refused to work in the
direction of a Common Fund, France worked for conciliation.
The French Minister of Economics and Finance proposed a
compromise half-way between the global demands of the '77'
and Kissinger's 'case-by-case' approach: there would be
case-by-case negotiations and an individual fund for every
product agreement. Once four or five individual funds existed, a common fund would be created to coordinate the activity of these funds. It would be financed by the cash surpluses of specific funds and by loans from the World Bank and
the IMF. In suggesting this 'umbrella fund' less ambitious
than the '77's' project but less disturbing for the free-
marketeers, France was the first large industrialized country
(along with The Netherlands, Sweden and Norway) to agree
to the idea of a central mechanism acting as a buffer pool
of individual commodity organizations. Contrary to the
United States, Great Britain, and especially West Germany
who expressed reservations until the very end, France voted
without an interpretative statement for Resolution 93 IV which
created the Integrated Programme for Commodities.
    Only a political will to avoid the failure of UNCTAD IV
allowed a partial harmonization of the positions within Group
B (the Western countries in UNCTAD) as well as among the
'Nine' of the EC. The same political will to avoid the failure
of the North-South dialogue led to the adoption of a reference
to the Common Fund at the end of the Paris Conference
(CIEC) in 1977. An agreement was reached on the principal
elements of the Common Fund in March 1979. France did her
best to maintain this political will and to bring the EC as such
to play a role in the negotiation.
    Both sides have made concessions on several important
points: the '77' agreed that the Common Fund would only
benefit the International Commodity Agreements (ICA) involving producers *and* consumers and that the Fund would draw
its main resources from ICA cash deposits and from loans.

'Group B' accepted the idea of a capital amounting to 555 million dollars at first to finance stocking operations (the '77' asked for 2 billion dollars plus a 4 billion dollar loan) and it agreed on a 350 million dollar account, the 'Second Window' which would stimulate production, processing and marketing of commodities in the Third World. In March 1980 France declared she would give 15 million dollars as a voluntary contribution to this 'Second Window': less than Norway (22 million) and The Netherlands (17 million) but more than the large free-market countries which still oppose the 'Second Window' and have offered nothing so far.

Up to now, little progress has been made in the establishment of the Integrated Programme. Contrary to the initial demands of the '77' the Fund will not be able to finance entirely the different commodity agreements; it will be able at best to encourage the conclusion of new agreements by lowering the contribution of the member States and by facilitating access to financial markets. But negotiations have yet to be concluded. For the eighteen core commodities involved (8) only ten had been discussed; of these ten, five of them were already regulated by international agreements. (9) The other five have not been discussed nor has any consensus been reached. Only agreement on rubber has been concluded.

The problem of restructing the commodity market still remains unsolved and the fundamental dilemma which lies at the heart of the question of stabilization has not yet been settled: should commodity *prices* be stabilized by an *ex ante* intervention (as the Integrated Programme for Commodities scheme does) or should export *incomes* be stabilized *ex post* (following the STABEX system)? The '77' favours the first solution. Non-interventionist countries prefer the second one which has the ideological advantage of not interfering with the determination of prices. At UNCTAD V in Manilla 1979, a German proposition for a worldwide STABEX was rejected by Group B. For the time being, France sticks to her preference for securing through commodity agreements a stabilization of prices on a long-term basis. She considers that these mechanisms allow more stable and secure supplies than a worldwide STABEX system would: it is a question less of mitigating the effects of the market instability than of deal ing with its causes. It is interesting to notice that France has been the first 'big' industrialized country to sign the agreement reached on 27 June, 1980, which established the Common Fund (on 4 November 1980, after Indonesia, Ecuador, The Netherlands, Denmark, Finland, Norway and Sweden). However, in the theoretical and practical competition which seems to have developed between the STABEX system and the

Inegrated Programme, it is not sure that the practical advantages of the former will not one day prevail over the symbolic appeal of the latter.

Considering the lack of progress at a worldwide level, France estimates and argues that the relations set up between the EC and the LDCs bring the developing countries involved a great asset in agricultural matters and that the Lome II convention is even 'better' than Lome I. Concerning the mineral raw materials, France focuses on negotiations for international agreements on the commodities which are most important to her: copper, tungsten and tin. As far as the other raw materials are concerned, the working papers for the Eight Plan suggest that France proposes and supports multilateral structures for information and agreement. Finally, France is more and more interested in the exploration and processing of minerals as well as in mining investments in the developing countries, either through bilateral cooperation or, on the European level, through the 'SYSMIN' system established by the Lome II convention. (10)

During this intense debate on the Integrated Programme and the Common Fund, the Third World claims for 'stable' and 'profitable' prices have been somewhat watered down. One would think that when France voted without reservation for Resolution 93 (IV) which aims at improving and maintaining 'the real income of individual developing countries' as well as 'protecting them from fluctuations in export earnings from commodities', she did it because the text was dim enough and the principle of price indexation of LDC's exports did not appear clearly endorsed. On this subject France was more elusive than the United States or West Germany who clearly opposed any stabilization in real terms, but it is impossible to draw the conclusion that she would accept an indexation system involving necessarily a rise in her import costs.

At the end of UNCTAD V the discussion on commodities seemed to be in a deadlock. A New International Order built upon the improvement of the terms of trade for all the developing nations seemed even more remote. France who had, for years, voiced many proposals on this subject added nothing new. A few months later at the UNIDO conference she did not offer much either when the '77' submitted the bill for their industrialization programme ... take it or leave it ...

Third World Industrialization and Technology Transfer

When voting, in 1975, for the 'plan of action for development and industrial cooperation' in Lima, France appeared much

more aware of Third World concerns than her Western partners. (11) It is also true, however that it was then a question of rescuing the Paris Conference and it was time for
mediation.

Basically the differences between France and the '77' are
nonetheless important. As far as France is concerned, the
question of industrialization must be included in the framework of both development and the North-South dialogue.
Consequently, a phenomenon which still benefits a limited
number of countries while ignoring other forms of development, agricultural ones for instance, should not be privi-
leged. The question of financing industrialization must be
included in the overall question of financing development.

In January 1980, at the Third UNIDO Conference in New
Delhi, the French delegation was ready to discuss these
issues. It was backed by a policy of industrial 'redeployment' initiated by the Barre government - no matter the
criticism this policy received domestically - which it intended
to present as 'a policy of economic adaptation aiming especially at allowing the Third World to get a share in the distribution of international industrial production'. (12) But the
figues submitted by the '77' did not leave either the French
delegation or the whole of Group B a leg to stand on. Industrial restructuring, fine! but the targets assessed by the '77'
for every branch (iron and steel, fertilizers, petrochemicals,
capital goods) were unacceptable. As for the amount required for a new international Fund for industrialization (300
billion dollars before the year 2000) to be run by the developing countries, it sounded like nonsense. The 'unrealistic'
drain from the 'already depressed' French economy would
lead to a 5 million francs yearly deficit. (13) The 'maximalist'
position of the '77' at UNIDO III was understood as the
announcement of a new deal before the Eleventh Special Session of the General Assembly which was to begin in August
1980 in New York. It expressed the growing impatience of
the Third World with the slow progress being made and also
a real misunderstanding of the problems generated by the
crisis in the industrialized countries.

France has no objection to the basic target of rising the
share of the developing countries in the world industrial
production - to at least 25 per cent. Several studies have
shown that this share grows quite slowly (7 per cent in 1973;
8.6 per cent in 1975; at least 9 per cent in 1979) (14) and
that the impact of LDC industrialization will not disturb the
industrialized economies very deeply for some while. (15)
Yet the process of Third World industrialization is admittedly
ineluctable. While this evolution - the effects of which are

already visible in daily life - arouses some fearful concern, official reports and authoritative spokesmen emphasize that this process must not be considered as a mere threat to the French economy. (16) On the contrary, the industrialization of the Third World may help the French economy start growing again, if the production structures are adjusted to the new constraints of world competition and if the opportunity offered by the needs and the potential markets of the Third World is considered. The major role played by the exports of equipment goods in equilibrating the French balance of trade is a good example.

Thus, the interest which France has in taking an active part in an unavoidable evolution is broadly understood but only recently has a coherent policy been defined. An 'opinion' adopted on 15 November 1978 by the French Economic and Social Council on 'The future of French Industry and the new international distribution of industrial production' emphasized that: 'concerning the investments in, and the technology transfers to the developing countries, the Council states that up to now neither the government, nor the professional organizations has a clearly defined policy.' The Council recommended the following policy: 'in a general manner, to encourage and facilitate investments and transfers in the LDCs, especially when the investments can contribute to France's active presence and to the promotion of French products of all kinds.'

In the present current of thought concerning the policy of redeploying the French economy, technology exports appear as an essential component of the trading and industrial strategy. The reasons are first of all political: transfer of technology as the effective transfer of industrial know-how has become one of the basic demands of the Third World. French enterprises could not expect to continue selling manufactured goods to developing countries if they did not accept exporting techniques too. In particular, one cannot sell industrial products to the Third World while denying it the means of industrialization. (17) For the experts of the Ministry of Industry, the old dilemma - either exports of products or supply of technology - is pointless: a country will no longer be able to export products if it does not export technological know-how at the same time. This new French attitude also meets economic requirements in so far as the transfer of technology supports exports. By creating a receptive environment for French products and side-effects as well, the sale of knowledge is a means of penetrating foreign markets.

Beside big companies which have been practising some

kinds of technological transfer for a long time (ELF in Nigeria, Creusot-Loire in India, CFP in Abu-Dhabi, etc.), small and medium-sized industries are being officially incited to play a growing role in this trend. Through a policy of incentives, French officials wish to overcome the reluctance of French enterprises which, contrary to their German, Japanese or Italian counterparts, still do not like the idea of transferring technology outside their traditional and well-known markets (mainly Maghreb and French-speaking Africa). (18) France's view on the role of small and medium-sized industries in the developing countries concurs with the views presently endorsed by UNCTAD or UNIDO. (19)

Thus France has no trouble in adopting a mediating attitude in international fora even on the principle of strengthening technological capabilities in the Third World, all the more since France holds an intermediate position in the international technology trade. She does not belong to the small group of industrialized countries whose balance is always showing a surplus nor is she a net technology-importer. Her main technology transfers are done with western countries and she has the interest of a country which receives transnational firms and buys technology at the same time. (20) However, her interests as an industrialized country differ from those of the '77' on the conditions of the transfer of techniques and know-how. Whatever the goodwill of diplomats may be, the managers of French enterprises who know how costly the development of their processes is will have some difficulty in admitting that technology is part of the 'common heritage of mankind'! For them the transfer of technology means paying off research and breaking through new markets, it is never a goal in itself and the purpose is certainly not to sell techniques which will be used by others to penetrate one's own markets! For this reason, the discussions about the rules which would lower the net cost of the transfer of technology are difficult. In particular, the French oppose the propositions of the '77' calling for the commercialization of manufactured goods made with the help of imported technology.

But, beyond the present debate about the obligations which a Code of Conduct adopted at the UN (21) would impose upon the governments accepting it, the question of the binding power of such a Code seems unsolvable. The demands of the '77' for a legally binding code are opposed by professional organizations in France. For the CNPF (National Centre of French Management), whose influence on the matter is considerable, the problem of technology transfer is an industrial one which must be treated as such and

cannot be solved by international regulations and institutions. Furthermore, while acknowledging the interest of
some provisions of the Code, the enterprises refuse to give
up their contractual freedom and to submit their technology
transfer contracts to the rules of this Code. (22) It should
be added that the French government is probably all the
more willing to take the wishes of the top management into
consideration as its 'decontrolling' policy pursued for the
past two years aims at transferring to enterprises numerous
responsibilities which were traditionally those of public
authorities. This is not favourable background to international measures which might impose regulations on enterprises.

One would imagine that the French government would
have tried to make up for the evasive responses it gave in
the fields of trade and technology by increasing its amount
of Public Aid for Development. Such a move would also have
mitigated the contradiction between its wish to remain a 'preferential interlocutor' for the Third World and its actual
policy. There again budgetary constraints did not permit
any significant gesture on behalf of the poor countries.
'Conceptual' diplomacy must strive to compensate for the
weakness of 'material' allowances.

Public Aid and Development Finance

At every given opportunity France pledges her will to meet
'as soon as possible' the objective adopted by the United
Nations to allocate 0.7 per cent of the GNP to Official
Development Assistance (ODA). She claims to rank fourth
among the main donors. In fact French public aid is about
0.6 per cent of GNP, but this honourable performance is
misleading because more than 40 per cent of this aid is used
for overseas departments and territories. Nevertheless, it
is necessary to point out a noteworthy change in this trend:
after a perceptible and sustained decrease in the amount of
public aid granted between 1970 (0.66 per cent of GNP) and
1978 (0.59 per cent), the whole of the ODA in the 1979
budget increased by 12 per cent. It affects 14 ministerial
departments, but, of a sum of 6,863 million francs, 6,739
million is controlled by three departments - Cooperation,
Foreign Affairs and Economics - and half of the credits
(3,444 millions) goes to the Ministry of Cooperation and is
assigned to Africa. (23) This trend reversal is largely due
to an increase in the French contributions to the EC and to
a noticeable rise in the bilateral transfers, together with a

more active presence in multilateral institutions. Thus
France has raised her capital subscription in the World Bank,
and entered the African Bank for Development where she
ranks fourth. She participates in all the regional Banks and
their funds; she has decided to be a founder member of the
International Fund for Agricultural Development. (24)

In contrast with her long-standing reservations about
multilateral aid, this new behaviour is a political gesture.
When representatives in Parliament worry about a trend toward multilateralization which is contrary to the Gaullist tradition of independent and 'sovereign' assistance, they get
the following explanation: 'Where international organizations
are financing concrete programmes and projects for example
in the field of technical assistance, we receive benefits in
form of consultations, equipment purchases, subcontracting
which amount to a multiple of our initial contribution. (25)
For the United Nations Development Programme it is true
France ranks tenth among the contributors but third among
the beneficiaries. In contributing 5.74 per cent to the first
five replenishments of ODA, France 'has obtained up to
now, on the average, a little more than 8 per cent of the
orders for goods and services ODA deals with. French
enterprises from the public works branch (water, transportation, electricity, education) are in a particularly good
position and get an especially large amount of the project
orders financed by ODA in Africa.' (26)

At a time when the budgetary contraction called for by
the Finance minister is an obstacle to an increase in public
aid higher than the increase in GNP, as wished by the
Foreign Affairs, this type of mercantile argument put forward for domestic purposes is not to be neglected. But,
beyond the economic benefits expected from the feed-back
effect, the political stakes are high: it is a question of
attaining credibility in the North-South negotiations and,
especially, to slow down the deterioration of aid to Africa
and to rescue the most seriously affected countries. (27)

Because of her commitments and responsibilities on the
African continent, France is particularly interested in the
latter question. Of the 45 Most Seriously Affected Countries
(MSACs) listed by the World Bank, half are African; and of
the 31 Less Developed Countries (LDCs) 21 are Africa.
France who, for budgetary reasons, estimates that she cannot undertake an important action by herself, has done her
utmost to initiate a joint action which would be geographically limited enough to be effective and would not dissolve in
the ocean of deficiencies in which the poorest countries are
immersed. This involves bitter discussions with other

industrial countries who are also concerned about helping the poorest countries but do not have the same geographical interests: in particular, France and Great Britain disagree on the question of including India among the MSACs.

A first attempt at a concerted action in Africa was launched on a French initiative. In May 1976, at the end of a Franco-African summit, Valéry Giscard d'Estaing recommended

a great, daring and generous initiative for Africa and with Africa ... a Fund endowed with important resources must be created by the industrial States having historical ties with Africa, which the United States of America would be able to join ... the organization would be ordered around two elements: on the one hand, a council of donors; on the other, an exclusively African council of user. In order to bring about this project, France would consider the calling of a conference of donor countries, if the nations concerned agreed with the idea.

Progressively a concerted Action for the Development of Africa was implemented. Furthermore, at the end of the Paris Conference, the industrialized countries decided upon the granting of the exceptional amount of one billion dollars in aid for the poorest countries. The EC decided to distribute a 385 million dollar amount through ODA. France contributed 14.67 per cent of the total amount according to the plan established by the Council of Ministers on 3 May 1977. This percentage is less than that contributed by West Germany (30.93 per cent) and Great Britain (29.87 per cent). Finally, France asked several times that the funds dispersed by ODA and the World Bank take into consideration the 'basic needs and potential resources of the populations', emphasizing that a 'special effort' had to be agreed upon 'favouring the poorest countries, especially in Africa'. (28)

This insistence on the duty of solidarity with respect to the 'Fourth World' is characteristic of the French approach to the more general problem of financial transfers. France has only agreed to cancel the debts contracted through ODA of a small number of under-developed countries - and much later than many industrialized countries. This decision, announced on the eve of the Manilla Conference, concerned ten countries; Bangladesh, Benin, Burundi, Comores, the Central African Republic, Guinea, Upper Volta, Mali, Niger and Chad, and concerned 747 million francs. In presenting these measures at UNCTAD V, the French Minister of Economics specified clearly:

this financial effort that my country is going to accomplish must be understood as the recognition of the heavy economic burden that debts represent for the poorest nations, while they still have to enter the development process; but it is necessary to be aware of the fact that we cannot go beyond this point, especially as regards the adjustment of debts. (29)

Facing the Group of 77, which considers the measures of alleviating or adjusting debts as 'one of the key elements of the new international economic order', (30) the French position has always been to consider the problem as part of an overall development policy. According to the official doctrine, a simple gesture of debt cancellation makes no sense either in economic or financial terms, and the pertinent question is that of long-term financing for developing countries. On the question of how to finance the current debts of non-oil-producing developing countries, and how to channel new resources to these countries, there are two main points in the very technical propositions set forth by France in different multilateral conferences.

Firstly, France considers that it is necessary to increase the volume of loans granted by the IMF and to make them more attractive. A better distribution of IMF resources, in particular, would grant the developing countries a larger share. France also favours some liberalization of the lending conditions (repayment period, rate of interest, etc.). Her goal is to make the IMF more adapted to the needs of the developing countries and thus to avoid a proliferation of new funds which would be non-cumulative and ineffective. The new pressures on the balance of payments of many developing countries (45 million dollars in 1979, 60 billion dollars in 1980) will make IMF intervention all the more necessary as private commercial banks, the main sources of financing between 1974 and 1978, seem less eager to play this role as the limits of risk have been reached in certain countries.

Secondly, like the other industrial countries, France insists on the importance of oil prices in the external deficit of non-oil producing countries, a statement which makes her (along with her Western partners in the OECD) subject to the accusation of dividing the Group of 77. She emphasizes the negative impact of the increase in oil prices on official assistance for development. She asserts that the OPEC countries have an 'historical responsibility' for the world economic balance for the years to come and that they must assume this responsibility. (31) One of the big questions on the agenda in the French administration is how to induce the

OPEC countries to direct their surplus - which, up until now, has essentially been used as liquidities on international capital markets - toward productive investments in Third World countries, particularly in Africa. To this end, in Nairobi in 1976, France proposed an international system of guarantees intended to lead the flow of international liquidities toward beneficial projects in developing countries. Such a system would have the advantage of a better regularization of the flow of oil revenue surpluses, while establishing more solidarity between lenders, borrowers, and guarantors. Generally, France seems to put more faith in recycling oil revenue surpluses for development than in official aid, and no longer wants to proclaim any financial plan which does not provide an impetus for oil producers to participate.

THE EXPLANATION OF THE RESPONSE

> The whole problem of the North-South dialogue - in relation to the decision-making process in Western countries can be summed up by the question of how to find a link between long-term stakes, which although very important to everyone are often both intricate and vague (such as peace and security), and much more short-term goals capable of mobilizing the main actors involved in the actual development of this dialogue. (32)

This quite relevant remark is particularly true in the case of France. France is perhaps more acutely aware of the long-term consequences of the North-South imbalance than her Western counterparts, but she also feels more threatened than they do by the current changes which take place in her international environment. This dual logic appears clearly in the international negotiations on the issues discussed above: each time the starting point was 'interdependence' and 'mutual benefits' and on each issue the moment of truth was reached when diverging conceptions of the NIEO opposed each other.

For French officials in the Ministry of Foreign affairs, the political and intellectual setting which determined, in 1974-5, the response to the demands for a new economic order is still valid: France must pay attention to the demands of the Third World and a NIEO must be founded which would substitute 'rationality' and 'justice' for the dangerous game of power politics, putting an end to the scandalously growing gap between the masses of poor countries and the minority of industrialized nations. The disorder which the economic

crisis brought to light would be redressed by balancing 'exchanges', 'activities' and 'currencies'. As far as the
'technical' ministries (Treasury, Economics, Industry) and
the economic agents are concerned, the New International
Economic Order is something quite different: it is not a system of global regulation which should be built up for a long-
term period and which should roughly meet the requirements
of the Third World, but the NIEO refers to the dramatic
change in the world geographic economy which is presently
taking place, and the future of France till the end of the
century is at stake. These two visions are not incompatible,
but they imply a different order of priorities. (33)

The expression 'New International Economic Order' is not
a mere motto. It is taken very seriously. The working
papers of the Plan Commisariat and of the Ministry of Industry are significant in this respect: they all take for granted
the new logic of an ineluctable global geo-political turn-
around to which France must adapt herself. The French response to the NIEO is to be found not only in speeches,
negotiations and votes in international institutions. To get
an accurate picture it would be necessary to present the
whole process of re-examination, reorientation and 'redeployment' in which the country is engaged showing the difficulties at every level: disagreements between the Foreign affairs and the Treasury, labour struggles, top management
lobbying, doctrinal disputes, etc. The French response
indeed is incrementally defined through the interrelation between the claims of the Third World and this major challenge
she has to face: the challenge of the other industrialized
countries in a context of exacerbated competition.

A Narrow Way for Action

In the negotiations surrounding the construction of a 'New
Order' France has only limited means. She does not control
the rules of the international game either in the monetary
field or in the commercial field. As far as financing capacity, industry or technology are concerned, she often lags
behind her Western competitors. In many fields the economic
weight of the United States, Germany, Japan, and sometimes
Great Britain, gives these countries a stronger bargaining
power than France has.

Also, on the political level, France's margin of manoeuvre
is narrow. Most of the subjects under discussion lie within
the competence of the EC. This is an advantage but it also
involves uneasy diplomatic exercises. In the UN, experience

shows that progress is best made when there is a triangular
- '77', USA, EC - agreement. Whenever the Nine manage
to agree on a common position, their bargaining power is
high. Their economic strength, the soundness of their civil
service and their political weight make the EC a major partner in negotiations. Giscardian diplomacy cared about this
European dimension even more than that of its predecessors.

Among the different options available in the NIEO debate
(34) France has deliberately chosen that of tightening up
European links. In a way, this choice strengthens her diplomatic position towards the Third World: France has all the
more credit as she is expected to support the Third World's
requests vis-à-vis the influential members of the EC. But
this position of go-between, which the country has held for
more than ten years (since UNCTAD I in 1964 until the Paris
Conference of 1975-7), has its own limits. Either the French
position is different from that of her influential partners
without reducing the internal divisions inside the Community
(as the problem of primary commodities discussed at UNCTAD
or that of industrial investments negotiated at UNIDO shows):
the EC is not able to make substantial new proposals and
France spoils her credit in dead-end negotiations. Or France
adopts a lower profile to favour a compromise, but the solution then appears as a European one and group negotiations
do not show the shades of the different partners' positions.
As the North-South dialogue is marking time, a third attitude
seems to prevail: the answer to the stiffening of the bargaining position of the '77' is a stiffened position of Group B and
France has no longer a distinct profile inside this group.
Just like the other members of the OECD she first pays
attention to her growth rate.

The NIEO: Change of, and Challenge to Growth

While the Third World calls for a reform of the regulations
and structures of international trade and for 'massive transfers' of resources to developing countries, France keeps in
mind the main constraint which is presently pressing hard on
her economy - that of foreign trade.

All the working papers preparing the Eight Plan (35) and
a recent parliamentary report stress that: 'the external balance of the French economy is a major concern, unanimously
and deeply acknowledged by executives in all spheres
whether political or administrative, be it in the labour, business, agricultural or diplomatic sectors.' (36) Since 1958
France has chosen to follow an open trade policy. The

relationship established between growth and integration into the international market (a policy strongly opposed by the French Communist party, a fraction of the Socialist party and some economists) has made the securing of external equilibrium the first condition for the maintenance of the standard of living and employment. But the first oil crisis in 1974, and above all, the oil shocks in 1979 and 1980 have seriously disturbed this equilibrium. France, whose oil imports were 3.54 per cent of her GNP in 1974, now devotes 4.17 per cent of her GNP (for a nearly equal volume) in 1980. (37) In 1979, energy expenses, the main cause of the balance of trade deficit (83.8 billion francs) was nearly double the global deficit (42.4 billions). (38)

In such a context, to better understand the stakes involved for France in the reform of international trade, in the increase of official assistance for development and a better transfer of technology, one has to keep certain data in mind.

First, the French market structures and balance of trade are significant: the greatest deficits are with the large industrialized nations and the oil producers, while surpluses (apart from Switzerland and the United Kingdom) come from the Third World and developing countries.

> Nearly one-fourth of France's imports come from developing countries in the form of energy-related products, food products and raw materials; these countries absorb a quarter of French exports in the form of manufactured goods. It is the importance of this balance which makes positive French trade with this part of the world even if the oil imports bill does not allow an equilibrium to be reached. (39)

Of all the Western countries France is the least open to the Third World. In 1978 LDCs provided 4.1 per cent of her imports in manufactured products, two times less than Third World industrial exports to West Germany and Great Britain, and five times less than the exports the United States and Japan. (40) In return, the industrial exports of France have been seven times greater than the manufactured deliveries coming from developing countries (for West Germany or Great Britain, sales to LDCs are 4.5 times greater than the purchase of manufactured products). Thus, the Third World, provider of energy and raw materials, is also an important customer for French exporters. (41)

Second, the geographical structure of French exports shows the weakness of the French position on Third World markets. On the one hand, the commercial preponderance of France only exists within the limits of her former colonial empire. On the other hand, out of seventeen of its best clients, ten have a per capita GNP under 340 dollars. This situation is worrying for two reasons: the geographical re-deployment of sales, which is vital, runs against keen com-petition from West Germany, Japan and the United States. These trading powers are much better prepared than France by a traditionally active presence on international markets, and, for the first two, by a better adaptation of the indus-trial production to international evolution. But, France will also encounter growing competition from new industrialized nations, and from the South-South circuits which are now emerging. Furthermore, France, who has sustained her sales through an extensive effort of exports subsidies, has an increasing number of clients among countries whose bal-ance of payments is largely in deficit. The situation can be summarized as such: France lends in francs, while she bor-rows in dollars, and her debtors are less solvent than her creditors.

Third, although the French market remains for the most part closed to Third World products, the industrialization of developing countries is a challenge and raises a large debate among the main economic actors, government and enterprises. An important report published by the Plan Commisariat in 1978 has evaluated the employment losses due to imports from the Third World. It shows that the industrial balance of trade between France and the Third World has on the whole benefited French industry and employment, leading to a net gain of 100,000 jobs. However, two points moderate this broad positive statement. In some branches of industry (e.g. textile, leather, footwear), and some regions where business is concentrated in a small number of products, competition from the Third World has caused bankruptcies, lay-offs and severe regional imbalances. (42)

This 'Berthelot Report' is interpreted in two ways in France. Some, like the Ministry of Foreign Affairs, stress the main conclusion of the report, pointing out the French interest in encouraging the industrial development of the Third World in order to ensure middle-term growth which means employment and higher standards of living. The re-presentatives of the regions hurt by the crisis and the vic-tims of 'intersectorial reallocations' take another stance! They are all the better understood as this restructuring leads to dramatic upheavals. Finally, in a country which has a long history of protectionism, the temptation to protect one-self against foreign products is stronger than the impulse to invest on external markets and to develop keen competition.

CONCLUSION

The economic crisis that France faces is too hazardous for
her to have a clear idea of what a suitable 'new order'
should be. Over the years, the French response to the
NIEO developed progressively. It is more precise about
what the 'new order' should not be than what it should.
Along with the other industrialized countries, France has
fought a minor but highly symbolic battle about the article
which should precede the acronym. France's insistence on
'a' NIEO and not 'the' NIEO means that the content of the
new order is still to be defined and that everything is not
negotiable. In spite of her efforts to be open-minded in the
multilateral debates, she opposes the Third World countries
both on substance and on procedures.
    Contrary to the '77' for whom all parts of the NIEO are
tightly linked together, (43) France does not want an overall
change in the international economic system. Instead she
calls for concerted and successive 'adjustments' in the main
fields. France does not believe in the virtue of plenary meetings although she accepts playing that game. She prefers a
restrained dialogue between a limited number of states or
regions.
    While the Third World repeatedly questions the IMF and
the World Bank privileges, France supports these organizations, even if she wants them to pay more attention to the
new problems of developing countries. (44) She also opposes
the creation of an International Committee on Debt which - if
not substituted for the Paris Club (Creditors' Club) - could
more closely associate the Third World to its decisions. As
for the redistribution of wealth, there again France agrees
on the principle but holds that she has reached the limits
of her capacity. She suggests (referring to the oil producing countries) that 'a positive approach of interdependence
implies that the distribution of surplus wealth be estimated
among all the international community members and that procedures be possibly settled in order to correct the accumula-
tion process which only benefits a few.' (45)
    Notwithstanding the 'mondialist' themes discussed in
1975, France supports in practice the creation of a new
'international' order, the finality of which is to implement a
balance between the different economic areas, i.e. OECD
countries, OPEC countries, semi-industrialized countries,
other developing countries, planned economy countries. In
1964 France stressed that the '77' should not be considered
as a whole, she now stands for a 'differentiated' policy.
With regard to trade, France favours the general principle

of promoting Third World exports. There is no question of
formally challenging the developing countries' vested interests such as the Generalized Scheme of Preferences, partial
exemptions, non-reciprocity and so on. But France favours
trading regulations which differ according to the level of
development of the countries involved. A 'differentiated'
application of principles and a stronger selectivity would re-
strain the competition of manufactured products from the
Third World which hurts several national branches, at least
temporarily and thereby give the industrialized countries
some time for adjustment. Then it should be understood
(and this is a reference to countries such as Mexico, Argentina, South Korea, Taiwan or Singapore) that 'gradually, as
a certain industrialization level and a real export capacity are
are reached, the common rules of GATT should be endorsed.'
Of course such an attitude runs against the interests of the
Group of 77, the only strength of which lies in the political
weight of its cohesion.

The French view on international trade which, though
formally favouring free trade, calls nevertheless for 'some
organizing of free trade', seems to favour regional arrangements. UN bodies are useful for promoting ideas and preparing for changes but the economic process of adjustment
to Third World development can only occur if the concert
with close partners helps to harmonize and reduce the costs
for adjustment. A new dimension for regional cooperation is
now seriously taken into consideration: the 'Euro-Arab-
African trilogue'. This venture is supported at the highest
level and is presently mobilizing some of the brightest minds
in the French administration. Only an ill-disposed commen-
tator would see it as a clever system permitting the European
countries, thanks to Arab petrocurrencies, to help African
states develop so that they would be better able to buy European exports. The scheme is presented as a 'political' one,
as a sort of 'Chart of Solidarity' or an 'Euro-Arab-African
Helsinki' to be founded upon six principles - non-interven-
tion, respect for boundaries, anti-colonialism and anti-
apartheid, an anti-hegemonic clause, the free flow of men
and ideas, security through development.

French public opinion is rather helpless in these matters.
There is no debate in the media or in Parliament about the
two main points involved: the French economic adjustment to
the NIEO challenge and the general policy regarding the
Third World. The first lesson taught by the opinion polls
is how poorly informed the French are. (46) However 50
per cent of the population are interested in the subject.
They are not really adverse to public aid nor to the allevia-

tion of debts for the poorest countries (43 per cent agree with the idea; 36 per cent are against it). They are quite realistic, 55 per cent of the respondents estimate that the reason why France is assisting developing countries is 'a concern for French economic and political interests' while 22 per cent ascribe public aid to 'a concern for helping the poorest countries'. Concerning the direct impact of imports from the Third World on employment, the French public opinion is divided, 45 per cent of the respondents think that these imports cause significant unemployment whereas another 45 per cent totally reject this interpretation.

This split is significant because it is parallel to the split which divides the left on a connected problem - does the working class benefit from the surpluses earned by industrialized countries thanks to the existing trading system? (47) Another intense debate puts those in favour of a self-contained development against those who support a larger integration in the international market, those who refute the new international division of labour and those who are searching for a way to adapt to it. This debate has not only divided the left - Communist Party, the general Confederation of Labour (CGT, close to the Communist Party) and a part of the Socialist Party on the one side, and on the other the majority of the Socialist Party and the French Confederation of Labour (CFDT, closer to the Socialist Party). It does not only concern the Third World question. It has divided experts and government, it involves the overal economic choices of the former Barre administration. We could not possibly summarize it here. (48)

Actually, the men in power have already made up their mind and the hard core of their policy regarding the Third World aims at making trading partners out of the developing countries. Thus the question is less of creating a new order than of rearranging the present one, and rather of speeding up North-South exchanges than changing the character of these exchanges. From this point of view of a well-understood self-interest, the search for a NIEO is mainly the search for patterns of behaviour which would permit the survival of the existing system while avoiding an international trade war due to wild-cat unilateral protectionist policies, and preventing a collapse in the international financial system under the weight of the debts of developing countries. The undemonstrable assumption being that a beneficial 'efficiency' for the North would go together with 'justice', as the Third World requires with some good reason.

Notes

1   J. Sauvagnargues, Minister of Foreign Affairs, at the
    seventh emergency session of the United Nations, on
    5 September 1975.
2   Statement made by M. Giscard d'Estaing, on 20 Decem-
    ber 1974. On this subject see: Zorgbibe, Charles, 'A la
    recherche d'un Nouvel Ordre économique mondial; La
    France: les initiatives d'une puissance moyenne',
    'Revue française de Science politique', August 1976,
    pp. 724–734; and 'La diplomatie giscardienne ou les con-
    tradictions du 'mondialisme', 'Le Monde Diplomatique',
    March 1978, p. 3.
3   Lecture given by Valéry Giscard d'Estaing on Le nouvel
    ordre économique mondial, at the Polytechnical Institute
    on 28 October 1975, 'Bulletin de l'Economie et des
    Finances', January–March 1976, pp. 5 f.
4   Hugon, Jean-Pierre, 'La politique française d'approvi-
    sionnement en matières premières minérales, p. 152 in
    'Matières premières et échanges internationaux', Claude
    Mouton et Philippe Chalmin, eds., Paris Economica, 1980.
5   The rate of global dependence on all raw materials is
    estimated to be 55 per cent, agricultural- and energy-
    related raw materials excluded.
6   Cf. 'Matidères de base, approvisionnement et compétiti-
    vité', Report given by the working group to the General
    Commissariat of the Plan in Paris, 'La Documentation
    française', 1979, pp. 37–39.
7   Statement made by Mr. Fourcade, Minister of Finance,
    in 'Le Monde', 11 May 1976.
8   Coffee, cacao, tea, sugar, cotton, jute, rubber, hard
    fibre, copper, tin, banana, meat, vegetable oil, tropical
    timber, iron ore, bauxite, manganese and phosphates.
9   Coffee, sugar, tin, olive oil and cacao.
10 This was the case for copper which had the 'honour' of
    opening the preparatory meetings specified by Resolution
    93 (IV). Cf. Legoux, Pierre, Les Nègociations inter-
    nationales sur le cuivre: mars 1976–october 1978, pp.
    253–259 in 'Matières premières et échanges internation-
    aux', op. cit.
11 Resolution adopted with 82 votes for, 1 vote against
    (United States) and seven abstentions (Belgium, Canada,
    West Germany, Israel, Italy, Japan, United Kingdom).
12 André Rossi, head of the French delegation at UNIDO on
    January 23, 1980. Also, see his statement about the New
    Delhi Conference in 'Le Figaro', 15 February 1980.
13 'Le Monde', 12 February, 1980.

14 'ONU, Chronique', April 1980, p. 28.
15 Pisani, Edgar, 'La France dans le conflit économique mondial', Paris, Hachette, 1979, pp. 288-289.
16 Cf. Stoffaes, Christian, L'industrie française et les défis de la concurrence étrangère, 'Problèmes Economiques', 14 February 1979, pp. 3-11; in particular, see: Berthelot, Yves, and Tardy, Gérard, 'Le défi économique du Tiers monde', Paris, La Documentation française 1978, 2 volumes.
17 Ministry of industry, 'Les transferts de technologie aux pays en développement par les petites et moyennes entreprises', Report given by the working group headed by Alain Weil, Paris, La Documentation française, March 1980, pp. 19-21, 112.
18 Cf. the Dakar Club Conference on 'la coopé ration industrielle et commerciale avec l'Afrique', held in Lyon on 7 June 1979, where the lack of information of the leaders of the PMI on technology transfers was obvious. Account given in 'Le Monde', 16 June 1979.
19 Cf. Judet, Pierre, Par rapport à la revendication du Tiers monde en matière d'accès à la technologie: positions et propositions françaises, pp. 279-306 in 'Le défi économique du Tiers monde, op. cit.', Appendixes.
20 Cf. Bizec, René-François, Le Code de conduite pour les transferts de technologie dans la construction du nouvel ordre économique international, in 'Un Code de conduite pour le transfert de technologie', Paris, Economica, 1980, pp. 8 f.
21 For a good presentation of the complex institutional framework in which the works are going on cf. Langlois, Alain, 'Les Nations Unies et le transfert de technologie', Paris, Economica, 1980, p. 222.
22 Ibid., Daudet, Yves, and Temy, Bernard, 'Le but et le role du Code de conduite', pp. 67-68, as well as Bonassies, Pierre,'Les transferts internationaux de technologie et le droit communautaire',p. 149.
23 Source: 'Actuel développement', 1978, no. 27.
24 With a very modest contribution (25 million dollars), France has a 'weight' which is inferior to that of Holland or Sweden; on the creation of IFAD see 'Annuaire français de droit international', 1977, pp. 650-654.
25 Stirn, Oliver, Secretary of State for Foreign Affairs, in a speech before the Senate, 24 November 1978, 'Journal Officiel', Senate Debates, pp. 3668 et 3675.
26 General Report by the Finance Commission on the government financial bill for 1979, Tome III, appendix 10-I, Senate, 'Documents', No. 74.

27 It was calculated that aid to French-speaking countries
    was twice their oil imports bill in 1973. It represented
    a third of their oil imports bill in 1979.
28 Monory, René, Minister of Economy in a speech given on
    September 25, 1978, et annual meeting of the Governor's
    Council of the IMF and the World Bank.
29 Monory, René, in Manila, on 8 May 1979.
30 Cf. the Council on Trade and Development Session at
    UNCTAD in March 1978, mainly devoted to the Third
    World endebtedness.
31 See speech given by René Monory in Manila on 8 May 1979.
32 Bressand, Albert, in an important article, Six dia-
    logues en quête d'auteur, 'Politique étrangère', June
    1980, p. 314.
33 Speech by Valéry Giscard d'Estaing, on 28 October 1975,
    often repeated by French delegates in international eco-
    nomic conferences.
34 Cf. Perrin de Brichambaut, Marc, L'architecture d'un
    nouvel ordre et les options de la France, 'Economie et
    Humanisme', March-April 1976, pp. 49-50. Thress scen-
    arios are proposed: 1) A strengthening of European
    solidarity; 2) An independent France playing a case by
    case bilateral game, and 3) the 'mondialiste' game fully
    played. A report by the group led by Jacques Les-
    ourne, has listed a hierarchy of the following solidari-
    ties: European solidarity ('before all others'), the
    whole of developed countries with a market economy, the
    middle East and Africa, and the newly industrialized
    countries, 'Demain la France dans le monde', La Docu-
    mentation française, Paris, 1980, pp. 169-170. It must
    be noted that there has never been a scenario which
    evoked the splitting of European communities; was it
    censorship or self-censorship?
35 The Eight Plan will cover the period between 1981-1985.
36 Pisant, Edgar, 'La France dans le conflit économique
    mondial', op. cit., p. 10.
37 Source: 'Conjoncture', a monthly bulletin published by
    the Banque de Paris et des Pay-sBas, July 1980, p. 99.
38 Source: 'L'Expansion', July-September 1980, p. 9.
39 International economic and external exchanges Commit-
    tee, Report by the Third World group, April 1980, p. 22.
40 Source: Lemperiere, Jean, 'Trente graphiques compara-
    tifs sur les échanges entre pays industriels et pays en
    développement, ;a concurrence sur les divers marchés,
    le rôle du Tiers monde comme débouché', Report given
    on March 15, 1980, pp. 56-57.
41 An example: in 1979, with a budget deficit of 38 billion

francs for industrial products in trading with rich countries, France reaches a budgetary balance with a surplus
of 65.8 billion francs in trading with countries outside
OECD.

42 Berthelot, Yves, and Tardy, Gérard, 'Le défi économique de Tiers monde', op. cit.

43 See Bedjaoui, Homammed, 'Pour un nouvel ordre économique international', UNESCO, 1978, p. 295.

44 Monory, René, in Manila, on 8 May 1979.

45 Ibid.

46 Opinion-poll by IFOP 'Frères des Hommes, published in
'Les Français ont-ils peur du Tiers monde', Paris, May
1979.

47 Cf. Beaud, Michel, Bernis, Gérard de, and Masini, Jean,
eds., 'La France et le Tiers monde', extracts from the
conference held at Vincennes in 1978 by the Third World
Economists' Association, Grenoble, Presses Universit-
aires de Grenoble, 1979, Part two, as well as Boucquet,
Jean-Pierre, Developpement et nouvel ordre économique
mondial: un point de vue syndical, 'CFDT Aujord'hui',
January-February 1979, and 'Les socialistes et le Tiers
monde', Paris, Berger Levrault, 1977.

48 For example, see the special editions of 'Tiers monde'
magazine, April-June 1976 and January-March 1979, and
the synthesis by Coussy, Jean, Extraversion économique
et inégalité de puissance. Essai de bilan théorique,
'Revue française de science politique', October 1978,
pp. 859-898.

NORWAY:

THE PROGRESSIVE FREE-RIDER OR THE DEVOTED INTERNATIONALIST

H.O. Bergesen

> It is in our relations with the poor countries that
> we as a people are put to the decisive test of
> whether we are internationalists or not
> *Knut Frydenlund, Minister of Foreign Affairs in
> April 1975.* (1)

INTRODUCTION

From the very start the Norwegian government has taken a
positive stand on the demands for a new international economic order. In general, Norwegian authorities share the
LDC view of the world economy:

> It is recognized that the existing international economic
> system produces effects which are detrimental to the less
> developed countries. The free market mechanism has not
> led to equitable results, but has on the contrary served
> to widen the disparity between the rich and poor coun-
> tries. There is therefore a need to establish coordinated
> regulating measures in the international economy, not
> only to achieve better stability, but also to contribute to
> greater justice between nations and continents in the dis-
> tribution of resources and incomes. (2)

As this quotation indicates, the Norwegian government envisages a future world welfare state displaying two related
goals: effective international political management of world
markets and fair distribution of the goods produced in the
international economic system. The government is in favour
of increasing economic interactions between the industrialized
and developing countries, but emphasizes that growing

148

interdependence requires much closer political cooperation if the international economic system is to become reasonably stable and equitable. The new order is therefore often referred to as a 'political necessity'. (3)

Norwegian foreign policy decision-makers have not only given Third World demands verbal support, but have also given the North-South negotiations high political priority. The achievement of the new order has been termed 'a central dimension in Norwegian foreign policy.' (4)

THE NATURE OF THE RESPONSE

The Aid Response

Norway is one of the leading aid donors among the OECD countries, and it was one of the first rich countries to reach (in 1976) the UN goal for official development assistance (ODA) of 0.7 per cent GNP. Aid appropriations increased very rapidly in the 1970s from 0.32 per cent of GNP in 1970 to 0.93 per cent in 1979 (2.1 billion kroner). (5) The annual average percentage increase in real terms 1970-78 was 18.3; the second highest of all DAC countries. This is a remarkable performance in relation to the OECD average (0.35 per cent of GDP in 1978). According to the latest long-term economic plan, the government now intends to increase the aid appropriations to 1.3 per cent of GNP by 1985. (6)

Norwegian aid has for a long time been distributed in two roughly equal halves: one to bilateral programmes, the other to multilateral agencies. This fifty-fifty principle, which is quite unusual among OECD countries (the average multilateral component is 34 per cent), (7) has been largely maintained during the rapid increases in the total aid budget, even if there has been a slight relative growth in the share devoted to bilateral programmes recently. As a result, Norwegian contributions to UN development funds have increased very rapidly, which reflects in practical terms the country's overall commitment to strengthen the UN system. The main recipients are UNDP and IDA (the World Bank). As to the quality and content of Norwegian aid, it has two important advantages from a Third World perspective, it is given on a 100 per cent grant basis and is, in principle, untied to purchases of goods and services in Norway. So, on the whole the Norwegian aid performance conforms very well with LDC demands, both in quantitative and qualitative terms.

There is no doubt that Norwegian aid has a very strong idealistic element. In the words of former Prime Minister

Nordli: 'Norway provides (development) assistance from an attitude of solidarity with the poor countries, not to obtain political or economic advantages, or to apply pressure on the recipients'. (8)

In recent years, however, a few cracks have appeared in this image. The first relates to the tying of aid. In general terms, the government still adheres to the principle of untied aid, but it has stressed that purchases should be made from Norway whenever 'appropriate', i.e. when Norwegian goods are 'not substantially less advantageous for the recipient in price and quality than similar deliveries from other countries.' (9) But the government has added another, new provision, as it has stated that three quarters of the total commodity assistance (which makes up 25 per cent of all bilateral programmes) should consist of Norwegian goods. The remaining quarter will be used for purchases from developing countries. Simultaneously, the government has fixed the commodity assistance to the present level, whereas it used to be a flexible account in the bilateral programmes.(10) Both measures are intended to increase the purchases of capital goods from Norway. There is little doubt that this policy implies introducing tied aid in an informal manner in the bilateral assistance.

In a similar way, the government is eager to increase Norwegian deliveries to multilateral aid programmes. It has recently increased substantially appropriations for so-called 'mixed credits' which will be used for the co-financing of projects with the World Bank and the regional development banks in order to obtain a larger share of the contracts for Norwegian export industries. (11) How this policy will work out in practice remains to be seen, but these credits have already taken such a large share of the total aid budget that there was a real decrease in the bilateral transfers to the main recipient countries in 1981 for the first time since the introduction of the bilateral programmes.

This shift of emphasis is also clearly seen in the government's policy to promote private exports and investments in the Third World. (12) It plans to step up state loans for Norwegian firms investing in joint ventures in developing countries. An existing guarantee facility for export credits will probably be extended. According to the government there has never been any doubt about the development character of these measures. (13) It is taken for granted that these private transactions will have a positive effect on development. The main, official argument behind these schemes is that such transfers are strongly requested by Third World governments. (14) There is no doubt that these

state support measures have a positive developmental effect
in the sense that they are wanted by the recipient governments and are in line with general UN resolutions. It is
equally clear that they have been deliberately used also for
quite different purposes. In his annual report of 1979 the
director of NORAD confirms that 'the special facility (for
export credit guarantees to LDCs) has to an increasing extent been used to promote Norwegian economic interests.' (15)
This trend is reinforced by the tendency to extend the geographical coverage of the support measures for private
transfers. The traditional 'concentration principle' in Norwegian bilateral aid (16) is clearly an obstacle to the stimulation of exports and investments as the most promising markets are in the newly industrializing or more 'advanced'
LDCs, not among the poorest countries. It seems like the
government is now prepared to deviate from the concentration principle whenever commercial considerations warrant it.
This diffusion is already apparent in the distribution of export credit guarantees: in 1979 hardly any of the effectuated
credits went to the main recipient countries or any of the
least developed countries. (17)

Even if the main part of Norwegian aid still follows established guidelines aimed at eliminating absolute poverty, the
trend towards a gradual commercialization is evident both in
recent practice and policy statements. How far this tendency will go remains to be seen, but the purely idealistic
formulation of the basic goals for Norwegian aid is clearly
being eroded. (18)

Trade Policy

In the basic parliamentary report of 1975 mentioned above,
the government committed itself in general terms to increasing trade with developing countries and improving their
access to the Norwegian market. It was noted that 'Norway
itself has an interest in a planned reduction of the obstacles
to world trade and has together with other industrialized
countries taken on a special responsibility to improve LDC
access to their markets.' (19) The report mentions several
possible additional liberalization measures such as the removal of goods from the exemption list of the GSP (see below)
and the abandonment or extension of import quotas. However, the government retains the right to introduce special
measures whenever necessary to protect internal regional or
industrial interests, though such measures can only be of a
temporary nature.

Following these general commitments, Norwegian authorities have introduced several measures to increase imports from developing countries. The Norwegian GSP, which came into force in 1971, includes in principle duty-free imports for all LDC manufactures, excluding agricultural commodities and some sensitive industrial products of which the most important are textiles, clothing, footwear and bicycles. The 28 least developed countries have been granted full customs exemption for all commodities from 1976. The practical effect of these preferences have been rather limited as LDC imports to Norway from the outset were to a large extent duty free. (20) An OECD study showed that 92 per cent of all LDC imports to Norway are duty-free (in 1979), which is considerably higher than the Western average, (21) but it must be added that these imports constitute a much smaller share of total imports and consumption in Norway than in most Western countries. (22) It is also a fact that the value of Norwegian imports of clothes and textiles from LDCs per capita is substantially lower than in Sweden and somewhat lower than in the EC. (23)

Nevertheless, on paper Norwegian trade policy conforms quite well with the NIEO demands. Two important caveats must, however, be noted. First, the government has not succeeded in realizing its own ambitious goals for trade liberalization. As early as 1977 Under-Secretary for Foreign Affairs, Thorvald Stoltenberg, the main architect of Norwegian NIEO policy, took the position that the industrialized countries must 'as a minimum be willing to give the developing countries equal opportunities to compete with imports from other industrialized countries.' (24) In practice, Norway still discriminates against Third World countries compared with the EC/EFTA area. Since the latter countries can offer access to their markets in return, they have obtained trade concessions that the LDCs have not. The free trade flows with Western Europe has, in addition, increased political pressure on LDC imports.

Second, the Norwegian exemptions from the GSP hit the very two sectors where LDCs have most to gain, textiles and agriculture. The most acute problem in Norwegian foreign trade policy in recent years has been the regulation of low-price textile imports from developing countries. Because Norway has been unable to reach agreement with Hong Kong on import quotas, the country - as the only OECD member - is not a party to the present Multifiber Agreement, which regulates textile imports. The Norwegian practice has been openly criticized in international fora and is now a major embarrassment to the government. The Minister of Foreign

Affairs has openly admitted that concrete domestic economic interests 'forced us to compromise our (NIEO) principles' in a case like this (UD-informasjon, no. 11, 1980, p. 22). The official purpose of the exemption list is to protect Norwegian industry from low-price LDC competition. The actual effect of this protection is, however, rather dubious. A recent study of the tariff schedule and trade statistics shows that the LDC share of total imports is very low. (25) It is therefore suggested that the protective effect for Norwegian industries is minimal and in many cases zero.

With regard to agriculture, tropical products are in general imported duty-free, but whenever an LDC commodity represents a possible threat to domestic producer interests restrictions are imposed. This was made very clear recently when a number of large food importing and retailing organizations tried to launch a special market promotion campaign for LDC agricultural products under the label of a 'developing country shelf.' (26) This plan had to be cancelled because of bureaucratic procrastination and outright opposition. (27) When this was brought to the attention of the public, the responsible politicians suddenly welcomed the project and promised to give the organizers the necessary support. The real effect of their intervention is still not known as the case has yet to be settled. Even if they are able to obtain import licenses for these specific products, similar import schemes will again run into the same problems in the future if there is no general change of policy.

It should also be noted in this connection that the special agency set up to stimulate LDC trade, NORIMPOD, did not intervene on the side of the importers. This indicates that the agency is so closely tied to special governmental and commercial interests that it can hardly work independently and effectively on behalf of Third World importers. (28)

Industrial Policy

LDC demands for market access are closely related to their arguments for structural adjustment of the industrialized economies. If they are to take over markets now supplied by Western producers, Western economies have to adjust their basic structure to this new division of labour.

The Norwegian government at an early stage recognized this close connection between trade liberalization and internal adjustment: 'It is only through a conscious and future-oriented liberalization and adjustment policy that it will be possible to live up to (our) trade commitments *vis-à-vis* the

developing countries and at the same time prevent unwanted
consequences for certain industries and regions.' (29) As a
practical follow-up measure the government proposed a new
fund for internal industrial adjustment which will be made
necessary by future liberalization of imports from developing
countries. The need to prepare for such restructing of
domestic industry has subsequently been underlined on
several occasions.

However, in practice little has been done. The adjustment fund has been put on ice and the Minister of Foreign
Affairs in February 1977 had to admit that 'we have not primarily kept the NIEO goals in mind in the formulation of our
industrial and trade policy'. (30) This understatement
alludes to the fact that the government has not only failed
to implement positive adjustment measures, but has actively
pursued a counter-recession policy aimed at preventing the
type of industrial adjustment that the LDCs have demanded.
The government is, in principle, still in favour of restructuring, but in practice it spends billions of kroner every
year to maintain the existing industrial structure.

Shipping

This area relates both to trade, structural adjustment and
international regimes, but it is so important to Norwegian
NIEO policy that it deserves separate treatment.

Traditionally shipping has been one of the largest export
branches in the Norwegian economy and an extremely important source of foreign exchange earnings. In recent
years the combined effect of the vast oil revenues and the
international shipping crisis has diminished its role considerably. Nevertheless, the Norwegian commercial fleet
is still among the largest in the world and is certainly not
insignificant to the domestic economy. (31)

The main characteristic of Norwegian shipping in a world
context is its dependence on international markets: over 90
per cent of the fleet is engaged in trade between foreign
countries. It is easy to appreciate therefore that the main
threat to Norwegian shipping interests is protectionism by
any form of cargo-sharing. As Norway itself has little external transport to or from the country by sea, it has few
cards to play with in future deals between senders and recipients of ship cargo. This is the main reason why the Norwegian government has consistently opposed the UNCTAD
code of conduct for liner conferences which includes a cargo-
sharing formula of 40-40-20 for sender, recipient and third

country vessels respectively. This is considered grossly un-
fair as it would exclude Norwegian shipping from 80 per cent
of the market and would give preferential treatment to
industrialized countries with small and inefficient fleets at
the expense of more competitive third nations, like Norway.
However, after a compromise solution was worked out within
the EC and OECD, prohibiting cargo-sharing in seaborne
trade within the West, this problem may have been overcome. (32) Together with most Western countries, Norway
has now declared that it will ratify the code.

The principal Norwegian argument in this area has always
been that free competition and the resulting efficiency in
world sea transport is in everybody's interest, as it mini-
mizes costs. Norwegian authorities have subsequently
argued that there is no conflict of interests between Norway
and the Third World as both parties stand to lose from protectionism in the form of cargo-sharing. Norway has offered
the developing countries technical assistance and training
programmes to support their efforts to establish their own
commercial fleet – as an alternative to international regulation.

The crucial question is whether the Norwegian policy in
this field is consistent with its general pro-NIEO position.
It is often purported that rejection of the cargo-sharing
scheme is contrary to the principal Norwegian attitude. In
my judgment, this argument is not well founded. Norway
has never supported direct market intervention of this type
as part of the new economic order. But the Norwegian
government has consistently advocated political management
of international market forces, underlining the need for
better insight into the actual working of the market, in particular possible monopolistic tendencies. This general standpoint is absent in Norwegian shipping policy. The government prefers to take it for granted that free competition
exists in international shipping markets.

The credibility of Norwegian arguments becomes even
more tarnished when Norwegian officials quietly tells the
UNCTAD secretariat to limit its activity in the shipping area.
This is clearly contrary to the country's general efforts to
strengthen the role of international organizations in the implementation of the NIEO. In effect, Norwegian policy in
this case has come to resemble to a remarkable degree the
behaviour of other large economic powers. (33)

International regimes

From the very start of the NIEO debate, Norway has been

one of the chief advocates of new UN regimes to regulate or manage the world economy. In this Norway has often been in outright opposition to the majority of Western states. This is most clearly seen in the commodity area where the Norwegian government right from the start wholeheartedly supported the UNCTAD Integrated Programme for Commodities and the establishment of the Common Fund. As the first Western country, Norway at UNCTAD IV in 1976 pledged a contribution of $25 million to the Fund. The government has later invested large personnel resources in the commodity negotiations in an attempt to compensate for the smallness of the country's objective weight in this field. (34) When the negotiations on the Common Fund finally led to an agreement in June 1980, the government expressed its great satisfaction at this 'magnificent result', (35) even if the final deal fall far short of original Norwegian (and Third World) ambitions. Norway has also participated very actively in individual commodity negotiations, even when its self-interests at stake have been very limited.

The Norwegian government has taken a similar stand favouring a strong international regime in the negotiations on a code of conduct for transfer of technology and for transnational corporations. However, it has not given the same priority to these issues, acting mainly as a member of the Nordic group whose spokesman in these rounds has been Sweden. Norway has put less effort into these negotiations and has not openly opposed the main OECD line, which is contrary to any effective international intervention in the markets dominated by TNC (transnational corporation) oligopolies.

In the controversy between the old Bretton Woods institutions and UNCTAD in the field of money and finance, Norway has taken an outspoken position in favour of LDC demands for institutional reform. This was clearly reflected in the decision to participate in an *ad hoc* Group of Experts on the Evolution of the International Monetary System, which was established by vote at UNCTAD V. This has been particularly sensitive as Norway was the only Western country to participate - as an observer - in the first meeting of the group in 1980. The large majority of Western countries have severely criticized this group for interfering with the work of the IMF, and the Western boycott of its work will certainly continue. This makes Norwegian participation all the more controversial, particularly as only a few other OECD countries have hinted that they might follow the Norwegian example. There is a clear, substantial difference of opinion between Norway and the majority of Western countries in

this case. The former asserts that the development of the
monetary system is so closely related to international trade
issues that it falls within UNCTAD's mandate, whereas the
latter want these questions to be dealt with by the IMF
exclusively. A similar difference is evident in the debt
area where Norway sympathizes with LDC pleas for new
institutional arrangements, again expanding UNCTAD's
influence, which has been flatly rejected by the large Western debtor countries. As Norway itself has no outstanding
ODA debt it has played a very low-key role in these negotiations.

The Law of the Seas

Within the wide range of issues treated by UNCLOS III two
questions are particularly important in this context: the
powers invested in the UN deep seabed regime, the International Seabed Authority (ISA) and the delimitation of the
border between the 'common heritage of mankind' and
national jurisdiction over the seabed In accordance with
its general ideological outlook, Norway has consistently and
actively advocated a strong and effective international seabed regime. It has, in principle, favoured an ISA with
regulatory powers vis-à-vis the mining industry parallel to
those of national governments over their continental shelves.
It is also typical that Norway has devoted considerable personnel resources to these negotiations and has probably
attained a degree of influence which exceeds its very limited
objective interests in the deep seabed regime. (36)
    As to the delimitation of the jurisdiction of the ISA, Nor-
way has advocated a clear-cut jurisdiction as far as possible.
(37) Norway has asserted that the coastal states can claim
rights to the continental shelf beyond the 200 nautical mile
economic zone, whenever the geological circumstances warrant it. If this formula is accepted as international law, the
Norwegian continental shelf will cover most of the seabed between the Soviet Union in the East and Greenland/Iceland in
the West. So, in the North Atlantic, the common heritage of
mankind may be well taken care of by a strong ISA, but its
scope will be very limited compared with the common property
of the Norwegian people.
    Judged as a whole, Norwegian positions with regard to
the NIEO regimes have been very close to those of the developing countries, as Norway has advocated both reform of
existing institutional arrangements (like the IMF-UNCTAD
relationship) and establishment of new management schemes

in formerly unregulated areas, like commodity trade, TNCs and the deep seabed. The only exception is the delimitation of the scope of the ISA, where Norway in effect has subordinated its principal, internationalist stand to national economic and security interests.

Disregarding the shipping controversy this is the only case where international regime formation or institutional reform in the NIEO debate touches directly upon tangible Norwegian interests.

THE EXPLANATION OF THE RESPONSE

Ideology

The general Norwegian approach to the NIEO is a clear reflection of an egalitarian ideology that is widely held throughout the whole of Norwegian society, including all major political parties. (38) The dogmatic version of economic liberalism has never really taken root in Norway. There is no disagreement on the principle that the state has both a right and duty to intervene in economic life to ensure an equitable distribution of income. (39) Several internal markets are thoroughly regulated, e.g. the whole food and fish sectors. In short, Norwegian NIEO policy represents an attempt to transfer the main elements of this welfare system, which has worked quite well internally, to the global level.

The growing gap between rich and poor countries is considered a constant threat to the stability of the world economic system, and this can only be overcome in a new and more quitable system. In addition to this economic rationale, the Norwegian government has always underlined that the rich countries have a moral responsibility to alleviate poverty and stressed Norway's solidarity with the poor people of the world. This combination of an egalitarian ideology and a feeling of moral duty explains the contents of the Norwegian policy in the regime negotiations under the NIEO and its aid performance, but to account for the intensity of Norwegian activism in these areas a third ideological factor must be introduced. This is the peculiar missionary trait in Norwegian attitudes to the outside world. The Norwegian people - and to varying degrees its political leaders - have always had a feeling of holding a set of unique values that must somehow be brought out to the rest of the world. At its worst, this is pure nationalist self-cultivation on the world scene. At its best, it can take the form of genuine international solidarity. A small country's efforts to promote global political management of the world economy can seem rather naive from a power political perspective, but from a Norwegian point of view it is just a natural combination of self-content (with a domestic system) and a missionary's incurable desire to bring his wisdom and experience out to the world.

Foreign policy interests

As a small country with very limited international economic power resources at its disposal, Norway has a clear self-interest in international regimes providing more stability and order in the world economy. International management, formal or informal, is more reliable and therefore preferable for the small – than unilateral or bilateral (ab)use of power by the strong. This small-state interest, combined with the egalitarian ideology, explains the general Norwegian support for international political management of the world economy. (40)

According to Norwegian political leaders, the new order is necessary to prevent not only economic conflicts, but also military ones. The alternative to peaceful cooperation between North and South is deemed to be an international class struggle where the poor majority rises against the affluent minority.

Nonetheless, neither ideology nor foreign policy orientation – both very general explanatory factors – can account for the rather sudden shift in Norwegian NIEO policy in the period 1974-6 (during the preparations to UNCTAD IV), when the country became a leading advocate of LDC demands within the West and one of the front-runners in the group of like-minded countries. Even with the benefit of hindsight it is still very difficult to explain this change. One important factor behind it seems to have been the rising expectations following a series of new oil discoveries in the North Sea (see below). Another possible explanation lies in Norwegian non-membership in the EC after the negative popular vote in 1972. This may have worked in different ways: since Denmark joined the EC the same year, the Nordic group was drastically weakened which made passive participation in the NIEO debate through this forum more difficult and less attractive. Staying outside the EC may at the same time have given the Norwegian foreign policy leadership a sense of political isolation which could be compensated for by seeking a role in the North-South arena. (41)

Foreign Economic Position

The main reason behind the change in Norwegian NIEO
policy in the middle of the 1970s was probably the prospects
of large oil revenues and the expectation that the country
would soon become a major exporter of capital as the domestic economy could not absorb the rapid inflow of foreign exchange earnings. This had both an economic and a political
impact. It improved the government's freedom of action
enormously, making increases in foreign aid an attractive
option even from a financial point of view. Simultaneously,
the prospects of becoming a large oil exporter apparently
gave both the general public and the foreign policy leadership a sense of Norway having reached a higher status in
the international system. It was suddenly no longer simply
a small, peripheral nation. The whole country developed an
awareness of having a voice, and of being listened to, in
international relations. The egalitarian ideology provided
the background and the emerging NIEO debate the opportunity for this new self-assertion to be expressed in the North-
South arena.

In the last half of the 1970s it became evident, however,
that Norway was not after all invulnerable to the general economic recession. At the same time the inflow of oil revenues
was delayed due to technical difficulties and reduced because
of growing costs. This explains why the aid appropriations
stagnated in the late 1970s.

Falling demand in important Western export markets following the recession is the main reason underlying the gradual commercialization of Norwegian aid. Stagnating exports
to traditional markets led to overproduction at home and subsequently to export drives in new markets in the Third
World, subsidized with public funds, partly drawn from aid
appropriations.

Public Opinion

Several recent polls and surveys have shown that there is
wide popular support for the rapidly rising aid appropriations. The opposition to aid is small and probably decreasing. On the other hand, there is no strong demand for continued growth. (42) In line with the ideological outlook
described above, most respondents in a recent survey mentioned moral responsibility as the main reason for development assistance. It is also interesting to note that a clear
majority of the Norwegian people is opposed to customs and

other restrictions on imports from developing countries. (43)
This indicates that the public is more development oriented
with regard to trade policy than the political leaders.

The public opinion studies confirm that the egalitarian
ideology and feeling of solidarity described above is deeply
rooted in popular attitudes. This is also reflected in party
positions. In fact, Norwegian political parties outbid each
other in attempts to display a pro-development image before
the national elections in September 1981.

Non-Governmental Organizations

As a consequence of the dominant popular attitudes several
church, youth and humanitarian organizations are active in
the public debate on North-South questions. Their activities probably serve to reinforce the overall pro-development
sentiments. Their main function with regard to policy-
making is that the government knows that it will be criticized
from this quarter if it gives up its principal positions in
international negotiations.

The main asset of this group is its wide political support
covering some parts of all the major parties. However, it
has very limited economic resources at its disposal and can
therefore hardly follow up on the many complex NIEO-related
questions. The commitment of these organizations to development issues also varies considerably as many of them work
with a wide scope of political problems. So they remain a
rather diffuse grouping that may be able to set some broad
outer limits for the decision-makers, but has limited influence on concrete decisions.

Sector Economic (Corporate) Organizations

Most corporate organizations have no general concern with
the NIEO but they take care to protect their interests whenever necessary. The combined forces of labour unions,
employers and local politicians have effectively opposed
trade liberalization towards LDC imports that compete with
Norwegian industries. (44) The related internal adjustment
fund was, apparently, blocked by the trade union leadership. In the food sector, LDC imports competing with Norwegian products are stopped by the strong agricultural
lobby.

With respect to shipping the influence of domestic interest groups, in particular the powerful Norwegian Shipowners'

Association, is equally clear. As mentioned above, the government has not in this case followed up its general commitment to political management of international markets and even tried to curtail UNCTAD's activities. This deviation can only be accounted for by the strong corporate interest effectively organized through the Shipowners' Association. The influence of the sector economic interests is also visible in the gradual commercialization of Norwegian aid policy, which has been described above. While this used to be an area where policy was exclusively guided by the peculiar Norwegian mixture of moralism and international solidarity, it is now evident that domestic economic concerns are being more heavily felt.

This does not necessarily mean that Norwegian aid policy will fail to achieve NIEO objectives. The developing countries themselves have, after all, continuously asked the West to encourage private investments in the Third World. But this trend in Norwegian policy definitely signals a shift in emphasis, according higher priority to internal economic interests at the expense of recipient needs. This probably reflects a corresponding change in the underlying political forces. The sector economic corporate interests seem to strengthen their position in relation to more general, long-term concerns. Even with the strong public opinion backing that the altruistic element in Norwegian aid has, it appears to be politically very difficult, or impossible, to avoid corporate inroads even into this policy area.

Decision-making Structure

The dominant corporate influence on policy is further reinforced by the fragmentation of the public decision-making structure. Officially, the Ministry of Foreign Affairs is responsible for the overall follow-up of the Norwegian NIEO policy, in particular those commitments that the government has accepted in international fora. When the NIEO negotiations do not directly touch upon specific Norwegian interests, this Ministry takes charge of policy-making and can therefore follow the official foreign policy line. This is why the pure pro-NIEO position comes out so clearly in negotiations on international regimes where Norway is economically indifferent. The main constraints are then scarce personnel resources within the Ministry and reactions abroad, especially among the Western countries.

In trade, shipping and monetary matters, the Ministry of Foreign Affairs has a much more peripheral position in the bureaucratic decision-making. These areas fall under the mandate of the Ministry of Trade and shipping, which has primary responsibility for both internal policy (e.g. customs regulation) and international negotiations in these fields. This Ministry is much more attentive to the demands of its counterparts in the private sector and much less influenced by the political pressure from the developing countries. Typical of this controversy is the dispute between the two ministries over the role of UNCTAD in trade negotiations and in monetary policy. As might be expected, the Trade Ministry favours the old institutions like IMF and GATT with which it has dealt for decades in a business-like manner, while the Ministry of Foreign Affairs is willing to accept an increased role for UNCTAD in these fields. The decision to participate in the UNCTAD monetary expert group represents a minor victory for the latter ministry. However, in that case it was not opposed by an alliance of bureaucratic and corporate interests. Whenever that happens, as in trade, shipping, agricultural and industrial policy, the Ministry of Foreign Affairs becomes impotent.

CONCLUSION

This analysis shows that two explanatory factors, ideology and foreign policy, account very well for Norway's general positive attitude to the NIEO and to a large extent for its aid policy. Public opinion serves to reinforce the effect of these factors.

However, when it comes to implementation of the new order in domestic politics, the influence of sector economic interests is clearly seen. Strong corporate opposition is the main reason why the government has largely failed to realize its own goals in practice. Either the government has been unable to impose the necessary changes on the strong sector interests, or it has been unwilling to run the political risks of so doing. It is hard to tell what efforts have in fact been made in this connection. Judging from public sources, the Ministry of Foreign Affairs, which is primarily responsible for the follow-up, has not made any impressive attempts to counteract the sector economic forces. This may be due to lack of political leadership, but it can also be a consequence of the Ministry's position in the policy-making process.

This analysis leaves no doubt that the corporate interests prevail in Norwegian NIEO policy whenever they are mobilized (45) (which means whenever they have an important

stake in the NIEO debate) - even when they run counter
both to the government's overall approach and to public
opinion in general.

If Norwegian NIEO policy is judged on the basis of the
internal costs the country has been willing to bear, the
record of achievements is very limited. In fact, the aid
increase is the only major result, and, as I have pointed out,
even here the practice has become more dubious. It may
also be added that compared with the state revenues following the increases in oil prices since 1973-4, which have hit
the poor countries very badly, the Norwegian aid record is
not in fact all that impressive.

Does this mean that Norway is simply a free-rider that
presents a progressive image abroad without bearing its
share of the costs? Is its internationalist stand in UN fora
just a rhetorical phenomenon? These questions can best be
answered on the basis of two contradictory propositions:
— The free-rider hypothesis: A free-riding country will
   only accept NIEO demands as long as they do not involve
   any serious political or economic costs to itself.
— The devoted internationalist hypothesis: A country
   following an internationalist NIEO policy will support
   international management even when it is contrary to
   domestic, political or economic interests in the short run.
As far as internal follow-up is concerned, this analysis shows
that apart from ODA, Norwegian behaviour has conformed
very well with the free-rider hypothesis.

As to the negotiations on international regimes under the
NIEO, most of these institutional changes have either no
direct or very limited impact on Norway. From a cynical
perspective the country can therefore afford to take a progressive stand, as it can rely on the big Western powers to
stop dangerous LDC initiatives. The Norwegian government
has consistently spoken out in favour of international political management of the world economy as a vital element of
the new order. The credibility of this position is, however,
seriously weakened as Norway itself takes a different stand
whenever its own interests are at stake (e.g. in the shipping controversy and in the negotiations of the geographical
scope of the ISA). Such action also conforms to the free-
rider hypothesis.

The description of the Norwegian response also shows
that the internationalist hypothesis cannot be completely
written off. Norwegian behaviour demonstrates genuine concern for a more equitable and stable new institutional order.
The country has invested considerable personnel resources
in negotiations on issues where it has only a general, long-

term interest in international management, and it has used
its manpower consciously to promote NIEO demands as far as
possible within the Western Camp. This is most evident in
the UNCTAD commodity negotiations. In the negotiations on
international regimes, the Norwegian pro-NIEO position has
certainly not been cost-free. Open advocacy of the new
institutional order and international political management has
brought Norway into intense diplomatic confrontation with
other Western nations, with which it has traditionally had
the closest and most friendly relations, in particular the US
and Britain. Today Norway is in many respects in a fairly
isolated position within the OECD. For a small country with
no diplomatic tradition this is in itself a major political cost.
(46) This shows that the Norwegian internationalist position
is not based on pure rhetoric. The country has paid a
heavy diplomatic price for its activism.

Thus, even if the somewhat naive missionary has been
unable to impose his message in his own parish, he has at
least stuck by his message to the world, even at the cost of
being left alone.

Notes

1 'UD-informasjon', (the official newsletter of the Ministry of Foreign Affairs) No. 20 1975, p. 10, my
   translation.
2 Quotation from Report to the Storting (Parliament) No.
   94 (1974-75) on 'Norway's Economic Relations with
   Developing Countries', 25 April 1975. (This quote is
   taken from the official English translation of the
   report, p. 21, while the subsequent ones are from the
   original Norwegian as the translation covers only the
   first part.) Henceforth, the document is referred to
   simply as parliamentary report no. 94.
3 The term has been used by the Minister of Foreign
   Affairs several times, cf. for example 'UD-informasjon',
   No. 2, 1980, p. 22.
4 Under-Secretary for Foreign Affairs, Thorvald Stoltenberg, 'UD-informasjon', No. 7, 1979, p. 6.
5 1 US dollar roughly equals five Norwegian kroner.
6 The government intends to spend the funds within the
   1 per cent limit for traditional aid purposes, while the
   additional appropriations will be used primarily 'within
   the framework of bilateral economic relations between
   Norway and the developing countries', e.g. support

for private investments and increasing use of 'mixed credits'. (The long-term economic programme 1982-85, p. 24.)

7 Figure for 1978 from 'Development Corporation 1979 Review', OECD, Paris, 1979, p. 82.

8 'UD-informasjon', No. 14, 1976, p. 29.

9 Quotation from parliamentary report No. 35 (1980-81) entitled 'Norwegian cooperation with the developing countries in 1979', p. 23. This is the latest government policy paper on development issues. Henceforth referred to as parliamentary report, No. 35.

10 Ibid. pp. 23-24.

11 Norwegian relations with the Inter-American Development Bank provides a similar example: As long as Norway is not a member of the bank, Norwegian companies are excluded from its contracts. After intense pressure from business circles the government has recently proposed to join the bank and intends to draw the necessary funds (18 million kroner per year) from the aid budget.

12 This has traditionally been a very small part of Norwegian aid, claiming only 3-4 per cent of the budget. The new plans are outlined in parliamentary report No. 35, pp. 21-26.

13 Minister of Foreign Affairs, Knut Frydenlund, in 'UD-informasjon', No. 2, 1980, p. 18.

14 This is the only concrete requirement in the otherwise very vague and general guidelines established for state loans and guarantees. (Cf. the NORAD booklet on these measures 'NORAD og naeringslivet'.)

15 NORAD Annual Report 1979, p. 7.

16 Norway has selected nine so-called main recipient developing countries. Of the total bilateral aid 63.7% was concentrated in this group of countries. (NORAD Annual Report 1980, p. 4.)

17 Cf. the report of the (state) Guarantee Institute for Export Credits 1979 (Parliamentary Report No. 68, 1979-80, p. 18).

18 This tendency towards commercialization has been moderated by parliamentary opposition.

19 Parliamentary Report No. 94, p. 60.

20 In 1977 the GSP covered only 2.8 per cent (189 million kroner) of the total imports from developing countries eligible for preferential treatment (66 countries in 1979). Of this figure seven countries accounted for 86 per cent, Korea alone for 33 per cent. Total duty-free imports from the GSP countries were 6.1 billion

in 1977, i.e. 89 per cent of total imports from these countries. (Source see note 22.)

21 'OECD Observer', January 1978, pp. 30-37.
22 Imports from developing countries to Norway have remained around 10 per cent of total imports through the 1970s. In the manufacturing sector the share is only 4.5 per cent, compared with an OECD average of 8 per cent. In relation to Norwegian domestic consumption, LDC imports are also insignificant: In spite of a relatively low level of self-sufficiency in manufactures, LDC imports account for only 2 per cent of consumption. This share is, however, higher for certain products, such as clothing (8.6 per cent) and textiles (3.9 per cent). (Lotsberg, Kari: 'Virkninger for norsk økonomi av endringer i handelssamkvemmet mellom Norge og utviklingslandene' (Effects on the Norwegian economy of changes in the trade relations between Norway and the developing countries), Ministry of Foreign Affairs, Oslo 1980).
23 The exact figures for 1979 are: Sweden - $60 per capita; EC - $40; and Norway - $38 (reported in a letter from the Trade Ministry to the foreign relations committee of the Storting dated 27 October 1980).
24 'UD-informasjon', No. 37, 1977, p. 9. The statement was repeated in a slightly different wording two years later ('UD-informasjon', No. 7, 1979, p. 12). On both occasions, however, the Under-Secretary spoke to an audience of foreigners.
25 The LDC share is below 1 per cent for half the product groups on the exemption list. It is above 10 per cent in only 4 cases (out of a total of 37). (Eide, Nils Torbjoern: 'Beskyttelseseffketen for norsk industri av at det kreves toll på import fra utviklingsland - en ökonomisk analyse' (The protective effect for Norwegian industry from duties on imports from developing countries - an economic analysis), preliminary, unpublished manuscript, 1981).
26 The commodities included were processed, in some cases also packed, in the developing countries and imported directly to Norway. The organizers deliberately picked producers with an attractive social profile, such as coffee growers in Tanzania and an Indian honey-producing cooperative in Guatemala.
27 The main problems - apart from all the red tape - turned out to be honey and corned beef imports. In the first case the Department of Agriculture refused to give an adequate import license, fearing competition

with Norwegian producers. In the second, sanitary pro-
provisions were invoked regarding the artificial flavor-
ing of the imported meat.

28 After a parliamentary review of its organization,
MORIMPOD may get a more independent position.

29 Parliamentary report No. 94, p. 62.

30 'UD-informasjon', No. 9, 1977, pp. 5-6, corrected in
'UD-informasjon' of 18 February 1977, p. 1.

31 The net foreign exchange earnings of the Norwegian
commercial fleet was 6.9 billion kroner in 1979. For
international comparison: The Norwegian fleet makes up
5.8 per cent of the world total (1979), the UK 6.6 per
cent and the US 3.9 per cent (Figures from Momenter:
Norsk og internasjonal skipsfart, Norges Rederfor-
bund, May 1980, pp. 34 and 12).

32 For more details see Knudsen, Olav: 'The NIEO at Sea'
paper presented to an ECPR workshop on the Western
response to the NIEO in Florence, 1980.

33 By virtue of its sizeable commercial fleet, Norway can
be considered a large economic power within this
issue area.

34 As a consequence of this activity, a Norwegian ambassador, Martin Huslid, was appointed chairman of the
ad hoc Intergovernmental Committee for the Integrated
Programme for Commodities.

35 Ambassador Huslid used this expression in a statement
to this committee at the opening of its final session, on
29 September 1980. (Quote from UD-forum 9/80, part
II, p. 4.)

36 Again, a Norwegian official was appointed to a key
position in the negotiation process, as ambassador
Jens Evensen chaired the so-called action group of
experts which served as a mediating forum in a critical phase of UNCLOS III.

37 The following treatment of this point is based on the
analysis presented by Østreng, Willy: 'Norway's Law
of the Sea policy in the 70's', The Nansen Foundation,
Oslo 1980.

38 This ideology has to a large extent been formed by the
strong social-democratic forces in modern Norwegian his-
history, but it has also deeper roots to the pre-
industrial agricultural communities.

39 However, this is not coupled with prominent left-wing
activism, as might be expected. In fact, the political
left is weaker in Norway than in most West European
countries.

40 However, when a proposed international regime runs

counter to concrete Norwegian (sector-economic or
national) interests, this principle can be compromised,
cf. the shipping controversy and the delimitation of
the ISA.

41   For a further - even more speculative - discussion see
Holm, Hans Henrik: 'Skandinavisk u-landspolitikk:
hvorfor så forskellig?', (Scandinavia development
policy: why so different?). 'Politica', 1, 1979, 100-124.

42   According to several recent polls 70-80 per cent of the
population is in favour of development aid, while 10-20
per cent is against it. Around 50 per cent think that
the present level is appropriate, 20-40 per cent (depending on the formulation of the question) say it is
too high and around 10 per cent that it is too low.
These figures have apparently not been influenced
noticeably by the actual rise in aid appropriations.
Ringdal, Kristen: 'Folkemeininga og den tredje verda'
(Popular Opinion and the Third World), Oslo, 1979,
p. 141 and 144.

43   Idem.

44   Some sector organizations do have an interest in trade
liberalization, but they have not made their voice
effectively heard in this struggle.

45   The main factor explaining this outcome seems to be
corporate control over strategic resources in the
policy-making process (such as expertise, capital,
votes, political support) and their ability to concentrate their lobbying on specific sectors presenting
concrete, short-term demands.

46   At the same time Norway has, naturally, registered
diplomatic gains with many Third World countries.

SOVIET UNION:
THE RELUCTANT PARTICIPANTS

C.W. Lawson

INTRODUCTION

The emergence during the 1970s of a reasonably unified
group of less developed countries (LDCs) articulating a
set of rather disparate economic demands, presented both
advanced capitalist and centrally planned economies (CPEs)
with a series of difficult policy choices.   While neither the
East nor the West has made any major concessions to the
creation of a New International Economic Order (NIEO)
their different responses reflect and illuminate their respective political and economic structures.
    In this paper, I will examine the Eastern responses to the
NIEO, setting them against the general experience of CPE-
LDC economic relations, and attempting to reconstruct the
policy principles and processes which determine them.
I will argue that although there were some political advantages in making more significant concessions, the bargaining strength of LDCs *vis-à-vis* CPEs was less than in
relation to market economies, and the moral demands for a
redistribution of economic power were easily rejected.
Thus CPEs' responses to the NIEO embodied a mixture of
qualified support for the principles of the system but
little or no specific encashable proposals.   Their attitude
and actions are precisely in character with their previous
policies and trading arrangements.   Such consistency,
assisted by the limited concessions of market economies
suggests that the policy creation process operated in a
fairly standard way.   The lack of specific information on
that process implies that our discussion of policy formation
will be rather tentative.
    The remainder of the paper is divided into three sections.
Section two describes the Soviet and Eastern European

Responses to the Group of 77s' proposals and indicates why
Yugoslavia and Romania have neither followed nor wanted to
adopt the Soviet stance. Section three then provides an
assessment of the political and economic determinants of the
response. The overall results of the study are reviewed in
a concluding note.

THE NATURE OF THE RESPONSE

Faced with an unusual degree of cohesion by LDCs in their
demands for a redistribution of economic resources and political power, and at least initially for a restructuring of international institutions, the Soviet Union as the dominant bloc
power responded very cautiously. As Western responses
might require counteracting or at least equivalent offers,
and Chinese influence demanded that LDCs should not be
antagonized, some stand was required. The timing of LDC
demands was rather inconvenient, for an underlying expan-
sionary Soviet policy was already in operation which would
soon require direct or indirect involvement in three African
countries as well as considerable commitment of materials to
reconstruction in South East Asia. This all occurred against
a domestic economic situation where agricultural difficulties
and declining growth rates made detente and arms limitations
an increasingly attractive if not essential policy.

   In responding to the original 'Declaration on the Establishment of a New International Economic Order', to the
'Programme of Action' and the 'Charter of Economic Rights
and Duties of States', it would have been convenient for the
Soviet Union and other Eastern European States to have presented a joint policy position. But by the spring of 1975
such a position was impossible. Despite Yugoslavia's associate membership of CMEA, political differences and her position amongst the non-aligned group explain her membership
of the Group of 77. Romania's situation was rather different, although her actions were totally consistent with the
independent political and economic line she had been pursuing inside CMEA and the Warsaw pact since the early sixties.

   Romania joined the Group of 77 at Manila in 1977, and at
the Colombo conference was allowed to take part in all the
meetings and activities of the non-aligned states. Whatever
the reason for the strategy, whether it was an attempt to
gain a negotiating edge with CMEA, or to benefit from MFN
concessions for LDCs, she has maintained her independent
stance, and along with Yugoslavia did not sign the joint
statements presented at UNCTAD IV and UNCTAD V. In

view of the joint response, which is discussed below, it is
also interesting that Ceausescu of Romania and Dolanc of
Yugoslavia were the only leaders to mention NIEO by name
at the Twenty-fifth CPSU congress in 1976. (1)

In practice this lack of total group agreement has not
greatly hindered the policies of the remaining members,
although it has meant that CMEA as an institution has
played a very minor role in the process. By 1979 CMEA had
relations with over sixty international organizations, and
since 1975 it has had official status in the UN and its
agencies. (2) Although it has played a minimal role in the
response to the NIEO, it has examined the questions involved and its meetings would seem to be the ideal place for
those members who have signed the joint statements to coordinate their plans. Thus at the Fifty-Fourth meeting of
the Standing Commission for Foreign Trade (Moscow, 11-12
April 1979) where most delegation heads were Ministers of
Foreign Trade or their deputies, the Commission reviewed
the forthcoming UNCTAD session and met with its Secretary-
General, G. Corea. (3)

The signatories of the joint statements to UNCTAD IV and
UNCTAD V have maintained a consistent response to the
NIEO, both through time and between countries. (4) They
have repeatedly blamed the industrialized capitalist countries for the difficulties of LDCs, and stressed that LDC-CPE
relations are qualitatively different from those between the
West and South. Having adopted this stance they are then
able to argue that most of the provisions of the NIEO need
not apply to CPEs, either because CPE-LDC relations are not
exploitative, or because CPEs have already implemented the
changes. As LDCs have begun to question these arguments
so the tone of CPE replies has become sharper.

The Commodity Response

The response to the integrated programme for commodities
provides an excellent illustration of these attitudes. The
joint statement to UNCTAD IV begins its remarks on this
question by stressing that consumer as well as producer
interests must be protected, and that while improved terms
of trade for LDCs are justified, they must devote more
energy to the control of foreign capital. Priority should be
given to the least developed countries and they were 'in
principle favourably disposed' to a link between export and
import prices for LDCs. But compensatory financing facilities 'cannot be seen as an effective means of perfecting the

structure and organization of commodity markets'. (5) They were willing to agree that LDCs should enjoy better access to the markets for primary and processed commodities, but as far as CPEs were concerned access should be limited to 'national undertakings'. In other words they were not willing to allow multinationals better access to CPE markets. Buffer stocks were viewed as alternatives to long-term bilateral agreements, and they urged that participating members should have the choice of which method they used.

In the period after UNCTAD IV, CPEs showed no more interest than developed market economies in constructing a commodity system which involved substantial resource transfers. While they participated in the preliminary agreement on the Fund which was stitched together in March 1979, like the USA they were reported to be unhappy with the outcome. (6) For both countries the voting or share distribution was the problem. In later, more detailed negotiations, they criticized but eventually accepted the proposal that they provide 17 per cent of the Fund's first window of $250m of non-fee capital, although receiving only 8 per cent of the votes on the Fund's Council. (7) Along with similar Western reservations these disagreements delayed the adoption of the Fund's Articles of Agreement until June 1980. As the Fund is also dependent on the formation of its associated commodity agreements, it remains to be seen whether CPEs will raise further difficulties over their creation, or over the actual, and long-postponed inauguration of the Fund.

Although such arrangements are not obviously totally unacceptable to CPEs, they fall well short of the preferred variants. An Hungarian assessment of UNCTAD V provides interesting evidence of some objections to earlier proposals. Nyerges (1979) criticizes the LDC approach to raw material problems, because oil and other commodities in strong market positions were not on the agenda. Hungary, he claims, would like to conclude agreements for thirty-six important raw materials, not just for the eighteen in the original integrated programme. Echoing the joint statement to UNCTAD IV, he suggests that the preferred regulatory device should be contractual obligations by the participants, including a specification of maximum and minimum prices rather than export quotas or countervailing funds. Indexation is rejected because it could lead to Western inflationary processes being transmitted to the Hungarian economy. The preferred version of the agreement would obviously involve a smaller outlay than LDC proposals, and in net terms might well be highly advantageous to Hungary.

The Trade Response

The position on LDC exports of manufactures and semi-
manufactures, tariff reductions and non-reciprocity is more
complex. The 1976 joint statement offers more long-term
agreements 'without reciprocity in respect of preferential
measures but based on normal and equitable terms and without discrimination.' (8) Indeed by the mid-1970s several
CPEs had introduced Generalized System of Preferences
(GSP) schemes. The USSR had abolished customs duties on
LDC goods in 1965. (9) Bulgaria reduced duties on some
LDC goods by 30 per cent in 1972, further reduced all such
duties by 50 per cent in 1976/77 and abolished them in
1978. (10) Czechoslovakia began the same process in 1972
by 50 per cent reductions on almost all LDC goods, and continued the reduction and abolition of duties, particularly for
the poorest LDCs, during 1978. (11) By 1979 Hungary had
instituted preferential customs tariffs for eighty-four
developing countries, covering about six hundred products
of which one hundred were totally exempt and the remainder
subject to reductions of between 50 per cent and 90 per
cent. (12) The concessions apply automatically to those
LDCs in contractual obligations with GATT, and the thirty
poorest LDCs are totally exempt.
    The problem with such concessions is that by themselves
they are virtually worthless. Except in Hungary there is no
freedom of choice by the domestic user of the product and
hence a lower tariff need have no effect on the volume of imports. (13) Nevertheless CPEs have tried to use these concessions as bargaining counters to obtain Most-Favoured-
Nation (MFN) status with LDCs. In effect they have interpreted the 'normal and equitable terms and without discrimination' to mean actual or effective MFN treatment. Only in
this way can we reconcile the statements made to UNCTAD IV
and Bogomolov's authoritative claim that 'the socialist countries ... cannot accept ... the demand that (they) should
accord to the Third World countries unilateral advantages
on the non-reciprocity principle.' (14)
    If there has been a change in attitude, and there is some
circumstantial evidence to suggest this, then the most likely
reason is the feeling that CPEs are still quite heavily discri-
minated against in international trade. The joint statement
to UNCTAD V is more insistent on this issue than was the
joint response to UNCTAD IV. Reporting on the outcome of
the conference the Soviet chief delegate, a deputy minister
of foreign trade, wrote that while the socialist countries,

supported those propositions in the Arusha Programme which ... (were) just ... and were truly conducive to equal and mutually beneficial international cooperation in economics and commerce ... But, first of all, there have to be measures to remove discrimination and any artificial barriers in world trade, and to eliminate all inequality, coercion and exploitation in international economic relations. (15)

The conference resolution against protectionism is singled out for particular criticism because it 'is one-sided, protecting only the interests of the developing countries. The socialist countries believe that international measures against protectionist tendencies can be effective only if they are not confined to the interests of one group of countries.' (16)

This comment reflects a general and long-standing desire on the part of the CPEs to widen UNCTAD discussions to include East-West trade, and particularly the issue of discrimination. For although several CPEs belong to GATT, the group as a whole has no obvious arena where it can negotiate on this question. In the face of Western opposition, since the mid-1950s they have been advocating the creation of a World Trade Organization where political and economic issues would not be formally separated. (17) UNCTAD and GATT membership are clearly inferior substitutes - which explains why the Soviet Foreign Trade Minister, N.S. Patolichev, suggested to UNCTAD IV that the organization itself should extend its terms of reference and evolve into a World Trade Organization. (18) Lack of progress in this direction can be attributed as much to LDC fears that the focus of discussion will move from their problems, as to Western opposition.

The Aid Response

Despite their lack of progress towards the creation of a world trade organization the Soviet bloc has continued to link questions of East-West trade and security with their ability to satisfy LDC demands. In addition they have been careful to distinguish their position on aid and debt repayments from that of the West. They are opposed to debt cancellation although some members, for example Hungary, have indicated a willingness to discuss debt questions on a bilateral basis. (19) On aid they clearly and unequivocally reject any responsibility for LDC backwardness and so do not recognize any moral claims for aid as recompense. The joint statement to UNCTAD IV declares that

it (is) unfounded to appeal to (us) to share the responsibility and material costs of eliminating the consequences
of colonialism, neo-colonialism and the trade and monetary
crisis of the capitalist economy. (20)

It follows that

There can be no grounds whatsoever for presenting to
the Soviet Union and other socialist countries the demands
which the developing nations present to the developed
capitalist states, including the demand for a compulsory
transfer of a fixed share of the gross national product to
the developing nations by way of economic assistance. (21)

This stand has been the cause of some friction between
CPEs and LDCs. Reporting on UNCTAD V, Manzhulo rather
tartly noted that 'the Group of 77 again included in its draft
several elements, being fully aware of the fact that they are
unacceptable to the socialist countries, beginning with the
demand that 0.7 per cent of their gross national product
should be allotted annually as aid to the developing countries.' (22) The response of the Group of 77 is neatly en-
capsulated in the statement of their chairman, Mahmoud
Mesteri, who has been reported as saying that 'The OPEC
countries were not responsible for colonialism and they are
giving us a great deal of aid. And so must the Soviets.' (23)
The past level of CPE aid is difficult to assess because of
data unreliability and the fact that less developed CPEs receive substantial grants and loans, whose indeterminate size
prevents an accurate comparison with OPEC or Western donors. For non-Communist LDCs it is generally concluded that
CPE assistance is substantially less in volume, has a lower
grant component, and is virtually all tied on a bilateral basis.
Holzman suggests that for the Soviet Union the net aid out-
flow, (deliveries minus repayments), as a proportion of
gross national product peaked in 1964 at less than 0.1 per
cent and by the early 1970s had fallen to under 0.05 per
cent. (24) More recently this flow has increased, and it has
been estimated that in 1978 Soviet aid commitments at $3.7
billion were beginning to approach American levels. (25) In
both their aid and trade arrangements CMEA members tend
to concentrate on large or geographically close LDCs, pre-
ferring to trade with those where some degree of socialist
transformation, or at least non-capitalist orientation is present. The decision to trade is normally economic, although
the choice of partner may be political. Aid is a much more
clearly political decision. Moreover it is a political decision

taken at best against domestic political apathy, for as
Adler-Karlsson has noted,

> there is no reason to believe that foreign aid is more
> genuinely popular among the Eastern masses than among
> the Western ones. Especially after the anti-socialist poli-
> tical changes in Indonesia and Ghana, the Soviet foreign
> aid programme is said to have been exposed to a great
> amount of domestic criticism. (26)

The Transfer of Technology Response

The initial position on the question of technology transfer
was slightly more accommodating, although clearly one of
self-interest. The statement to UNCTAD IV suggested a
new code of conduct which was to apply to all countries, and
discriminate against none. While they were willing to discuss
new patent agreements this should be 'without prejudice to
the existing and proven international rules'. (27) More
positively the Thirtieth CMEA session (Berlin, July 1976)
responded to the NIEO by establishing a one billion trans-
ferable rouble fund at the International Investment Bank,
for economic and technical assistance to LDCs. It also
established a CMEA scholarship fund for LDC nationals to
train in Eastern Europe. The value of such training may be
greater than similar schemes in Western countries, for as
Patolichev claimed at UNCTAD IV and many have echoed
since, there is no permanent brain drain to Eastern Europe,
(28) although clearly trainees can later settle in the West.
The training as much as its location induces mobility.

The Response on Wider Issues

On some of the wider issues of the NIEO, the Soviet and
East European positions are predictable if more muted. They
have serious reservations about whether the NIEO will lead
to any long-term political and economic change within LDCs,
and may prove to be counter-productive. Thus Bogomolov,
the Director of the Institute for the Economy of the World
Socialist System, USSR Academy of Sciences, reports that
the CMEA countries

> emphasize the need for progressive social transformations
> and the mustering of internal potential for economic
> growth as the chief means for changing their economic

condition. (They) oppose the diverse utopian projects
for a worldwide redistribution of wealth which tend to
distract the Third World peoples from the vital tasks of
struggling for their national liberation and social emanci-
pation and for the utmost use on that basis of their internal potential for socio-economic progress. (29)

They formally support the cooperation and unity of LDCs,
but warn that its outcome must not be discrimination against
CPEs. This increased wariness of LDC solidarity reflects a
shift in Soviet perspectives since the beginning of the major
decolonization period in the late fifties. From viewing LDCs
as natural allies they have moved to a more pragmatic position, where nationalist governments are viewed not as auto-
matic but merely as potential allies, who may prove to be un-
reliable and costly clients. Ideological reliability is now more
highly prized and rewarded, and LDC proposals supported
less often and less vigorously. The fact that in the NIEO
debate Soviet support was sometimes for the South and sometimes for the North may have considerably reduced the
South's chance of success. But the importance of this
vacillation should not be overstressed. The advanced market economies dominate world trade to such an extent that a
South-East joint approach, although influential, could never
have been decisive on major issues.

Not only has the lack of consistent Soviet support
weakened LDC chances of success, but a similar process has
developed in relation to institutional changes. The Soviet
Union has been quick to realize the inherent danger of
creating or expanding international institutions dominated by
the LDCs; institutions within which they can 'use their
majority for all the international problems at their discre-
tion.' (30) The Soviet desire to extend the scope of the
NIEO debate to cover East-West trade has already been
noted, as has their hope that UNCTAD could evolve into or
spawn a World Trade Organization. In the face of Western
and LDC opposition such plans are unrealistic, and consequently the Soviet Union has opposed extensions of
UNCTAD's terms of reference and resources while its form
of operation is unchanged.

This set of wary and not completely consistent attitudes
reflects the caution of the reluctant donor coming to terms
with the uncertain solidarity of an emerging but not very
powerful economic and political grouping. How such a response developed is examined in the next section.

THE EXPLANATION OF THE RESPONSE

In providing an explanation of the Soviet and East European response to the NIEO it is essential to concentrate on two major sets of factors: the global position and strategy of the Soviet Union, and the role of trade and type of trade policy followed by centrally planned economies. It will be argued that the rather piecemeal approach of the Soviet Union is the result of changing perceptions and policies towards LDCs. However, the rather partial nature of the response is perfectly consistent with the past history of CPE-LDC economic relations, and indeed cannot be properly understood without considering that experience. We begin by outling the policy formation process and indicating recent trends in Soviet analysis of the world economy. Then, by sketching the changing roles of trade in a centrally planned economy, we describe the chief characteristics of CPE-LDC trade and indicate how the NIEO response fits into past patterns.

In examining the processes and principles behind policy formation towards the NIEO we will concentrate on the Soviet Union as the prime mover and coordinator of the bloc's response. Given the somewhat incomplete state of knowledge about the precise processes of policy generation, parts of the account remain rather speculative.

There is one major advantage and one drawback in examining foreign policy formation. The advantage is that participation in decision-making is a rather limited activity, probably involving only a small set of senior leaders, ministers and research institutes. Moreover the considerable periods of time which many of the top decision-makers have been in the post has led to a certain stability in actual policies. The drawback is that the sensitivity of foreign policy questions means that there is less open disagreement between expert advisors, which can be used to reconstruct the internal debates, than in some other policy areas.

There are three groups of institutions within the Soviet system which have direct interests in foreign economic policy, apart from the Politbureau. The first are the relevant Central Committee departments, particularly Foreign Cadres and the International Department. Second are those ministries with direct international interests, Foreign Affairs, Defence and Foreign Trade, and the State Committee for Foreign Economic Ties (handling the economic assistance programme), State Security, and Planning. This is a minimum list of potential actors, several of which, in particular the Ministry of Foreign Trade and State Committees for Planning and Foreign Economic Ties, appear to be more

concerned with policy implementation than formation. The
third group comprises the seven specific research institutes
which might reasonably be supposed to have contributed to
the NIEO debate. Specifically those of the World Economy
and International Relations, the Economy of the World
Socialist System (which is known to have produced a discussion document on CPEs and the NIEO), (31) Africa, Eastern
Studies, the Far East, Latin America, and the United States.
The heads of such institutes are not academics but 'persons
with substantial experience in the Central Committee apparatus or Ministry of Foreign Trade (and) who presumably retain a major policy interest and who presumably are appointed to their post because the leadership wants the institutes
to have such an interest'. (32)

As far as domestic Soviet actors are concerned these
three sets of institutions along with the Praesidium of the
Council of Ministers, the Central Committee and the Politbureau appear to exhaust the policy formation cast list. If
the issue of the NIEO was dealt with in a fairly standard way
then a temporary commission involving interested institutions and relevant specialists would have produced a draft
of operational responses. The draft would have passed
through the Central Committee and on an issue of this
importance it is hard to believe that some Politbureau involvement did not occur. How and where other bloc members were
involved is obscure. But it was suggested about that CMEA
meetings would provide an ideal forum for discussion, and
given the nature of the responses examined in the previous
section, it is unlikely that there were many serious disagreements between the signatories to the joint statements.
The concessions to the LDCs were so minor and the policy
pronouncements so general that individual CPEs had wide
powers of manoeuvre on all issues.

On the research institutes, recent work by Valkenier has
apparently established an important division of opinion, between those who still view the LDCs in the context of a world
economy divided between the Socialist and Capitalist camps,
with most LDCs as appendages of the latter, and those whose
perspective is that of an interdependent global economy.(33)
She convincingly argues that the second view has become
increasingly influential in the current process of strengthening the international economic linkages of the Soviet economy.
The proponents of this framework of analysis are more concerned with the economic rather than political aspects of
CPE-LDC trade, more interested in the development demands
of the domestic economy than in whether LDCs can hope to
develop while still trading with capitalist economies.

It seems likely that both views influenced the policy-making process on NIEO, but more recently disillusionment with the returns from supporting 'bourgeois national liberation movements' may have led to a return to emphasis on ideological reliability in Third World allies. (34) But whatever the precise influence of the alternative views, it is clear that some response to NIEO was required.

The main difficulty in framing a response arose from conflicting objectives and constraints. While the Soviet Union could gain some advantage from support for LDCs, and at the same time divide LDCs and the West, significant material concessions would damage domestic development policies. Yet failure to respond might enhance the credibility of China as a leader of the Third World.   On the other hand Soviet support might not be effective in gaining concessions from the West.   But as the Soviet bloc was interested in expanding rather than contracting its role in the world economy, it could hardly stand aside from the creation of new international institutions.   Then again such institutions tend to be dominated by the developed market economies or, in the case of many United Nations agencies, the less developed market economies.   So a natural option might be to continue the past policy of minimal involvement in such institutions. However, such a policy would constitute defeat by default, and remove still further from international discussion the key questions of East-West trade and the creation of a World Trade Organization which was what really interested the bloc.   The dilemma facing the Soviet Union is clear, for it 'has a growing stake in an international order which it fundamentally rejects but which it has *exceedingly little power to change*'. (35)   In this position its approach is understandable.   Rhetorical support, but few actual concessions; switching from support to one side of that of the other on different issues; refusing to extend the powers of UNCTAD when it is clear that the LDCs did not want attention diverted from their position; (36) a willingness to let the discussions drift into stalemate.

Despite such conflicting objectives the responses themselves are consistent with the past objectives and characteristics of CPE-LDC trade.   Indeed they cannot be separated from these facets of planning.   In a CPE we can distinguish four sets of roles for foreign trade; the static, the dynamic, the cooperative and the political. (37)   In the Soviet economy the static role of trade as a breaker of domestic bottlenecks, as a provider of temporary scarce inputs which are essential in fulfilling the domestic plan, has long since given way to trade as a dynamic growth-inducing factor.   This has implied a strengthening of foreign economic relations, and the development of long-term agreements with more and less advanced market economies. Concessions were granted in the expectation of reciprocal advantages. LDCs came to be viewed as actual or potential markets for machinery and manufactured good and suppliers of raw materials. The demands of the NIEO would effectively have worsened CPEs' terms of trade with LDCs, and were resisted for that reason.

The cooperative roles of foreign trade involve the development of economic, technical and scientific links with allies or sympathetic states. Inside the Eastern bloc the CMEA has been a major vehicle for furthering these aims. The political roles of trade cover its use as an arm of state power, and in relation to the NIEO this is the most difficult aspect to assess. The impression one gets analyzing CPE responses is that they distinguish between LDCs partly on economic, partly on political and strategic grounds. The categories, which are used separate out the poorest LDCs, follow conventional international practice. The remainder are divided into oil producers, those which are geographically close, important LDCs perhaps with large state sectors, and the remainder - which includes many middle-income states, particularly those in Central and South America.

Traditionally CPEs have expressed a preference for trade with LDCs having significant state sectors, although they have increasingly emphasized the convenience rather than the revolutionary potential of such long-term links. For example, in a recent article, Teodorovich recognizes that strengthening the state sector of LDCs may not assist and indeed may retard the development of socialist relations of production. (38) More normally such connections still combine the joint attractions of administrative convenience with the possibility of political development and influence.

In the context of the world and, more significantly, the growing bloc energy shortage, the concentration on trade with oil producers is understandable, while trade with large LDCs is partly a statistical phenomenon, partly a question of political influence. Extensive bloc relations with Brazil and Argentina are presumably examples of the former. Certainly there is no lack of awareness of the conservative nature of many LDCs' ruling élites. Not all would go so far as Malhassian (1978) in emphasizing that support for LDCs is limited to 'progressive and democratic forces', (39) but most would agree with Bognar (1977) that economic development will succeed in LDCs only if substantial internal changes and social reforms accompany the NIEO. While it might bring about some qualitative changes in the international conditions

affecting LDCs 'a genuine (real) new international economic
order can only be introduced when the revolution (socialism)
comes to power in the economically most powerful countries
and makes it possible to introduce an international division
of labour based on socialist principles'. (40)

CONCLUSION

In this paper it has been argued that the rather piecemeal
and tentative Soviet and Eastern European responses to the
NIEO can best be understood against the background of
their normal economic and political relations with LDCs.
There is no evidence that the responses marked any significant break with previous policies, nor were they intended to.
As we have seen, their standard argument is that in effect
CPEs were implementing the NIEO proposals before they were
drawn together in the United Nations Declaration. More
recently LDCs have begun to complain that such continuity
offers them no new advantages in trade and none at all in
aid.
    Although there has not been total bloc unanimity on the
subject, the interests of the different members have been
sufficiently close to present a reasonably united front. In
general they are less involved with LDCs and less vulnerable to economic pressures for them, than comparable
developed market economies; although energy shortages and
increased involvement in trade may remove this advantage.
The limited value of Western concessions has further
removed any pressure for significant Eastern responses.
Moreover, in studying the record the impression emerges that
CPEs are losing interest in forums like UNCTAD. It has
been shown in this paper that one of their main motives for
supporting the growth of UNCTAD was the hope that it
would develop into a World Trade Organization and provide a
forum for the discussion of the much more important problems of East-West trade. Failure to achieve this objective,
in the face of both LDC and Western hostility, has led to a
concomitant weakening of interest in the organization. In
this field the basic objectives of all CPEs are to secure reliable sources of supply of raw materials and markets for
manufactured goods and machinery and to participate in
trade in the most efficient growth-inducing way. Little in
the NIEO favours these objectives and so a cool reply is
understandable.
    If McCulloch is right in suggesting that 'It now appears
that representatives of the North and South have agreed, at

least tacitly, to turn the New International Economic Order
into a rescue operation for the old political order' (41) not
even a Soviet and Eastern European shift in perspective to
an interdependent global economy is likely to produce more
extensive concessions.

Notes

I am grateful to the participants in the ECPR Florence Workshop on the NIEO, and particularly to my discussant Jim
Caporaso, for providing helpful suggestions on an earlier
draft of this paper. Philip Hanson, Carl McMillan and David
Kemme also suggested improvements – but as usual all errors
of omission and commission remain my own. Research for
this paper was completed under SSRC grant HRP 7417/1.

1   Knirsch, P., The CMEA Attitude to a New Economic
    Order, 'Intereconomics', 13,5/6,1978.
2   'Foreign Trade', 1, 1979, p. 9.
3   'Foreign Trade', 7, 1979, p. 8.
4   The signatories were Bulgaria, Czechoslovakia, East
    Germany, Hungary, Mongolia, Poland and the USSR.
    These statements are undoubtedly Soviet policy, but, as
    will be argued, in almost all respects they coincide with
    the identifiable interests of the smaller bloc members.
5   Joint statement by the socialist countries at the fourth
    session of the United Nations Conference on Trade and
    Development. Supplement to 'Foreign Trade', 9, 1976,
    p. 8.
6   'Economist', 24 March 1979.
7   'Guardian', 6 November 1979. A further $150m. was to
    be raised for the first window by a per country admis-
    sion of $1m. It is intended that the second window,
    which is to finance marketing, export promotion and other
    non-stocking activities, should have $70m. from direct
    governmental contributions (UN 'Chronicle', 27, 7, 1970,
    pp. 65-66).
8   'Foreign Trade', 9, 1976, p. 11.
9   'Foreign Trade', 7, 1979, p. 38.
10 Malhassian, E.M., 'Economic Relations of Bulgaria with
    the Developing Countires,' in E. Dobozi, ed., 'Economic
    Cooperation Between Socialist and Developing Countries',
    Budapest, Hungarian Scientific Council for World Eco-
    nomy, 1978.
11 Angelis, I., 'Some Issues Concerning Economic Relations
    between the CSSR and the Developing Countries', in
    Dobozi, ed., op. cit.

12 Orosz, A., 'Gazdasagi Kapcsolataink a Fejlodo Orszago-
    kkal', Budapest, Kossuth Konyvkiado, 1978.
13 Naray argues that save for Hungary, MFN treatment is
    not applicable to CPEs because of the state monopoly of
    foreign trade and the ineffectiveness of tariff conces-
    sions. See Naray, P., A Legnagyobb Kedvesmenyes
    Elbanas Elvenek Alkalmazasa a Kelet - Nyugati Keves-
    kedelemben, 'Kulgazdasag', 21, 10, 1977.
14 Bogomolov, Zubov and Medvedev confirm this interpreta-
    tion when they state that 'MFN treatment is an essential
    condition for normal trade, political and economic rela-
    tions between countries rather than a special privilege.'
    They report that MFN clauses, with the usual exemptions
    in favour of neighbouring countries, customs unions and
    LDCs, had been included in over eighty of the ninety-
    one inter-governmental agreements signed by 1974. See:
    Bogomolov, O., 'The CMEA Countries in the Changing
    International Climate,' in Fallenbuch, Z. and McMillan,
    C., eds., 'Partners in East-West Economic Relations:
    the Determinants of Choice', Elmsford, NY, Pergamon,
    1980, p. 16; and Zubov, G. and Medvedev, K., Princi-
    pal Trends in the Soviet Union's Trade and Treaty Rela-
    tions, 'Foreign Trade', 4, 1976, p. 23.
15 Manzhulo, A. and Krasnov, G., International Forum on
    Trade and Economic Problems: Results of the Fifth
    UNCTAD Session, 'Foreign Trade', 9, 1979, p. 21.
16 Ibid., p. 22.
17 Kostecki, M.M., 'East-West Trade and the GATT Sys-
    tem', London, Macmillan, 1979.
18 He actually said: 'We ... do not opt out (of) a possibil-
    ity of transforming (UNCTAD) into a World Trade
    Organization, with its terms of reference covering also
    GATT problems.' See: Patolichev, N.S., Statement by
    the Head of the USSR Delegation to the Fourth UNCTAD
    Session, 'Foreign Trade', 7, 1976, 00. 2-9.
19 Nyerges, J., Az V. UNCTAD - Magyar Szemmel, 'Kul-
    gazdasag', 23, 4, 1979.
20 Op. cit., p. 14.
21 On the Restructuring of International Economic Relations.
    Statement by the Soviet government to K. Waldheim, UN
    Secretary-General, 4 October 1976, 'Foreign Trade',
    12, 1976, pp. 2-5.
22 Manzhulo, op. cit., p. 22.
23 'Guardian', 22 October 1979.
24 Holzman, F.D., 'International Trade under Communism:
    Politics and Economics', London, Macmillan, 1976,
    p. 195.

25 Cooper, O. and Fogarty, C., 'Soviet Economic and Military Aid to the Less Developed Countries 1954-78, in US Congress Joint Economic Committee, 'Soviet Economy in a Time of Change', Vol. 2, Washington, GPO, 1979. Actual deliveries were lower at $0.4 billion. Given the time lag in shipments this is not surprising. In the same year arms agreements at $1.8 billion were well below the trend. A substantial part of aid-generated deficits are believed to be covered by hard-currency arms sales.

26 Adler-Karlsson, G., 'The Political Economy of East-West-South Co-operation', Wien, Springer-Verlag, 1976.

27 'Foreign Trade', 9, 1976, p. 16. This suggests that only minor concessions were contemplated.

28 Patolichev, op. cit., p. 5.

29 Bogomolov, op. cit., p. 15.

30 Sofinsky, V., An Important Factor of Democratization of International Relations, 'International Affairs', (Moscow, September 1977, p. 124.

31 Fedorenko, N., Economic Science in the Tenth Five Year-Plan Period, 'Voprosy Ekonomiki', 7, 1978.

32 Hough, J.F. and Fainsod, M., 'How the Soviet Union is Governed', Cambridge, Massachusetts, Harvard University Press, 1979, p. 399.

33 Valkenier, E.K., The USSR, the Third World, and the Global Economy, 'Problems of Communism', 28, 1979.

34 I am indebted to Philip Hanson for this point.

35 Legvold, R., The USSR and the World Economy: The Political Dimension', in Legvold, R., ed., 'The Soviet Union and the World Economy', NY, Council on Foreign Relations, 1979, p. 2.

36 Western nations have also opposed such an extension, although for rather different reasons. Many declined to answer a recent UNCTAD questionnaire on aid and boycotted UNCTAD meetings on IMF reform. ('Guardian', 11 August 1980.)

37 For an extended discussion of the changing roles of trade within CPEs, See: Lawson, C.W., 'The Stability, Structure and Direction of Communist Foreign Trade, 1960-72', Phd. Thesis, University of London, Chapter One, 1979.

38 Teodorovich, T., The USSR's Role in Building up the State Sector of the National Economy of Developing Countries, 'Foreign Trade', 2, 1979.

39 Malhassian, op. cit., p. 207.

40 Bognar, J., 'The Fight for a New System of International Relations', Budapest, Hungarian Scientific Council for World Economy, 1977.

41 McCulloch, R. North-South Economic and Political Rela-
    tions: How Much Change?, 'Harvard Institute of Econo-
    mic Research', Discussion Paper 645, August, 1978,
    p. 4.

SWEDEN:
THE JANUS FACE OF PROGRESSIVENESS

B. Nygren

INTRODUCTION

The increase of oil prices in 1973/74 created a state of uncertainty in the industrialized countries. The decisions of
the Sixth Special Session of the United Nations General
Assembly, which adopted the Declaration and Programme of
Action on the Establishment of the New International Economic Order, must be seen in the light of this unclear situation. (1) Politicians endorsed a comprehensive programme
for changed international relations - probably without having
a real grasp of what the programme contained, nor what
could be the result of the decisions made. The Western
world was taken by surprise. They did not object openly to
the programme. Decisions on the Declaration and Programme
of Action were made by consensus. However, many explanations of votes were made. Endorsing the programme was
maybe only an act of gaining time while the real impact of
the increases of the oil prices and the resulting change of
economic relations emerged.

THE NATURE OF THE RESPONSE

In Sweden, politicians from all camps declared their support
for the New Order. The NIEO 'gained wider support than
there had been cause to expect. The concept soon became
something of a holy cow; its legitimacy was left virtually un-
challenged and there was hardly any discussion of its content either.'(2) The wide NIEO concept did surely lend itself to many different kinds of interpretations. Some believe that the recommendations aim at a kind of international
planned economy. This view is based on the fact that some

188

of the proposals suggest the need for considerable market
intervention. Others read the texts as a recommendation
for continued capitalist growth and, in so doing, base their
remarks on what is said about liberalizing trade, capital
movements and other transactions. In the first spate of
enthusiasm some groups also imagined that the UN resolution embodied a plan for a world society that would econo-
mize more with non-renewable resources. (3)
Summarizing drastically, but not altogether unfairly, one
can say the Sixth Special Session of the General Assembly
recommends an integrated, though not yet fully spelled out
programme to give the developing countries a larger share
of the world's resources and power. This is meant to take
place by means of continued rapid economic growth within a
framework for a stabilized and liberalized world economy. In
other words simply, as Amuzegar (14) pointed out, a 'new
deal' for the poor countries in the world. It is thus not a
matter of a new and different world order. The demands of
the developing countries are really quite modest. (6)
The NIEO programme did in fact contain few new elements. It was largely a compilation of proposals made by the
developing countries over a long period of time in different
international organizations. What was new was the framework for the proposals and the setting for this international
conference. The decisions of the Sixth Special Session gave
momentum to the international negotiating machinery. A
great number of international conferences followed. The
general principles laid down in the new order were then to
be transformed into concrete action and that would show the
strength (or lack) of political support for the NIEO.
Probably the decisions of the Sixth Special Session also
contributed to a change of the Western world's concept of
the developing countries. During the sixties, developing
countries were discussed mostly in connection with development assistance whereas other measures affecting the
developing countries received little attention. Now, the
developing countries had shown that they were no longer
passive recipients. They claimed a bigger share of the cake.
The rise in oil prices and the subsequent NIEO debate presented the developing countries in a new light, namely as a
group capable of translating words into action. (6)

From Idealism to Pragmatism

Recent economic difficulties has shown that Sweden is not
that progressive, permissive, affluent, middle-way welfare

democracy it appeared to be in the sixties. As time has
passed, it has also become clear that international solidarity
which was regarded as the prime motive for our concerns
for the Third World, was not as deep-rooted and widespread as one would have thought judging from official
declarations and the public debate. When Third World demands have collided with the Swedish interests, solidarity
has had to give way to self-interest. Commercial interests
have gained influence over the Third World policy. New
slogans such as interdependence and mutuality of interest
are gaining ground. Idealism as a dominant feature of Third
World policy is fading away while a more pragmatic approach
is more evident.

It seems clear that the fundamental changes in the world
economy which became apparent during the last part of the
seventies, and which resulted in a slowing down of economic
activity in Western Europe, had a substantial effect on
Swedish attitudes towards the Third World. The public
debate turned away from international issues and became
more inward-looking. As the affluence of our society, which
so long was taken for granted, has proved to be fragile,
solidarity with the Third World hardly ever appears in
speeches made by politicians. How to overcome the present
economic crisis is what concerns the politicians and people.

In 1976 a 44-year-long period of Social Democratic
governments ended. First a centre-liberal-conservative
government was established, which fell on disagreement on
nuclear energy. A liberal minority government took over.
Following general elections in the autumn of 1979, a new
coalition government was formed. After 1976 development
cooperation has been the responsibility of a liberal minister.

No doubt, the changes of governments have had an impact
on Third World policy. Decisions such as the one to terminate aid to Cuba or to join the Inter-American Bank would
most likely not have been made by a Social Democratic
Government. However, as is indicated by the examples
given below, on the whole, the Third World policy of the
Social Democrats does not differ all that much from that of
the governments after 1976. The change of policy cannot be
explained solely by the changes of government.

How these changes in attitudes and thinking have resulted
in a changed policy, will be demonstrated by brief discussions on the aid level, commercialization of Third World contacts and action taken by the government in connection with
proposals on massive transfer of resources. However, before that, a brief review of the conditions during the ' progressive' sixties is made in order to provide a background

to the changes in policies and attitudes that later took place.

The Progressive Sixties

During the late sixties public interest in conditions in the Third World grew. A strong opinion in favour of the developing countries emerged. Demonstrations were held in favour of a more generous aid policy when the parliament was to discuss a new bill laying down the principles for official development assistance. (7)

All political parties gave their support for a rapid increase of development assistance. Surely, there were differences of opinion as regards suitable means of transfers, whether aid should be tied or untied, what channels to use, bilateral or multilateral, what countries to assist, but, on the whole, an increase of development assistance was never in dispute. In 1962 the objective of reaching one per cent of GNP in development assistance was first pronounced in a government bill. In 1968, the government decided that it would be a reality within a five-year period, and in 1974 the objective was attained.

Was the increase of development assistance an act of genuine solidarity or did some elements of self-interest also play a role? Government bills on aid policy do emphasize the moral motive for aid. In the presentation of the bill of 1962 the Prime Minister Tage Erlander said that 'assistance was an expression of a feeling of moral duty and international solidarity'. Such feelings did stem from 'a deeper understanding of the fact that peace, freedom and prosperity are not exclusively national, but something more universal and indivisible.' (8)

Solidarity or self-interest - sometimes the distinction is difficult to make. In both bills mentioned, development assistance is seen as a means to promote a peaceful development in the world. It is said that more equitable economic conditions may be a prerequisite for peaceful international relations. Therefore, it is in accordance with Swedish interests that 'political independence, which most developing countries have acquired recently, be given an economic base and a social content, which is a prerequisite for a democratic development of society and for real national independence.'(9)

The programme for development assistance expanded. Development aid increased from 0.12 per cent of GNP in 1962 to 0.38 per cent in 1970. By 1974 the 0.7 per cent target was reached. (10)

No doubt, the progressive image Sweden got through the generous aid policy matched the objectives of the foreign policy at the time. Sweden's being the first nation attaining the 0.7 per cent target, being the largest per capita contributor to the UNDP and being politically supportive of the Third World demands rendered Swedish politicians attention and appreciation from the Third World in international fora. That underlined the policy of non-alignment and added weight to a small nation eager to play a role on the international arena.

Aid Level

Following the attainment of the 0.7 per cent target, Swedish aid as a percentage of GNP has increased quite slowly. In 1974 it amounted to 0.94 per cent of the GNP (11) No further increases are envisaged. On the contrary, it could even be reduced. During recent discussions on Sweden's economic problems, it has been indicated by the conservative party that according to their opinion aid may have to be cut, though slightly, as part of the grand retrenchment programme which is being carried out in order to decrease the budget deficit of Skr. 55 billion by Skr. 7 billion. Also, aid is no doubt a burden on the balance of payments, which in 1980 ran into a deficit of more than Skr. 20 billion.

The government may have difficulties in explaining why aid should be left untouched, when, as is already announced, cuts have to be made in the social welfare budget. And the question may be put why Sweden, in the light of the new economic difficulties, should continue to have such an outstanding ODA performance among DAC member countries, when the ones with more prosperous economic outlooks make little or no effort to increase their ODA budgets.

Of course, a decrease of the aid level would not pass without reactions. In an article in the newspaper 'Dagens Nyheter' a leading official from the Swedish Development Authority (SIDA) has discussed the changed principles for development assistance during recent years. In his opinion the most important thing is to maintain the level of aid. Should changes be required, the content first has to be looked at.

If one argues that the Swedish crisis economy requires a changed direction of development assistance, I would prefer an increased part being tied (delivery of goods from Sweden) to the mixed forms of assistance. Tying of aid

results in increased exports ... Tied aid can be used for
cooperation with the poorest countries. Mixed forms
favours in particular the better offs among the developing countries. (12)

Such a change in aid policy may also be acceptable to the
Social Democrats. In their Programme on Development Cooperation from 1978 it is said that

there is hardly any need to establish a new (quantitative)
goal. Efforts ought to be made in order to, concomitantly
with growing resources, raise the level. Of greatest
importance is however to improve the quality of Swedish
assistance and direct it more clearly towards agreed
objectives. (13)

Commercialization of Contacts

A number of measures have been taken during recent years
which have aimed at increasing commercial contacts with the
Third World. Often such measures have been justified by
using formulations of the demands from the Third World,
such as the UNCTAD II slogan 'Trade not aid' and the 25
per cent industrialization goal formulated at UNIDO II in
Lima in 1975.

In response to demands for increased trade, a system of
preference for products from developing countries was
adopted in 1972. The range of goods covered by the system
was widened in 1974, and the system is now applicable for
all manufactured goods, except textiles, shoes and leather
products. In accordance with the Swedish agreements with
the EEC and EFTA, Swedish duties have to be lowered for
imports from these countries.

Thus, products where many developing countries are
very competitive are in fact burdened by higher duties than
imports from other countries. Concern about employment in
Sweden, maintenance of a minimum level of production for
security reasons, good relations with nearby influential industrialized countries, have thus proved to be more important than responding to Third World demands.

Textiles is certainly a case in point. Sweden has the
highest import penetration among industrialized countries.
It is also true that the textile and clothing industries have
shrunk to a very low level. However, while imports from
EFTA and EEC countries, except Portugal, are completely
free, imports from developing countries are strictly

regulated through bilateral agreements concluded under the umbrella agreement, the Multifiber Agreement.

In connection with the Multilateral Trade Negotiations, Sweden offered reduction of duties on tropical products, which among other things meant that the tariff on coffee was abolished. Following that measure, 90 per cent of total imports and 99 per cent of imports from the least developed countries are duty free.

The Social Democrats have taken a very cautious stand regarding increased trade with developing countries. They reason that efforts by the developing countries to increase production will also result in increased exports. Responses to demands from the Third World for improved access to markets in industrialized countries require that the structure of industry be changed. 'But such change of structure of industry in the industrialized countries must be planned if it is to materialize in socially acceptable forms,' (15) The Social Democrats are thus not prepared to work for improved market access unconditionally. They disapprove of international competition which allows exploitation of labour in developing countries and demand that an agreement be concluded within GATT on a social clause.

> The Social Clause means that the members of GATT are demanded to pursue policies aimed at full employment in order to benefit from the rules of trade. It further means right to prohibition of export of dangerous work places in order to protect the employees. The Social Clause requires employers not to exploit people living in societies with high unemployment by offering them conditions which are obviously unacceptable and below minimum level of existence. In order to achieve this, stronger influence from the trade unions over trade policy as well as trade union representation in GATT ... is required. (16)

As another means to stimulate trade with developing countries, a Swedish office for promotion of imports from developing countries was established in 1974. This office, IMPOD, serves developing countries by providing information about the Swedish market, barriers to trade etc., and, to a certain extent, assists in marketing. The effects of the activities of IMPOD could be a stimulation of price competition and a facilitated introduction of goods previously not marketed in Sweden. Thus, the activities are not only a form of assistance to exporters in developing countries, but they are also of benefit to Swedish consumers. Interestingly enough, the entire costs of these operations are financed from the aid budget. The allocation is, however, quite small, namely Skr. 3.5 million, compared with the total of Skr. 5,015 million for the fiscal year 1980/81.

The establishment of IMPOD was not particularly controversial in Sweden, but the office set up to foster industrial cooperation was more debated. Industrial promotion was seen as a significant expression of new tendencies in development cooperation. The Swedish Fund for Industrial Cooperation with Developing Countries, SWEFUND, should, according to the Commission appointed to make an inquiry into the field of industrial development cooperation and to look at conditions for establishing such a fund, promote the formation of manufacturing companies in the poorest developing countries by stimulating transfer of capital and know-how from Swedish industry. (17) For that purpose, the fund is allocated Skr. 33.7 million from the 1980/81 aid budget. The Commission also proposed that the capacity of the Swedish International Development Authority (SIDA) to handle assistance in the field of industry should be strengthened.

The aid budget thus appears to be utilized more and more for activities with mixed objectives - activities not only to satisfy the traditional objectives for development assistance, but also to satisfy objectives for internal Swedish economic policy. The latest example of a measure of such character is a proposal for establishment of a system for mixed credits for Swedish exports to developing countries. (18) Formerly the recipients got their equipment or whatever the loans were meant to finance, as gifts. Now, the government wishes to introduce a credit system. In a report by a government commission it is said that there is a demand from the Third World for this form of assistance, expressions of which could be found *inter alia* in the UN resolution on the NIEO. 'Many developing countries consider today that they would benefit more from increased financial resources at a cost lower than the market cost, than from transfers in the form of gifts.' (19)

It is indicated in the report that such a system for soft credits can be compared with lending from international and regional institutions such as the World Bank, the Asian Development Bank or the Inter-American Development Bank. 'These banks provide credits on soft terms *inter alia* for financing of imports of capital goods in connection with development projects. The credits may be used only for purchases in the countries which are members of the Banks.' (20) In a parallel manner, a Swedish system for mixed credits would, according to the proposal, only apply to exports from Sweden. Although it is said in the report that subsidized exports will result in an ineffective allocation of resources, the report still finds it justified to use such means in order to help increase exports. The reason for that is mainly the substantial external deficit of the Swedish economy. Also, it is pointed out that markets in the OECD countries can be expected to grow slowly in the future. Therefore, it is important that Swedish industry finds outlets for their products in developing countries.

It is thus proposed in the report that a system of mixed credits should be introduced.

> Swedish mixed credits should be used on a selective basis and only be used when, in addition to developmental considerations, it is deemed particularly important to strengthen the market position of Swedish industry on one or more developing country markets or for the launching of new Swedish products. The beneficial credits should thus be used in order to finance such imports to developing countries which otherwise would not have materialized and which could be expected to result in future increased demand for goods and services from Sweden. (21)

Probably, the Swedish self-interest in development assistance has never been more clearly pronounced. The sum to be allocated from the budget for development assistance for this purpose is not particularly large (Skr. 60 million), but nevertheless this proposal is a significant indication of a change of policy.

It is remarkable that alternative ways of strengthening the ability of the developing countries to sustain their imports are not discussed in the report. The proposed system with mixed credits is compared with lending from international financial institutions, but the question is never raised whether in fact increased lending through such institutions would be of greater benefit to developing countries than the proposed Swedish system. Instead, considerable attention is devoted to similar credit systems in other countries. The risk of increased credit competition is recognized but not regarded dangerous enough to motivate the Swedish government to refrain from introducing a system with mixed credits. In principle, the Commission argues, such competition should be reduced and controlled. However, the Commission apparently feels that it is necessary to introduce this measure in order to be in a position to abolish it. (22)

It may be noted that the tendency in Swedish Third World policy towards establishing a kind of 'broader cooperation' with developing countries and having part of these new measures financed from the aid budget, is in line with the thinking of the Social Democratic Party. The Social Democrats propound that agreements for cooperation be concluded with developing countries and say that:

> the aid allocation may be used in this connection, but of course according to the fundamental principles for aid policy laid down previously in the report. The agreements will not have to be limited to countries fulfilling all the requirements for receiving Swedish aid, but may also be guided by other aims discussed above as means of the economic foreign policy. (23)

Massive Transfer of Resources

Some of the more controversial elements in the NIEO demands are the ones concerning monetary reform. As pointed out in the introductory chapter, the Third World is demanding increased influence in the IMF, increased transfers of financial resources and debt renegotiation. (24) Sweden has conceded the demand for debt cancellations, though, as pointed out in the chapter on the Federal Republic of Germany, only on a selective basis. The concession involves no great sacrifices, since the debts were negligible. The forceful criticism from the Third World of the methods of operation employed by the IMF has met little explicit sympathy by the government.

The Swedish attitude towards the IMF has been quite respectful. A cautious wording in the budgetary bill for the fiscal year 1980/81 reads:

> from the Swedish point of view, we welcome the increased interest within the IMF for the economic situation of the developing countries. The growing balance of payment and debt problems which the development countries are facing in the 1980s require increased preparedness. In that connection an extended cooperation between the IMF and the World Bank appear to be justified. Sweden consider it furthermore justified to support realistic proposals for increased influence for the Third World in these institutions. (25)

As regards the IMF, the Social Democratic Party has taken a more radical stand than the government. In their

Programme on Development Cooperation from 1978 it is said that:

> IMF's rules and methods of operations are to a large extent influenced by capitalistic values ... They (the IMF) often request as a condition for extension of loans that the countries limit the size of their public sector, discontinue social redistribution policies and allow foreign investments ... Social Democrats ought to give full support to a reform aiming at getting away from the present weighted voting system and introducing more democratic forms of decision-making. (26)

The Social Democratic Party also supports establishments of a link between SDRs and development finance. (27)

However, as regards an increase in the transfer of resources, the Swedish government has taken very active part in discussions on ways and means to achieve a flow of resources in addition to ODA. The ideas launched by the EEC Commissionary, Claude Cheysson, in 1977 aroused great interest in the office within the Ministry of Foreign Affairs responsible for development cooperation.

The Cheysson proposal was put forward at a time of stagnation of economic activity in the OECD countries. The underlying idea was that a 'massive transfer of resources' to the developing countries would enhance their purchasing power and that their increased demand would be directed towards the industrialized countries. Thus, resources lying idle due to recession would be used and that would give a boost to the economy of the OECD countries. This new 'Marshall-plan' would, according to Mr Cheysson, supply the developing countries with about US$ 10 billion during a period of 3-5 years. (28)

A Swedish paper on this matter was presented at the Second meeting of the Committee of the Whole in May 1978. When introducing the paper in the committee, the Swedish Ambassador said:

> Firstly, we do feel that massive transfers should be seen as supplementing not substituting regular ODA flows. Secondly, massive transfers of resources should not only be seen in a short-term economic stabilization perspective, or as a means of levelling out the present economic recession by increasing the low capacity utilization in the industrialized countries ... In this longer perspective such transfers would be aimed at supporting the industrialization process in developing countries and

increasing the production potential in industrialized countries. (29)

In this speech mutuality of interest was apparent as a theme. Solidarity now has to be subordinated to self-interest. Not as a principle, but in view of the fact that it is seen as the only way to solve prevailing problems.

The paper presented at the UN meeting did not contain any elaborate concrete proposal. In fact, it only called for studies to be made within the UN system of how such proposals could be formulated and what would be their possible effects. In spite of that very tentative and cautious approach, the proposal met with very limited appreciation from the Group of 77. No decision was made at the meeting to initiate the proposed studies. However, the Swedish government continued its efforts to push this proposal. At UNCTAD V held in Manila in May-June 1979, a more positive attitude was shown by the developing countries. Decision was taken to study the ramifications of such transfers.

The proposal on massive transfer of resources has been discussed in the Swedish press. One official from the government says in one article that: 'Solidarity and global justice simply have not been strong enough arguments for increased aid. Ideas on massive transfer of resources in which the self-interest is clearly declared may therefore be a realistic solution in order to change the paradoxical economic situation which prevails.' (30) But one development economist points to the necessity of questioning transfer of financial resources as a means that automatically generates development. He further says that:

> one of the lessons (from tied aid) was that the cheapest way of attaining two objectives - employment in Sweden and maximum transfer of resources to developing countries - is to devise on the one hand special employment generating measures in Sweden, and on the other allocate untied assistance ... Apparently clever attempts to reach two objectives with one measure have often proved to result in considerable loss of efficiency. Massive transfer of resources seems to be such a proposal. (31)

Meanwhile, reality has changed and so has the perception of the most important problems. Thus, the gist of the measures now being discussed are different from what they were a few years ago.

Under-utilized capacity is indeed still a problem. However, the growing financial imbalances have resulted in

attention being focussed on the delicate question of how to
manage the recycling process avoiding bank failures which
could threaten the whole financial system and thus the
economies of both industrialized and developing countries.

Massive transfer of resources have thus more and more
become the heading for a recycling operation. The government still puts much emphasis on this matter, but has so far
abstained from giving it a concrete content. This may also
be indicative of the change of policy and the change of conditions for formulating the policy. It is no longer only a
question of responding to demands and giving concessions.
The dependence of the industrialized countries on the
developing countries, particularly the OPEC countries, has
become apparent. Therefore, there are now a number of
areas within the NIEO framework where a foundation for real
negotiations has emerged. A New Order, not necessarily
identical with the NIEO of 1974, which will manifest the new
role of the developing countries, or at least some of them,
is bound to materialize. Such a change of the framework
for international relations will not come because the industrialized countries voluntarily and out of solidarity with the
Third World conceded their demands, but as a response to a
real shift of economic and political power.

THE EXPLANATION OF THE RESPONSE

In this section factors discussed in the previous part which
could explain the policy response of the Swedish government
to the demands for a New International Economic Order will
be summarized. When trying to get a clear picture of the
response to these demands and the different factors that
have influenced the response since 1974, it may be useful to
distinguish between the initial reaction and the response
that has emerged later.

The initial all-pervading positive reaction could be interpreted in different, not altogether mutually exclusive, ways.
The cynical explanation is that politicians, confused over the
undoubtedly quite unexpected determination of the Third
World, preferred to concede the high-sounding principles,
while waiting for the real implications to emerge.

It is also plausible that in some quarters a genuine support prevailed in favour of a programme that would result in
substantially better conditions for developing countries and
that many persons actually believed that the NIEO would in
fact result in a more equitable world order.

Probably both explanations of the initial reaction are true.

However, the historical background also has to be taken into account. Maybe, that is the most important explanation. During the sixties the development cooperation policy had been comparatively progressive and had had a wide political support. The initial positive reaction to the NIEO could thus be seen as nothing but a logical consequence of the development cooperation policy pursued until then.

However, over time the initial positive reaction was transformed into a more diluted, maybe lukewarm response to the NIEO. Explanations to that development could be found both internally and externally. The internal factors are not unaffected by developments in other countries and in international organizations. Thus, it has to be borne in mind that the passive and even negative response in other countries to the NIEO, and the inertia which has characterized the international negotiations machinery when the goals and objectives laid down in the NIEO were to be transformed to concrete measures, have of course had an impact on the Swedish response.

Among the internal factors which have had a bearing on the 'long-term' response, the development cooperation tradition could be seen as the only factor working in favour of a positive response, while other factors, such as change of public opinion, changes of governments, and, most importantly, the deterioration of the economic development, all have worked against it.

In principle, there has been political agreement on the fundamental objectives for the Third World policy. The rapid increase of the aid level, the principle of untied aid and the choice of major recipients of bilateral assistance are factors that have contributed in giving Sweden a position as one of the industrialized countries with the most progressive Third World policies. Though much space has been devoted above to demonstrating the changes of policy that have taken place, it is important to keep in mind that the government has always been anxious to maintain a progressive image abroad. 'Bridge-building' had been regarded as an important feature of foreign policy in the North-South context. Thus, if the government were to continue to act as a mediator between developing and developed countries, it had to tread cautiously not to lose credibility in any camp, and consequently dramatic changes have been avoided.

During the sixties, there was a strong opinion in favour of a progressive Third World policy. Later it changed, partly in response to changing economic circumstances. Thereby the pressure on the politicians to pursue a vigorous Third World policy eased. Decreased public interest in

Third World matters combined with changing economic conditions paved the way for the change of policy above labelled · 'from idealism to pragmatism'. In this connection it may also be appropriate to recall the rather disappointing results of aid transferred during the last decades. How to transfer aid in an efficient manner is a question that so far has not received a satisfactory answer. Growing doubts on the usefulness of transferring resources of which a large part never reaches its destination have probably also had an impact on the shift of emphasis in the development cooperation policy.

This shift of policy was of course also the result of changes of governments. Following the Conservative-Centre-Liberal take-over in 1976, no doubt, the business community increased their influence over the Third World policy. Business groups, which during the sixties had argued strongly but to no avail in favour of closer cooperation between business and aid authorities, now got a chance to present their arguments to politicians whose political stand made them more inclined to listen and respond favourable.

The very fact that business groups got easy access to the new government is however not a sufficient explanation and should not be over-emphasized when the shift of policy is to be explained. More important than the actual pressure exerted from business groups is probably the fact that the new government had a different view on the role of trade and investment in development cooperation. When the economic situation became a constraint to a continuously generous aid policy, the government had, from an ideological point of view, no difficulty in putting more emphasis on commercial relations with developing countries.

The change of government has made it possible to see both of the Janus faces of Sweden's Third World policy, but, as also the former prime minister Olof Palme has admitted, there have always been two faces. (32)

Notes

1   Anell, L. and Nygren, B., 'The Developing Countries and the World Economic Order', London, Frances Pinter, 1980.
2   The Secretariat for Futures Studies, 'Sweden in a New International Economic Order - a project presentation', Stockholm, Liber, 1979, p. 46.
3   Anell, L. and Nygren, B., 'The Developing Countries and the World Economic Order', op. cit., p. 124.
4   J. Amuzegar is an Iranian economist. He has *inter alia*

written 'Technical Assistance in Theory and Practice. The Case of Iran'.

5 Annell, L. and Nygren, B., 'The Developing Countries and the World Economic Order', op. cit., pp. 124-125.

6 The Secretariat for Futures Studies, 'Sweden in a New International Economic Order', op. cit., pp. 45-46.

7 Government bill on Swedish development assistance, 'Proposition 101', Stockholm, 1968.

8 'Swedish Cooperation with Developing Countries', White paper SOU 13, Stockholm, 1977, p. 222.

9 Ibid., p. 23.

10 Organization for Economic Cooperation and Development, 'Development Cooperation Review', 1973, 1978 and 1980.

11 Ibid., 1980.

12 Göransson, B., Bundet bistand att föredra i krisläge, 'Dagens Nyheter', Stockholm, 28 April 1980.

13 Socialdemokraterne, 'Arbetarrörelsen och en rätvisare världsordning' (The Labour Movement and a More Equitable World Order), Bôras, 1978.

14 'Swedish Cooperation with Developing Countries', op. cit., pp. 181-182.

15 (The Labour Movement and a More Equitable World Order), op. cit., p. 39.

16 Ibid., pp. 39-40.

17 'Swedish Cooperation with Developing Countries', op. cit., p. 77.

18 Report from interdepartmental working group, 'Blandade krediter' (Mixed Credits), Stockholm, 1980.

19 Ibid., p. 85.

20 Ibid., p. 80.

21 Ibid., p. 93.

22 Ibid., p. 94.

23 (The Labour Movement and a More Equitable World Order), op. cit., p. 56.

24 Resolution 3202, United Nations General Assembly, Section II.

25 Government Budget Bill, 'Proposition 100 - 1979-80', Appendix 6, p. 30.

26 (The Labour Movement and a More Equitable World Order), op. cit., p. 33.

27 Ibid., p. 34.

28 Rylander, S. and Jerlström, B., 'En ny Marshall-plan? (A New Marshall Plan?), 'Rapport från SIDA', No. 8, 1977, p. 1. In an UNCTAD-document possible effects of increased Third World demand on industry in the industrialized countries are looked at. The study

indicates that it is not likely that the total of increased Third World demand will be directed towards the industrialized countries, particularly not in industries such as ship-building, where many developing countries are competitive. UNCTAD TD/B/C.3/161/Supp.1, 29 April 1980.

29 Statement by Ambassador Thunborg, Sweden, in the Committee of the Whole on 3 May 1978.

30 Jerlström, B., 80-talet sätter u-hjälpen i nytt perspektiv, (The 80s put Development Cooperation in a New Perspective), 'Dagens Nyheter', 23 July 1980.

31 Goppers, K., Trots 20 års negative erfarenheter - Blind trö pa massiv u-hjälp, (In Spite of 20 Years of Negative Experience - Blind Faith in Massive Aid), 'Dagens Nyheter', 28 April 1980.

32 'In a sense Sweden does have two faces: we have a face that protects the interests of our citizens, and a face that provides assistance to the Third World.' Olof Palme in an interview in 'Third World Quarterly', Vol. II, No. 4, p. 646.

UNITED STATES:
WHO PAYS THE PIPER?

G.C. Abbott

In order to understand the American response, it is necessary to put the NIEO demands into perspective. Most of
the demands contained in the Programme of Action, the
blueprint for action, have all been heard before and on more
than one occasion. The arguments are thus well-known and
fully articulated in the literature. It would be quite wrong
therefore to assume that the Programme of Action represented a package of new demands. What it did was to aggregate
all the outstanding demands of the developing countries,
incorporate them into a single package and label it the NIEO.

It appears that the developing countries took the view
that negotiating individual issues was slow, painful and un-
coordinated. It was also unlikely to make a major break-
through on the problem of restructuring the world economy.
What was clearly called for was a more comprehensive global
or macro-approach covering a whole range of demands and
involving an equally large number of countries. By mobilis-
ing support on as wide a front as possible, it was hoped to
force the developed countries to make a number of concessions which would not have been possible otherwise. Basically, therefore, it was an attempt to mobilise political, ideological and international support in order to extract additional economic concessions from the developed countries.

The 1973 oil crisis provided the opportunity as well as
the justification for implementing this change of strategy.
Among other things it enthused the developing countries
with a new sense of purpose and power. For the first time
they became aware of the fact that it was possible to extract
substantial and lasting benefits from the developed countries
through the use of economic power and commodity cartelisation. Impressed no doubt, by the way the members of OPEC
had almost single-handedly brought the economies of the

industrial countries to a stand-still, they felt that the
time was right for an all-out collective approach for wresting
control of the international economy from these countries.

Accordingly, the Programme of Action called on the
developing countries to promote the use of commodity power
through cartels, producers' associations and similar organi-
sations in order to maintain or increase the price of individual commodities by restricting their supply. They were
also advised to engage in price-fixing, division of marketing
territories, centralisation of sales, pooling of profits and
other restrictive practices in order to free themselves from
the influence of market forces and earn above-normal profits
for themselves.

For their part, the developed countries were required to
introduce a number of sweeping changes in the existing
world trade and payments system specifically for the benefit
of the developing countries. They had created a world system which not only neglected the basic needs of the vast
majority of the world's population, but had established a
system of dependence and unequal exchange which, in turn,
was largely responsible for the vast disparities and inequalities in the distribution of the world's wealth. It was thus
unjust. It perpetuated international inequalities and was
incompatible with the common goals of international cooperation and development. They must therefore accept the
responsibility and moral obligation to establish a new order
based on peace, justice, equality, stability and concern for
the future of all mankind.

This then, is the context in which NIEO must be evaluated. On the one hand it called upon the developing countries to use their collective economic and political power to
gain control of the international economy. On the other it
accused the developed countries of corrupting, distorting
and exploiting the same system for their own ends, and
demanded that they institute a new order based on morality,
humanitarianism and common concern for mankind. NIEO
was thus about power, economic and political power, how to
get it, and how to use it to further group interests, with
one basic distinction. Whereas one group was advised to
seize it and use it to further its own interests, the other
was required to relinquish it in the interest of all humanity.

THE IMPLEMENTATION OF NIEO

However, the strategy for implementing NIEO was based on
a number of false premises, misplaced hopes and a lot of

wishful thinking. Aside from petroleum, the developing countries have no commodities which can be effectively cartelised. A brief look at some obvious possibilities will suffice. Although they account for over 50% of world exports of coffee, tea, cocoa, sugar, jute, cotton and rubber, their ability to form producers' associations to keep prices artificially high is limited by the relative ease with which these commodities can be replaced, or their consumption reduced.

Attempts in the past to lessen their vulnerability to adverse market conditions or to raise prices can only be described as moderately successful. The International Coffee Agreement expired in 1973 and has since been superseded by the Cafe Mundial, an association of producers controlling the international supply of coffee. The six major rubber producing countries have formed the Association of Natural Rubber Producing Countries with a view mainly to controlling supplies and maintaining prices within a specified range through the operation of buffer stocks. Their scope for effective action is however severely constrained by the existence of synthetic rubber and the current level of stocks held by the United States. A substantial proportion of this stockpile is clearly surplus to its own requirements, and could easily be released onto the world market with disastrous consequences for the developing countries.

Similarly, the tea producing and exporting countries have not been able to devise a satisfactory agreement for the coordination of production quotas and market shares. In many respects this inability to find enough common ground on which to base a comprehensive strategy exposes the brittle facade of uniformity and homogeneity which one tends to associate with the term the developing countries. They are not in fact, one group of countries, but several, and the poorest among them (i.e. those whom NIEO is supposed to benefit most) are also the ones that lack commodities which can be cartelised.

Turning now to minerals, the developing countries as a group account for more than 50% of the world's exports of bauxite, copper, manganese and tin. In the case of bauxite, Jamaica, Surinam, Guyana, Papua New Guinea and the Dominican Republic produce about 40% of the world's output. However this is not enough to give them the necessary power to control the world's supply. Australia produces about 28%, and given that the underlying philosophy of NIEO's strategy is to use cartels and producers' associations as one of the weapons in the confrontation with the developed countries, one must rule out the possibility of

any inter-group cartels in which substantial economic benefits accrue to the developed countries.

Further, the United States, which imports about 84% of
its needs, has huge reserves of aluminium-bearing clays
which could be used as a substitute, if the necessity arose.
The possibility of the International Bauxite Association
turning into another OPEC-type organisation is thus rather
remote. In fact, both Jamaica and Guyana have been able
to win substantial concessions from the mining corporations
on their own. Their successes must cast doubt on the overall efficiency and authority of this Association.

Between them, Chile, Peru, Zambia and Zaire which constitute the Intergovernmental Council of Copper Exporting
Countries (CIPEC), account for about 30% of the world's
output of copper and 50% of total exports. It is doubtful
though whether this body could develop into a major cartel
on its own. It would need additional members, several of
whom have already refused to join. Papua New Guina which
owns about 23% of the world's reserves is not interested in
becoming a member. In fact, most of the world's reserves
of copper is held by non-members. The United States alone
accounts for 22%. These are not the conditions which make
for effective cartelisation.

Notwithstanding the benefit of hindsight, the call for the
use of commodity power was in fact based on a false perception of their own economic power and position. The developing countries do not have the commodities nor the internal
cohesiveness to exercise the appropriate degree of monopoly
power on world markets. Differences in their cultural and
historical backgrounds as well as their diverse political and
economic philosophies deny them the necessary degree of
cohesion and discipline. Further, unlike the members of
OPEC they lack the financial reserves to cut back production without seriously endangering their own development.

It was also based on a false analogy. Petroleum is in
fact a special case. OPEC owed its success to a set of circumstances which do not obtain elsehwere, and to which the
United States contributed in no small measure. Its own
energy policy came badly unstuck just at the time of the
1973 oil crisis, thus intensifying the impact of the latter
event. Secondly, as the free world's largest consumer of
imported oil, it refused to cut back on imports, or to reduce
domestic consumption consistent with global supplies.
There were isolated instances of well publicised shortages,
but, by and large the American public was shielded from
the worst effects of the oil crisis. Consequently they took
a long time to adjust to the new situation.

Their actions contributed much to the uncertainty,
instability and tightness of the international oil market, and
enabled OPEC to use its monopoly power to maximum advantage. By the same token they frustrated for a long time the
activities of the International Energy Authority (IEA), the
organisation which the developed countries established for
the purpose of devising a coherent energy policy among
themselves. Those difficulties have more or less dis-
appeared. Petrol has been decontrolled in the United States
and prices allowed to rise to reflect market conditions. As a
result they have cirtually doubled over the last year, and
the Americans now have a different perception of the world
energy problem.
The point, though is, that much of the success of OPEC
(and conversely the early reverses of IEA) must be attributed to the failure of the U.S. Government to take effective
counter-measures to deal with the world energy problem.
By its actions, or more appropriately inactions, the United
States actively encouraged the false sense of economic
power which the developing countries experienced as a
result of the 1973 oil crisis. The vicarious sense of power
which many of them experienced from OPEC's success cannot however be realised in terms of their own potential,
which in a fundamental sense, exposes one of the basic fal-
lacies of NIEO. Although it is about economic power, and
it outlines a strategy for capturing such power and shifting
the international balance in favour of the developing countries, its basic model is unsound and impracticable. It also
depended on the United States, the country it identified as
primarily responsible for the injustices of the existing system, for its success.

NIEO AND THE DEVELOPING COUNTRIES

Aggregating all the demands of the developing countries
into a comprehensive package was clearly a mistake. It was
perhaps the surest way of strangling NIEO at birth. There
was no way in which any developed country, in particular
the United States, was going to concede to an overall package of demands in the interest of humanity. Governments do
not operate in this way. Few (if any) moralise about the
state of mankind, and fewer still see it as their duty and
responsibility to promote the welfare of the international
community. Governments exist first and foremost to protect
and promote the interests of their citizens, howsoever these
are defined.

Although these may be negotiated and/or are negotiable,
they are never conceded or compromised without a corresponding *quid pro quo*. In every concession there is
usually a counter-claim. This is a fundamental principle of
international diplomacy and foreign policy. Countries must
not only therefore be prepared to negotiate, more importantly, they must have something with which to negotiate.
Otherwise their negotiating position is hollow and unsustain-
able. This basic principle seems to have escaped the formu-
lators of NIEO's demands. They presented the developed
countries with a major package of demands, but offered
nothing in return.
What is more they are in no position to enforce any of
these demands. They are not a homogeneous group. Some
have very sophisticated industrial sectors. Others depend
on exports of a few primary commodities for their liveli-
hood. A few are rich in minerals and other natural resources, while many subsist on the margin of the international
economy. Their differences run even deeper in the field of
international relations. There are substantial political and
ideological differences between them. There are wars, border disputes and attempts to subvert and sabotage each
other's economic and political system.
As a group they are too weak and disorganised to be an
effective bargaining bloc, economically as well as politically.
NIEO tried to get round this particular difficulty by appeal-
ing to the necessity to alleviate the poverty of vast masses
of people. But humanitarianism alone cannot sustain a mean-
ingful relationship between free, independent and equal
nations long enough for the establishment of NIEO which,
insofar as it has a time dimension, was described as "part
of an historical process".
Some of NIEO's supporters have also made vague threats
of confrontation and disruption of the life style of the rich
countries if the legitimate demands of the developing countries are not met. A clear and unmistakable warning to this
effect was given by the Third World Forum.

> Historically, the rich have always underestaimated the
> political bargaining power of the poor just because
> their economic clout is so limited. We would urge the
> industrialised nations not to make such a mistake.
> Ultimately the real bargaining power of the poor is
> their ability to disrupt the life-styles of the rich
> whether through a wholesale confrontation or through
> limited unilateral actions. The rich can never afford
> to drive the poor to the ultimate despair and belliger-
> ence. (1)

The United States was not however, taken in by such rhetoric. It realised that the developing countries were in no position to carry out this threat, and saw no reason to concede any of the innumerable demands contained in the Programme of Action, or to change its traditional bargaining stance of negotiating from a position of strength. Any concession offered would have to be matched by a corresponding concession from the developing countries.

In the context of NIEO discussions, this boiled down to assurances regarding the supply and price of oil and a range of commodities. Incidentally, the other OECD members followed precisely the same line. Each attempted to negotiate individually with the members of OPEC in order to safeguard supplies through a series of deals. But this had nothing to do with the wider issues raised by NIEO, which in themselves were too vague and indeterminate to be reduced to a negotiable package. They had no political or economic clout, no means of bringing pressure on the developed countries to make concessions. In the final analysis they depended on humanitarianism which carries very little weight with most governments, as the Carter administration discovered when it attempted to make human rights a major foreign policy issue in its dealings with the developing countries.

Quite clearly therefore, both sides viewed the problem differently. While the developing countries talked of the need for a new order and hinted vaguely of their political and economic power to change the existing system, the United States saw the situation firstly, as the outcome of the oil crisis, and secondly, as an attempt by OPEC to establish itself as a major political and economic force in world politics. Whereas the former required immediate short-term economic responses, the latter was potentially a more serious development involving fundamental changes in international economic relations, new political alliances and major shifts of foreign and economic policy.

Viewed in this light one begins to understand the American response to the NIEO demands, which were not about relieving poverty in the Third World. The vast majority of these countries stood to gain very little. NIEO was in fact the means by which OPEC hoped to establish itself as the leader of Third World countries as well as an effective international force. Its demands were therefore the price which the non-oil developing countries demanded for falling in behind OPEC. By a strange inversion of logic these were addressed not to OPEC, but to the rich industrialised countries (the OPEC countries), with the heaviest costs obviously falling to the United States.

THE U.S. DEPENDENCE ON THE DEVELOPING COUNTRIES

While some developed countries may have decided to go along with the assertion that NIEO was a genuine attempt to get a better deal for the poorer countries, the United States refused to go along with the idea. It took a much tougher line. NIEO was not about poverty but power. It was absolutely necessary therefore not to make any concessions which would either jeopardise its own position economically as well as politically, or benefit its rivals. Its response was thus not to NIEO as such, but to a series of individual situations which started with the 1973 oil crisis but which were all seen as intended to promote and enhance the international standing of OPEC.

Unlike a number of other countries, the United States took the view that instead of strengthening their bargaining power, the oil crisis had in fact done immense harm to the economies of the developing countries. Obviously the members of OPEC had benefitted handsomely, but collectively the non-oil developing countries, particularly the poorer ones, had been weakened by it. They were in fact its principal casualties. They were therefore in no position to make demands, or effectively to disrupt the American way of life. A few figures will bear this out.

In 1978 the value of US exports exceeded $140 billion and its imports $182 billion. These totals are substantial by any reckoning and, taken out of context might suggest that the United States is heavily dependent on foreign trade to maintain present standards of living, and consequently highly susceptible to disruption from foreign sources. However, this would be a gross oversimplification of the true picture. Less than 10% of its gross national product (GNP) comes from the foreign trade sector. Further, most of its trade is conducted with the rich industrialised countries, principally Canada, Western Europe and Japan. Roughly the proportionate shares of its exports divide as follows: 62% goes to the developed market economies, 2% to socialist countries and 35% to the developing countries, of which about 24% is exported to the non-oil developing countries.

Imports follow a similar pattern with one additional important consideration. The united States is the most important single market for exports from the non-oil developing countries. In 1978 it took about 26% of their exports as compared with 24% for the EEC. Socialist countries and OPEC accounted for 6% each. Given this pattern, it would be pointless for the non-oil developing countries to try to mount a trade boycott of the American market in order to

force the U.S. government to accede to the NIEO demands.
They stand to lose too much. The pattern of trade is too
diffuse and spread over too many countries for a boycott to
be effective. All that would happen is, there would be a
considerable reshuffling and redistribution of trade to those
who are willing to take it up - and there are many would-be
takers!

The simple truth is that apart from a few strategic
materials to which the U.S. government already has assured
access through trade agreements, bilateral deals and
defence treaties, etc., a wide range of imports from Third
World countries is not absolutely essential to the American
way of life. If these were reduced there would be some in-
convenience but the economy would soon adjust. This basic
premise has largely influenced the American attitude to
negotiations with Third World countries. It enables the
Americans to bargain hard and long and to extract the maximum advantage without giving too much away. Further, not
having a history of colonial attachments they are less likely
to be swayed by such arguments as historical injustices and
exploitation, or to feel any deep sense of duty and moral
obligation to promote the development and welfare of former
subjects.

In a manner of speaking the Americans have less hang-
ups in their dealing with Third World countries than some
other industrial nations. They are more forthright and
open in their negotiations, and not easily moved by the
accusations and opprobrium of developing countries. They
have been accused of attempting to sabotage the UNCTAD
conferences, and of generally frustrating progress of a
number of trade and aid proposals going back to the First
Session of that organisation. Among other things, they
have stood firm on indexation and the link scheme, to mention just two proposals. They withdrew for a time from the
International Labour Organisation because of unfriendly and
pernicious ideological influences and developments. They
have also become distinctly disenchanted with IDA, the
branch of the World Bank which provides cheap credit to
the poorest countries.

ITS HEGEMONY OF THE WORLD SYSTEM

These developments must be seen as part of the overall
philosophy which they represent. The United States sees
itself as the protector of the Free World, the main bastion
of freedom against the march of international communism.

Its actions in the field of international economic relations and foreign policy must therefore be assessed in terms of their contribution to these ends. Its aid programmes for example, have always been strongly motivated by political and ideological considerations. The Marshall Plan was intended to aid the post-war recovery of Europe as well as to help its weaker Western allies resist communist aggression and internal subversion.

The singular success of that exercise encouraged its extension to those countries on the periphery of the Soviet Union as part of its 'policy of containment'. Later, when the developing countries were deemed to be in the throes of 'the revolution of rising expectations', the United States instituted a series of aid programmes in order to accommodate this revolution, but more particularly to prevent them from falling under the influence of the Soviet Union. Similarly, the Alliance for Progress was instituted as a direct result of the revolution in Cuba and the growing threat of Soviet influence and infiltration in the region. Once the threat to American hegemony subsided, the Alliance quickly folded.

Having taken on the role of the world's policeman, the United States saw its primary international responsibility as defending freedom, making the world safe from the Soviet threat and promoting international peace and prosperity, all of which were ultimately and inextricably tied in with its own security and hegemony of the system. Consequently, it expanded its activities into practically every corner of the globe, and foreign aid became the principal means by which these objectives were to be achieved in developing countries. It was used to buy friends and influence nations, destabilise unfriendly governments, prop up puppet regimes, secure votes in the United Nations and elsewhere, and a host of other purposes intended either to prevent Soviet penetration in Third World countries or to preserve its own hegemony.

Any threat to either of these foreign policy objectives was to be strenuously resisted. This in turn, provided the justification for American involvement and interference in the internal affairs of developing countries. The policy of containment thus gave way to the so-called 'domino theory' in which it was argued that the fall or take-over by the communists in any developing country would set off a chain reaction first among neighbouring states, and ultimately lead to the collapse of the free world enterprise system and all that it stood for, and the establishment of international communism.

However, the American involvement in Vietnam and South
East Asia proved a costly and unpopular mistake, and a
truly traumatic experience. It left the nation divided and
confused. There were those who argued that the policy was
right but the means inappropriate and/or inadequate.
Others demanded that the United States should relinquish
the role of protector and leave the developing countries to
sort out their own affairs, a policy which incidentally advocated cutting aid drastically as well as disbursing it more
selectively. Elsewhere it induced a sort of seige mentality
with Americans feeling let down by its allies in the
developed countries and reviled and defied in the developing
countries. Nevertheless, although the nation's psyche had
suffered a serious shock, at no time was there any basic
disagreement that the overall aim of US foreign policy was
to maintain its own hegemony and to resist the threat of
Soviet domination, which had shown itself to be capable of
taking on many forms.
Coming so soon after the Vietnam war it was almost inevitable that NIEO should have been seen as yet another
variant of that double plot. There was certainly enough
evidence pointing in that direction. The language of the
early NIEO debates was intemperate, emotional and blatantly
anti-American. Talk of Third World solidarity and socialism
served only to confirm the worst fears of many that NIEO
was just another attempt to establish socialism throughout
the developing countries. The exclusion of the Soviet Union
and other socialist states from any obligation and responsibility for establishing NIEO seemed to provide ample evidence to this effect. It remains one of the most obvious and
inexplicable omissions of the whole new order scenario.
Whatever the reasons for its omission, it aroused the
suspicions of many influential political and other pressure
groups, and generally lost a lot of public sympathy for the
plight of the poor countries. People got turned off NIEO,
and given the way the American system works with its
powerful lobbies and almost paranoic concern with defence
and security, any attempt by the government to concede any
of NIEO's demands would have been interpreted as a sign of
weakness, and strongly resisted. Governments can only go
as far and as fast as public opinion will allow, and in the
case of the United States, this was very much anti-NIEO.
Also the attitude of many developing countries did not help.
Given its overly political and ideological overtones the
United States were bound to reject NIEO. It would have
given rise to an entirely new political and international force
and threatened its own hegemony.

THE INTERNATIONAL ECONOMY

NIEO was supposed to change the international economy in a fundamental way. However, in retrospect, the timing was very badly off. At the time it was put forward the developing countries as a group were doing rather well. They were in fact growing faster than the developed countries. They had exceeded the rate of growth of output targetted for the First Development Decade. Exports were booming, particularly for minerals (not counting petroleum) manufactures and other industrial products. The terms of trade had moved in their favour mainly as a result of the boom in commodity prices of the early 1970s, and their reserves stood at healthy levels.

It is true of course, that many of them, particularly the poorest ones did not share in this prosperity. But they were not the ones making the running in the NIEO debates. In fact, they stood to gain very little from it. As already suggested, they have no cartelisable commodities and no mineral wealth to speak of. Their industrial structure is either weak, inefficient, or non-existent. Agricultural production had slumped badly, and most of them have difficulties feeding themselves. Any fundamental change in the way the international economy is run was thus unlikely to benefit them.

Further, any major benefits which they won from lining up behind the members of OPEC would almost certainly have had to be set against the existing trade preferences and aid flows which they receive from the United States and the other developed countries. Faced with these stark realities it is doubtful whether they would have gone along with the idea. They can therefore be left aside for the moment. The main point is that those who were making the most noise were precisely the ones who were doing best from the existing system. The charge therefore that they were being exploited cannot be sustained in the light of the evidence.

Secondly, the 1973 oil crisis was largely responsible for precipitating the world recession of 1974 to 1976. In 1974, for example, there was no growth in real output for the OECD countries as a whole. In 1975, the worst year of the recession, real output actually fell by about 2% from the preceding year. The fall in exports was even greater. They were down by about 5% while inflation averaged 11% for the group and unemployment was running at about $5\frac{1}{2}$%.

The recession hit the U.S. economy particularly hard in terms of lost output. In 1974 real GNP fell by 1.7% and again in 1975 by 1.8%, making it along with the United

Kingdom the only two members to register a fall in output in
the two years of the recession. Both the automobile and the
construction industries, the two most sensitive indicators of
the wealth of the American economy were very badly affected
by the recession. Output in the former slumped by 10%,
while the latter experienced a massive contraction which
resulted in lay-offs and helped to push the number of un-
employed to close on 7 million. On top of this, inflation was
running at the rate of 11%. These were not the type of economic conditions in which to start negotiations or to make
concessions which would have added to the country's domestic problems.

As it turned out the U.S. government was in fact preoccupied with trying to reduce the level of inflation, stimulate output, and to get the economy moving again, and so
reduce domestic unemployment. The economic benefits of
recovery would in turn spill over to the rest of the world,
including the developing countries. It would stimulate the
demand for their exports, increase their output and so provide employment overseas. The health of the world economy
in general and of the developing countries in particular this
depended on the economic recovery of the United States.
In the jargon of the day it was the "locomotive" which would
pull the international economy out of the recession.

On the wider international front, the old Bretton Woods
System had collapsed, after having provided the conditions
for an unprecedented period of post-war economic growth
and world prosperity. As a result world financial markets
were thrown into chaos. All the world's major currencies
took to floating, and there was intense speculation and much
uncertainty and instability in international currency markets.
Efforts to restore some degree of order and stability, and to
establish new parities failed. In addition, two devaluations
failed to stop the downward slide of the dollar, the linchpin
of the old system and a major reserve asset of most of the
developing countries.

Various attempts were made to devise a new world system, but these ran into all sorts of problems. Finally a new
system incorporating a number of changes and new elements
was adopted as the 2nd Amendment to the IMF's Articles of
Agreement. However, leaving aside the details of the new
system, two points are important. Firstly, the developing
countries played a full and effective part in devising the
new system, which in many respects reflects the extent to
which the developed countries went to accommodate them.

The members of OPEC in particular, secured larger
quotas consistent with the new found oil wealth. This in

turn gives them a greater say in the determination of policy, which is something the developing countries have always claimed is absolutely necessary in order to ensure that the system not only reflects their needs but actually caters for them.   So far though, the members of OPEC have shown very little inclination to use their new authority and power to bring about any of the fundamental changes which NIEO claims are necessary for relieving world poverty or integrating the poorer nations into the world monetary system.

Secondly, the United States was accused of establishing its hegemony over the old system, and also of using its position to exploit that system, including among other things, financing the Vietnam War.   Whether or not this is true, is not the point at issue here.   Like most broad accusations there is probably some truth in it, but one would need to go a lot deeper than present purposes require.   The point is, those countries which accused the United States of abusing its hegemony of the old system, later accused it of benign neglect in allowing the dollar to float downwards, thus wiping out a substantial proportion of their dollar reserve holdings.

In other words, when the United States was the world's banker it was accused of misusing its position to achieve its own international and foreign policy objectives.   When it relinquished that position it was immediately accused of failing to maintain the value of other countries' reserve assets. Obviously both charges cannot be valid at the same time. If the former is valid, then clearly it was right for the U.S. to relinquish its control of the world's monetary system. However, having relinquished that position, it cannot then be accused of failing to act as the world's banker.

The slide in the value of the dollar was also given as one of the main reasons for demanding the indexation of commodity prices as well as the subsequent increases in the price of oil.   It is not possible to examine the arguments in any detail in a short article, but briefly, the United States refused to concede the case for indexation on the grounds that it was unsound in theory and unworkable in practice.   In the case of oil, there was no reason to prevent the members of OPEC moving out of dollars and pricing their oil in one (or a basket) of their own currencies, or for that matter, in any other of the world's major currencies, in order to maintain its international purchasing power.   The fact that they choose not to must be presumed to be based on sound financial and economic reasons and not on America's use (or misuse) of the dollar.

SOME ASPECTS OF AMERICAN FOREIGN POLICY AND NIEO

The U.S. response to NIEO was not totally negative. At UNCTAD IV it put forward the so-called Kissinger Plan for the establishment of an International Reserve Bank for dealing with the world food problem and the need for an adequate and effective international stabilisation mechanism for world commodity markets. It was offered as an alternative proposal to the Common Fund which the developing countries and UNCTAD in particular regarded as absolutely crucial to the success of NIEO.

The scheme had a rather cool reception. Without going into details, there is no doubt that part of the reason for its defeat was that it was regarded as a bid by the United States for control of world commodity markets, and since this was precisely what NIEO was intended to break, there was no way in which the developing countries were going to agree to it. This was a great pity for two main reasons. Firstly, it meant that the proposal did not get a fair run. Neither its economic rationality nor financial feasibility was examined in any depth. Secondly, its summary treatment played a large part in determining the American attitude and negotiating stance in subsequent discussions on the Common Fund. These not only dragged on for an inordinately long time, but the final form and resources of the Fund were very different from the original proposal. The question is, did the developing countries gain more than they lost?

No research has as yet been done on this point, which may well hold the key to understanding the general hardening of the American position. For example, on the question of debt relief, the other issue which UNCTAD singled out as crucial to the successful launching of NIEO, the Americans dug their heels in. Notwithstanding the fact that most of the other members of OECD were prepared to make major concessions, the U.S. government stood, and still stands, by its original position that debt relief should be used sparingly and only in extreme cases, and then on a case by case basis. Obviously such a strategy is intended to keep the debtor on a short leash, safeguard American interests and investments, and to use the leverage which indebtedness gives to extract additional foreign policy and other concessions from the developing countries.

It did of course agree to the establishment of the $1 billion special Fund to help the most seriously affected and the least developed of the developing countries. It was however largely at its insistence that the disbursement of these funds was left entirely to the discretion and determination of the donor countries. The intention quite clearly was that there should be no general distribution, but that donor countries should keep control of operation, and use the additional funds as they saw fit. In the case of the United States disbursement has been on a limited and highly selected basis, and made contingent on a number of conditions aimed at increasing and enhancing American influence and presence in the recipient countries.

At UNCTAD IV the United States approved Resolution 94 (iv) which pledged the developed countries to quick and constructive consideration of individual requests for relief for developing countries suffering from debt service difficulties, in particular the least developed and the most seriously affected. It also accepted Resolution 165 (S-IX) of the Trade and Development in March 1978 which called upon donor countries to adopt measures to readjust the terms of past bilateral official development assistance (ODA) and bring them into line with current ODA terms, the so-called principle of Retroactive Terms Adjustment.

The terms of these resolutions left it up to the donors to decide what action to take, how far to go, and which countries to help. Accordingly, performance is very uneven. Some OECD members have gone further than others. A recent questionnaire by UNCTAD showed that the total value of bilateral debts outstanding at the end of 1977 amounted to $43.7 billion for the developing countries as a whole. Just over half of this debt was owed to the United States. The most seriously affected and the least developed countries between them accounted for about 50% of the total debt. The total value of the measures taken to readjust the terms of this debt retroactively was put at $5.7 billion, excluding any measures taken by the United States, for which no data are available. (2) In other words, the United States with more than half the total debt owing to it, took no action to readjust the terms of this debt. Alternatively, it failed to report the extent of such action, a most unlikely possibility.

The United States obviously takes a different view to that of the other OECD members. It sees debt relief and the leverage which it creates as an additional means by which to achieve its foreign policy objectives in Third World countries. It will thus be granted to the "good guys" and not to the "bad guys" (i.e. those who threaten nationalisation and expropriation of American assets, or engage in other hostile and unfriendly Anti-American activities). It will also be granted to countries in which American defence and security interests appear to be threatened, or the balance of world power is likely to be shifted against the United States. And, given that this is one of the primary objectives of NIEO, the U.S. government will in fact use debt relief to frustrate the new order and preserve the status quo.

In many respects therefore, the American stance on debt relief is an integral part of its overall policy on foreign aid. NIEO called for increased aid disbursements consistent with the developed countries' commitment to the 1% aid target. However, as the record shows, the proportion of its GNP which the United States disburse as aid has consistently fallen over the years. The Reagan administration is committed to further cuts and a more aggressive foreign aid policy. Among other things, this will result in hardening the terms and conditions of aid, a reduction in the level of multilateral aid and the contributions to international aid institutions, extracting greater advantages and commitments from recipients, and using aid more aggressively to counter the threat of Soviet invasion and major shifts in the balance of power in particular regions.

Evidence of this new policy has already begun to emerge. Recently, it was reported that President Reagan's foreign policy advisers had worked out a programme of development aid for the Carribean Basin nations which would allow these nations to sell their goods in the American market without any trade restrictions or requirement on their part to grant similar concessions to U.S. exporters. The programme also called for the establishment of a Carribean Basin Insurance Consortium to provide partial protection against political risks such as war damage and government expropriation.

The cost of this programme is expected to reach $350 million per year for the next three years with an additional $100 million per annum being contributed by other governments. The purpose of this programme is stated as helping the recipient nations to reach economic self-sufficiency, reduce poverty and redress the social imbalance and economic miseries "that make leftist propaganda so beguiling to the downtrodden masses". The U.S. government is anxious to avoid the charge of "Yankee imperialism" and "dollar diplomacy" and has accordingly been attempting to get the support of Canada, Mexico, Venezuela and Britain. However it has run into problems from its regional partners, many of whom feel that this programme, like its predecessor the Alliance for Progress, is mainly an attempt by the United States to counter the threat of Soviet infiltration in the region and to contain the growing influence of Cuba. Significantly, only Cuba and Grenada are specifically excluded from the programme. Nicaragua may also be excluded, but the inference is clear. The United States feels that its influence and interests in the region are threatened and are prepared to pour massive amounts of aid in the area to preserve its hegemony.

CONCLUDING REMARKS

This in a way sums up the American foreign policy response to developments in the developing countries. Its obsession with its own hegemony forces it to see these developments in terms of its own security and defence. Any increase in Soviet activities and interest in these countries invariably results in a massive foreign aid programme or other countervailing measures to head off that challenge. To a large extent therefore the Soviet Union calls the tune for American activities and involvement in the Third World. It does not however pay the piper. That burden falls on the developing countries which are basically seen as pawns in a larger game of international power politics.

OPEC and the Group of 77 tried to muscle in on the act when they called for a NIEO. However, the exclusion of the Soviet Union and other socialist states from any commitment and responsibility meant that the major cost of NIEO would have had to be borne by the United States. The United States refused to buy the package, principally because the socialist countries could not, and did not offer any creditable alternative.   Secondly, neither OPEC nor the Group of 77, individually or collectively, was in a position to enforce any of their demands. There was therefore no need for the piper to play his familiar tune. He did nevertheless, and his tune was strongly anti-NIEO. Again it was the developing countries which paid the price.

NOTES

1 Proposals for a New International Economic Order, 'Third World Forum Report', Mexico City, August, 1975, p.15.
2 For details of this questionnaire, see Report by the Secretary General of UNCTAD, Implementation of Trade and Development Board Resolution 165 (S-IX) on the Debt and Development Problems of Developing Countries, UNCTAD, TD/B/809, Jan. 1981.

THE OUTCOME OF THE NIEO DEBATE

H.O. Bergesen, H.H. Holm and R.D. McKinlay

THE OUTCOME: AN ASSESSMENT

We shall present our assessment by examining the achievements of the Third World on each of the three clusters of demands outlined in our introductory discussion of the origins of the NIEO debate. (1) This review will be concluded by an overall assessment of the success/failure of the NIEO demands as a whole.

Changes in productive structure

The primary objective of the first cluster was to relocate processing industries from the industrialized to the developing countries. In general terms the Third World has made considerable progress in its industrialization efforts in the last two decades. Its manufacturing output has increased manyfold since the 1960s (2) and manufactured products are now as important as primary commodities in its exports. (3) This expansion, however, is largely confined to a small number of developing countries - the newly industrializing countries. In fact, over seventy per cent of the growth in manufacturing value added and of the increment in LDC exports of manufactures in the 1970s was attributed to eight or nine countries. (4) In addition Third World industrial growth is heavily concentrated in a few product lines (e.g. clothing and leather) and often limited to specific processing activities with few spin-offs (e.g. assembly plants in electronics and heavy manufacturing). So in spite of apparent progress in LDC industrialization a recent UN review concludes the 'developing countries still play a marginal role as suppliers of manufactured products to developed countries.

The "vertical division of labour" ... continues to be the
dominant feature of trade relations between the two groups
of countries'. (5)
    In addition, the limited progress that has been made has
not been brought about by international negotiations, but is
rather the result of independently working economic forces.
(6) As a matter of fact, very little progress has been made
in the international discussions on the issue of structural
adjustment, as this is called in UN terminology. Third
World demands for some kind of consultative machinery
within UNCTAD have not resulted in any changes. The rich
countries have been reluctant to enter into substantive
talks on the issue, and certainly within the framework of
UNCTAD. (7) Evidently, the industrialized countries are
not ready to accept any international regulation of their
internal industrial policy. They want to retain the right to
support their ailing industries whenever necessary to maintain employment. In practice most Western governments
spend large funds to subsidize traditional industrial sectors,
such as textiles and shipbuilding – in spite of mounting
Third World protests. With regard to the competitiveness of
LDC raw materials in relation to synthetics, the Western
countries have not accepted any proposals for reform that
encroaches on the present working of market forces. So,
while the industrialized countries support Third World industrialization in general, they have never accepted specific quantitative goals or practical responsibility for implementing such targets. (8) This is the essence of the outcome of numerous rounds of talks on industrial reallocation
and structural adjustment within UNCTAD, UNIDO and ILO.

Changes in market structure and increased transfers

The second cluster of NIEO demands covers changes in the
structure of international market systems and increases in
financial transfers. Changes in market structure encompass
two main features: commodity trade and market access.
    Commodity trade has been the most contentious issue
within this group. The demands for radical reforms in international commodity markets has all along been essential to
the whole NIEO package. The Third World has given this
area the highest priority in their negotiating position.
Closely connected to it is the question of indexation, i.e.
the attempt to link Third World export incomes to world
inflation.
    In the commodity field the starting point for the

negotiations were UNCTAD's ambitious Integrated Programme for Commodities (IPC), which aimed at stabilization of commodity prices and LDC earnings and economic diversification in the producing countries. The centrepiece of the plan was a proposed Common Fund of about six billion dollars which should stimulate the formation of individual international commodity agreements (ICAs) through joint financing. It was envisaged that the Fund would 'play a catalytic role in facilitating negotiations of many more commodities than would otherwise be possible'. (9)

After endless rounds of negotiations an agreement on the establishment of a Common Fund was finally reached in June 1980. The result, however, turned out to be very different from the original scheme. The Fund will have an assured capital base of only $470 million consisting of obligatory governmental contributions. (About half the amount is to be provided by the West, one third by the LDCs, ten per cent by the Eastern bloc and three per cent by China.) In addition it is hoped that $350 million will be raised by voluntary contributions to the Fund's 'second window'. This account has been set up to promote processing and marketing of commodities by the producing countries. So the resources actually available to the Fund are around ten per cent of the amount originally envisaged.

The voting rights in the Fund give the Group of 77 49 per cent, Group B (the West) 42 per cent, Group D (the East) 8 per cent and China 3 per cent. On paper this may look like a major achievement for the Third World. However, all major decisions with important financial implications require a qualified majority of three-quarters of all the votes. This means that the largest Western countries in effect have a veto power over the future dealings of the Fund. The agreement also includes severe limitations on the use of these funds. LDC demands for full fungibility between the Fund and the connected ICAs, which is the crux of the whole idea of the pooling of resources, were eventually turned down. (10)

While the original scheme envisaged the Common Fund as a catalyst and initiator of individual ICAs, the result seems to be a fund dependent on them. Several independent observers have concluded that the Common Fund as it now stands is of little value to the developing countries. (11) This may be the reason why the LDCs themselves have been rather slow in ratifying the draft Articles of Agreement. Some of them have even expressed doubts of whether it is in their long-term interest to link ICAs to the Fund, and attempts have been made to de-link the Fund from UNCTAD. (12)

As to individual ICAs, very little progress has been made. By late 1981 only one new agreement - on natural rubber - had been concluded. Negotiations on cocoa, tin, coffee and jute have run into difficulties, and the talks on most other commodities are virtually stalled. In UN jargon: 'recent developments are not reassuring'. (13) The outcome reflects both Western opposition and increasing disagreement among the LDC producing countries themselves. The lack of progress in this area will have a further crippling effect on the Common Fund, since it has been made dependent on the formation of individual ICAs.

With regard to indexation, the LDCs have not achieved anything at all, as the West has flatly refused even to discuss the concept. In practice, most commodity exporting countries have experienced a continuing worsening in their terms of trade vis-a-vis the West, in the same period as these negotiations have taken place. (14)

As far as market access is concerned, the developing countries have fought a rearguard battle to maintain the concessions they obtained in the early 1970s, when the general system of preferences (GSP) was introduced. The multilateral trade negotiations (the Tokyo round) were dominated by the interests of the Western Countries. The developing countries obtained much smaller tariff cuts in the products of special concern to them than the average reductions. In addition, 'many industrialized countries have either placed (such products) on the exceptions list or have not yet offered any tariff reductions.' (15) On the positive side it should be mentioned that the GSP has been extended for an uncertain period of time and that the Western countries have been encouraged to improve the conditions of it. Practical results, however, still depend on the good-will, individually or collectively, of the industrialized countries. So in terms of tariff regulations the LDCs have hardly improved their relative position in the world trade system. In addition, there is good reason to believe that the new, creeping protectionism in the West, in the form of orderly market sharing arrangements, has dealt a severe blow to LDC export possibilities. (16)

As far as financial transfers, the second component of this cluster, are concerned, increasing development assistance from the rich countries has been a high priority issue for the Third World for two decades. The developing countries have consistently argued for the UN target of 0.7 per cent of GNP. (17) In spite of this, actual official transfers have stagnated and in some recent years even declined in real terms. On average Western ODA has

has levelled off at around 0.35 per cent of GNP, (18) which
is less than the proportionate level at the end of the 1960s.
Some of the Western donors have not even accepted the UN
target; the Eastern bloc, while accepting the target, de-
clines any responsibility for its implementation. Most donors
remain reluctant to accept long-term commitments in their aid
policy. In the words of the UN Assessment 'no major
advance has been made in attaining predictability and assurance of concessional finance', but there has been a certain
improvement in the terms of ODA flows. (19)

As to the distribution of aid among recipients, OECD
member states have increased the relative share of ODA to
middle-income developing countries at the expense of the
low-income countries, (20) which is also contrary to Third
World demands.

There has been a growing tendency in recent years to
link aid more closely to commercial considerations which includes both bilateral export credits and mixed credits extended through multilateral institutions (21) (such as the
World Bank and the regional development banks).

Another important Third World demand concerns increasing development assistance through multilateral agencies.
Here some positive results have been achieved. In the 1970s
this kind of aid increased very rapidly both in absolute
amounts and as percentage of total ODA. OECD contributions to multilateral development funds in fact grew by ten
per cent per year from 1970 to 1978/79 in fixed prices. The
multilateral share of total ODA increased from 16 to 27 per
cent in the same period. (22) As a result the World Bank
and the UN development agencies have been able to step up
their assistance and lending to the Third World very rapidly
in the last decade. (23)

The prospects for the 1980s are, however, much gloomier.
The fiscal conservatism that now prevails in most Western
countries has hit these institutions very badly. The situation is so serious that the World Bank estimates that it may
be unable to increase the real flow of concessional resources
to developing countries. (24)

With regard to the debt problem, the Western governments agreed after intense negotiations to improve retro-
actively the terms of ODA debt in favour of the poorer
LDCs, (25) but this scheme is full of loopholes and open to
widely differing interpretations. The large creditor countries maintain that they still have the right to decide uni-
laterally both the concrete terms of adjustment and the
coverage of LDC recipients. (26) According to a preliminary UNCTAD estimate, measures taken following this

agreement have effected ODA debt of more than $5 billion.
However, in 1978 the aggregate debt of developing countries
probably exceeded $300 billion. (27) The West has refused
to discuss LDC debt to private sources and has blocked any
move towards institutional change in international debt
policy.

In the monetary field some adjustments have been made
to meet Third World demands. The IMF has accepted, in
principle, the structural character of the balance of payments deficits of developing countries. The Fund has improved its terms of lending accordingly. It can now extend
the repayment period of ten years and it can provide financial support amounting to six times a country's quota. (28)
The controversial 'conditionality' provisions have been
eased, as the Fund does not supervise the short-term
adjustments as closely as it used to. (29) In addition, the
Fund has set up special arrangements to meet Third World
financial requirements. The Compensatory Financing Facility provides funds to offset fluctuations in LDC export incomes. (30) The Trust Fund, financed through gold sales,
has mobilized close to $4 billion in transfers and conces-
sional loans to developing countries. (31) Total financial
transfers from IMF to non-oil exporting developing countries
have gone up from 450 million SDRs in 1974 to 5.1 billion in
1980. (32) However, all these adjustments have taken place
within the established practices of the present world monetary system. These changes do not represent any challenge
to the status quo. Third World demands for more far-
reaching reforms of a principal character have been rejected
(or referred to further study) by the guardians of the
Bretton Woods institutions. (33) The UN Assessment concludes: 'Most of the international monetary objectives of the
new international economic order remain to be met'.

Changes in decision-making structure

A central point in the NIEO programme is the call for increased Third World participation in international economic
decision-making. This entails both reforming the old financial institutions, like the IMF, the World Bank and GATT,
and setting up new international regimes in areas presently
beyond international political control.

UNCTAD was planned to be the main instrument of such
institutional reforms. The LDCs have made numerous efforts
to enlarge the role of that organization particularly in the
field of trade and finance. This has been vehemently and

effectively opposed by the Western countries (with only
minor exceptions) insisting that the original mandate of the
Bretton Woods institution be kept intact. (34) They do not
want any UNCTAD interference in such delicate matters as
debt, monetary policy and trade regulations. As a result
the real negotiations in these areas still take place in the
old Western dominated institutions where the atmosphere is
more business-like and less inflicted by 'political pollu-
tion'. (35) UNCTAD's role has been reduced to that of a
'poverty commission'. It may carry out studies on the
misery of the poor and the causes of inequality, and discussions in UNCTAD bodies may put some political pressure on
the have-nations, but the nave-nots cannot force them to
negotiate within that framework.

The frustrated LDC efforts in this respect is most clearly
seen with regard to commodities and debt. (36) In a similar
way their plea for institutional reforms of GATT and IMF
has not given any significant results. Third World voting
shares in the IMF and the World Bank have increased very
slowly (37) and the basic structure of decision-making, so
heavily skewed in favour of the founding (Western) countries, remains unchanged. (38)

With regard to LDC demands for international management
of formerly unregulated areas, the results are rather mixed.
Some advance has been made in the formulation of codes of
conduct for transnational business transactions, (39) but it
seems impossible to reach agreement on binding operative
provisions and effective implementation procedures. There
is good reason to anticipate that any new rules, that can be
agreed upon, will be so vague and non-committal in form and
the implementation machinery so loose that the regime will
have more symbolic than substantive value.

In the Law of the Seas negotiations the developing countries have made real progress towards establishing an effective international organization with regulatory powers and
considerable Third World influence, the International Seabed
Authority (ISA). The large Western powers have, however,
ensured themselves veto power on all major decisions in the
ISA so that they can block any move contrary to their deci-
interests. Compared with the Bretton Woods institutions
this can still be considered a step forward for the Third
World, as the West is no longer in a position to control the
international bodies in questions, but only to prevent unwanted action. However, it remains to be seen, whether
there will be sufficient political support from the major
countries for this new institutional set-up. (40)

The Western countries have been more forthcoming with

respect to power sharing in other international institutions.
The International Fund for Agricultural Development (IFAD)
was set up in 1977 with a tripartite structure according one
third of the votes to the West, one third to the OPEC donors
and one third to the rest of the Third World. But the two
former groups retained control over the financial flows to
the Fund. It is typical that in such sensitive areas as world
food trade, the major economic powers have not shown any
willingness to share their influence over the market with the
have-nots. The numerous appeals and suggestions from the
developing countries and international organizations (FAO
and the World Food Council) for a world food security system
have been stranded on outright opposition (and to some extent internal disagreement) from the West and tacit neglect
from the East.

   We conclude, therefore, that the Western powers have
resisted all LDC efforts to set up new international regimes
with real power to intervene in the established functioning
of the world economic system. Sometimes the outcome of the
negotiations has been stalemate, while in other cases it has
been new but harmless UN talking-shops.

Overall Assessment

Success or failure can in general only be assessed by reference to a specified set of goals or objectives. From the perspective of the set of objectives defined by the NIEO protagonists, essentially a radical restructuring of the old economic and political order, we can only conclude that the
NIEO demands have largely failed. The major Third World
demands for industrial restructuring, market access, increased transfers and new 'rules of the game' have met at
best with indifference or at worst with outright opposition
from the North. The few adjustments that the North has
been willing to make has taken place within the limits of the
old economic and political order.

   In this context it is also important to note that the
achievements of the Third World over the duration of the
NIEO debate seem to follow a 'falling curve'. In the first
stage, covering the period from 1974 to 1976, at least some
agreement on principles was reached. Optimism about a
fruitful North-South dialogue abounded in many circles,
especially after the Seventh Special Session of the UN in
1975. This meeting produced a consensus text covering the
whole NIEO agenda, which, though deliberately vague in
wording, at least held out the prospect of substantial

negotiations in a conciliatory atmosphere. UNCTAD IV, in 1976, and the Conference on International Economic Cooperation, lasting from 1975-77, showed, as the negotiations on crucial issues dragged on from one meeting to the next, that this optimism was not firmly based in political reality. Nevertheless, the main participating countries still preferred compromise to open confrontation even though the compromise was always couched in vague terms and very clearly covered substantial differences.

By the UNCTAD V meeting in 1979 the preference for compromise over confrontation had waned. Many controversial issued were brought to the vote, thereby openly dividing the North from the South. UNIDO III in 1980 was an even more clear-cut failure. The positions of the North and South had become entirely irreconcilable. The so-called 'global negotiations' are the latest attempt to revitalize the 'dialogue'. Following, an extremely vague UN resolution, adopted in late 1979, numerous efforts have been made to reach agreement on procedures and agenda for this all-encompassing round of negotiations. During the Eleventh Special Session of the UN in 1980, however, the US, FRG and UK openly rejected a compromise solution on the outstanding issues. This move from compromise to confrontation both reflects and is a function of a shift of focus in the diplomatic debate from matters of substance to procedural issues. The shadow-boxing that takes place under the label of 'global negotiations' reflects a seemingly endless round of talks on procedure and agenda.

This change in the debate from compromise and negotiation to confrontation and a preoccupation with procedure has also been reflected in a 'falling curve' for the negotiating stand of the Third World. The Group of 77 has retreated from its original demands in order to obtain at least some minimal concessions from the North. In reality, the developing countries have given up negotiating for a new order in favour of a greater say in the old.

While, by the start of the 1980s, the NIEO demands from the perspective of radical structural change had largely failed, it would, on the other hand be oversimplistic to dismiss the NIEO demands as an unqualified failure. If we evaluate the NIEO achievements from a perspective rather less ambitious than the radical restructuring of the old international economic and political order, then the efforts of the Third World do not appear to have been entirely futile.

In the first place, Third World countries have been able to focus international attention on the economic issues most important to them. Second, they have in some cases forced the North, though mainly the West, to participate in discussion, if not negotiation, on such matters. Third, a number of new UN bodies have been established on Third World initiatives. This has created a bureaucratic machinery with a potential for handling NIEO issues on a technical level much more effectively than before. Finally, the West has been forced to make some increases in resource transfers, usually in the form of ad hoc operations like the CIEC special fund and IFAD.

Thus, from a perspective considerably less ambitious than the establishment of a new international order, it can be argued that the NIEO demands have achieved some degree of success. When these successes are evaluated, however, against the original Third World ambitions and goals for restructuring the world political and economic system, the successes appear very modest. Indeed their modesty only serves to highlight the scale of the failure of the original goals and ambitions. In this respect we find ourselves in essential agreement with a UN assessment which points out that: 'On most fronts ... negotiations to attain those (NIEO) objectives have yielded results that fall considerably short of their initial targets or they have shifted focus from bold changes to attempts at partial adaptation. Indeed in a number of fundamental aspects of the new international economic order, progress has been negligible.' (41)

THE OUTCOME: AN EXPLANATION

Our explanation of this outcome of 'negligible progress' is couched in terms of four sets of explanatory factors: the changing power of the Third World, the changing content and priority of issues on the international agenda, the changing constellation of key domestic and international Northern actors, and the principles governing the responses from the North to the demands from the South. We now outline the factors that make up each of these explanatory sets and indicate also how each set has contributed to the combination of modest success and more substantial failure that constitutes the 'negligible progress'.

The Changing Power of the Third World

We have argued earlier that one of the critical factors underlying the initiation of the NIEO debate was the increasing

power and influence of the Third World. The increasing
political mobilization and organization of the LDCs combined
particularly with the cartel power of OPEC in 1973/4 created
a situation in which the North felt under a very real threat.
Progressively, and especially after the conclusion of the
CIEC negotiations in 1977, the North perceived that the
Third World threat had decidedly diminished. The changes
in the Northern perceptions of Third World power manifested
themselves in several ways.

In the first place, it became clear that the initial fears
about Third World coercion based on cartel power were certainly overdrawn. Some of the early apprehensions of extensive Third World cartel action disappeared as it became evident that for all practical purposes it was impossible for the
South to establish effective cartels in raw materials other
than oil. Oil, it seemed, was the exception rather than the
harbinger of a new rule. Furthermore, even oil power lost
its image of invincibility. The coercion potential of oil-
exporting countries decreased to some extent as these countries integrated their surpluses on their trade balance into
the Western financial and industrial system. Despite
increases in aid from the OPEC countries, OPEC did not use
its surplus to create price support arrangements for other
commodities but rather placed their surplus funds in Europe
and the US. As a consequence the OPEC countries imposed
strains on their own future freedom of manoeuvre by gradually building up an interdependent relationship between
themselves and the industrialized North. More recently
the effect of energy conservation in the North combined
with a world recession has further reduced the demand
for oil. Finally, the OPEC countries did not develop
as the vanguard of the Third World cause. The action of
the Arab oil-producing countries in 1973 was motivated by
the hostility towards Israel and its supporters, and their
role in advancing the NIEO demands was in many respects a
by-product. Furthermore, the fourfold increase in prices
in 1973/4 created difficulties for the oil-importing Third
World countries, and thereby created a new dividing line
within the Third World coalition.

A second factor that has contributed to the relative decline in Third World power over the course of the NIEO
debate pertains to Third World unity. At the outset of the
NIEO debate the North perceived that it was confronted by
a coherent South whose unity was even further enhanced by
the newly found cartel power. As in the case of cartel
power, the perception of a united Third World was overdrawn. The Third World covers a vast array of differing

economic and political systems. Many Third World states
have been much more preoccupied with domestic or regional
problems than with issues such as NIEO. More importantly,
intra Third World conflicts, which exist in all regions, have
proved to be a major source of tension at most Third World
meetings. Indeed Nyerere makes a very realistic assessment
of the limited potential of Third World unity when he commented: 'The unity of the Third World is the unity of the
weak, a unity of opposition and a unity of nationalisms.' (42)

A third factor constraining the power of the Third World
is that the international system lacks the rules of authority
and mechanisms for sharing decision-making of democratic
national systems. The fact that the Third World constitutes
a majority, in number of countries or population size, does
not mean that they are automatically in any position to influence the rules of the system. In the international system the
the few and the powerful decide for the rest, and transforma-
tions like the ones that established democracy in the industrialized countries do not seem to be imminent in the international system.

Despite this, the Third World has tried to use the international institutions as sort of a world parliament where
things are voted through, and in this way symbolic decisions
have been made. The problem for the Third World is that
they are purely symbolic or merely involve the creation of
new international institutions, further studies of new empty
financial funds.

The Third World has moreover also a divided attitude
towards the implementation of the majority principle. On the
one hand this would give them effective power over the
international system; on the other hand, a fundamental
force in the Third World is the nationalism of the individual
countries. This nationalism has meant that most Third World
countries have been totally unwilling to relinquish any
national control to international bodies, and they guard their
national autonomy very carefully. As a consequence, the
Third World has built its case around the concept of sovereign equality - with all the contradictions that this entails.

A fourth factor that has a bearing on the nature of
Third World power relates to the widespread feeling in
1973/4 that the developing countries could withdraw from the
international system, and in this way endanger the stability
of the entire international order. Bergsten outlined a number of steps that the Third World could take: cartelization
by raw material producers, take-overs of multinational corporations and repudiations of debt obligations. (43) The
events of late 1973 and early 1974 indicated to many Northern

countries that this was a real possibility. In order to prevent the developing countries from opting out of the system,
it was thought that some accommodation was necessary.
However, once the shock of the period 1973/74 was over,
it became increasingly apparent to the North that secession
by the South was not really credible. Indeed in this context it is important to remember that the NIEO package itself was premised on the very obverse of secession. The
critical consequence for the South was that they lost the
leverage inherent in the threat of secession. In this context, it is obvious that the developing countries could have
done a lot more than they actually did. It seems hard to
understand why the Third World has not established its
own organization, with secretariat and research facilities,
that could improve the quality of the proposals from the
Third World. The Third World has also honoured all
existing obligations, patent rights, debts, etc., and there
has been little reason for the North to believe the utterances
about leaving the system or about internal Third World cooperation (collective self-reliance).

The potential for Third World power has, however, certainly not been eliminated. Many of the factors that were
responsible for obliging the North to become involved in
the NIEO debate still remain. The North continues to have
vital interests in the South, the movement towards increased
cooperation within the Third World is there to stay, and a
number of critical resources are still concentrated in the
hands of Third World countries. On the other hand, the
general growth in the coercion and influence potential of
the South relative to the North up to 1973/74 has definitely
stopped. Indeed the growing appreciation in the North over
the second half of the 1970s of the limitations of Third
World cartel power, of the difficulties inherent in Third
World unity, of the absence of mechanisms for translating
majority 'votes' into control and of the lack of credibility
of secession has contributed to a general decrease in the perception of the relative power of the Third World. This
changing calculus of Third World power has had a number of
effects on the NIEO debate.

In the first place, the Third World has clearly been unable to force through its demands. Thus, the original proposals for a Common Fund, for example, envisaged a large
fund that could intervene and control directly the markets
of individual commodities. The actual outcome, a small fund
with virtually no independent powers, clearly illustrates the
inability of the Third World to force through an accommodation of their central demands.

Secondly, the Third World could not keep up the original pressure for change that existed during the boom period of the North-South debate. Consequently the Third World had to accept tinkering, and in this way the whole concept of a NIEO was even further diluted. The differences within the Third World, and the inability of the Third World to stand united meant that the Northern strategy of dragging the negotiations along by technifying the discussion proved very successful.

Thirdly, the adoption of numerous highsounding principles in the boom period had to be followed by operational decisions, and this is where the decline of Third World power became most apparent. The Third World had to accept follow-up decisions of a watered-down nature, for example the Common Fund, or new purely symbolic decisions. The adoption of the growth targets for the Third Development Decade is a case in point. The developed countries finally conceded accepting a seven per cent growth target for the Third World for the next ten years, but everybody knows that this is without operational significance. (44)

Finally, despite all the factors that have produced a general stagnation in the North-South debate, the relative decline of Third World power is still not sufficient that the North can simply terminate the debate. Not only does the debate continue but every now and then some tangible results have to be produced. As we have argued above, however, the Third World achievements tend to follow a 'falling curve' and this 'falling curve' seems to correlate very well with the general decline of Third World power.

The Changing Content and Priority of Issues on the International Agenda

In discussing the origins of the NIEO debate, we have argued that the focus on development issues provided one of the key rallying-points for the mobilization and organization of the Third World. Progressively the Third World managed to push these issues to the forefront of the international agenda. The most outstanding success of the Third World in this context was the convening of the Sixth Special Session of the UN in April 1974 to discuss the demands for a New International Economic Order. This was the first Special Session in the history of the UN to be convened on the initiative of the Third World and it was the first to deal with a topic other than security. Since then three special sessions have been devoted to the economic

problems of the Third World as have numerous meetings of
UN bodies and other international organizations. The high
point of attention was the period 1974-77 when CIEC ended.
Since then development issues seem to have attracted less
attention of the international community and are awarded
less priority within national systems. This decrease in
attention and priority has been manifested in three different
ways.

First, the debate on the NIEO has overlapped with the
severest recession since the 1930s. Northern governments
have been far less concerned with the problem of how to
accommodate Southern demands than with coping with the
threats to the health of the domestic economy in the form of
such problems as inflation, unemployment and balance of
trade difficulties. Externally, the preoccupation with domestic recession has resulted in attempts to expand exports and
reduce imports. Consequently new types of restrictive
trade arrangements have appeared under the disguise of
'orderly market arrangements' or 'voluntary export quotas'.
The attempt to keep down inflation at the same time has led
to a form of interest rate war that has pushed up interest
rates in all the industrialized Western countries. The consequences for the Third World have been drastic: reduced possibilities to export goods to the North and increased interest
burdens from financing their foreign debt. Thus, while the
problems for the Third World increased as a consequence of
Northern preoccupation with recession, concomitantly the
willingness of the North to do something about them decreased.

Secondly, the North seemed to feel that the monetary
chaos, envisaged by many after the breakdown of the
Bretton Woods system in 1971, was no longer an imminent
danger. The international exchange of goods, capital, and
services seemed to be able to continue and to increase despite the breakdown of the fixed exchange rate system and
the gold-backed dollar. Certainly some problems still
remained, as seen in the discussion over the substitution
account in the IMF, but on the whole the feeling that immediate drastic reforms had to be instituted was no longer pre-
valent among the industrialized countries. At the same time
that the Third World increased its pressure for radical reforms of the international monetary system, the North
seemed to become more and more interested in preserving
the status quo in this area. Even countries that normally
supported the Third World, such as Sweden, Denmark or
The Netherlands, ended up being very reluctant to support
reform proposals for the international monetary system.

Thirdly, towards the end of the decade, a number of specific events turned the pecking order of international priorities completely upside down. The events in Iran and in
Afghanistan transformed the international agenda back into
a situation where security issues were once again awarded
the highest priority, and the developing countries seemed to
be of interest only as battlefields in the struggle between
East and West. This reordering of priorities may of course
change, but it seems more than just a passing phenomenon.
If this is the case, then the entire development debate will
gradually be transformed, and the discussion of a NIEO may
become a historical phenomenon.

The combined effect of the changing content and priority
of issues on the international agenda has had a number of
effects on the NIEO debate. First and most obviously, the
salience accorded to the development issues has decreased.
The reception of the Brandt report in the North is a case in
point. The Soviet Union has stated that it had nothing to do
with the report and disclaimed the proposals contained in it.
The report was published shortly after the invasion of
Afghanistan, and Willy Brandt himself has openly admitted
that it proved extremely difficult under those circumstances
to appeal to the enlightened self-interest of the developed
countries. The change of administration in the USA meant a
further increase in the priority given to security issues and
decreased receptivity towards Brandt type proposals.

Second, the establishment of a sort of ad hoc regime in
the international monetary field had the effect of creating a
pronounced reticence for concessions on the part of the
North. When collapse was not threatening there was no reason to accommodate demands for changes in the system. In
the field of international monetary reform there was also a
pronounced scepticism towards change, since the cost of a
potential disruption of a temporary modus vivendi seemed for
the North to outweigh the benefits of discussing the Third
World demands for a complete overhaul of the entire Bretton
Woods system.

Third, the impact of the recession underlined this general
scepticism in relation to change, and protectionism and
export promotion entered into the overall policy of the North
towards the Third World. One immediate consequence was
the commercialization of aid policy by the North, for example
by tying aid to procurement in the donor country, or by
stimulating private enterprises to engage in trade and investment in the Third World.

On the other hand, while the effects of the recession, the
decreasing concern with the collapse of the international

monetary system and the increasing preoccupation with
security issues have generally had a negative influence on
the NIEO debate from the perspective of the Third World,
there have been some counter pressures. The very fact
that the NIEO negotiation process has been started and that
a bureaucratic momentum has been gained means that it will
be difficult to disregard totally these issues in the future.
Especially within the development field there seems to be a
multiplier effect of international discussions. Once a set of
international conferences has been started, they lead to
more and more discussions on more and more issues. Conferences all call for new conferences to discuss this or that
problem and create new organizations or funds that call
their own meetings and do their own studies. In this respect, the issues of the NIEO is maintained on the international agenda.

Nonetheless the balance of pressures of the change in the
priority of issues on the international agenda has been in
the negative direction as far as the Third World is concerned. In this respect, the changing agenda fits with the
'falling curve' of Third World NIEO achievements and again
as such has contributed to the outcome of negligible progress.

The Changing Constellation of Key Domestic and International Northern Actors

Some of the invariant ingredients of political debate are
political mobilization, participation and coalition formation.
It is no coincidence therefore in discussing the origins of
the NIEO debate that we called attention to the process of
the mobilization and organization of the South. Or again,
in discussing the relative decline of Third World powers, we
pointed to the failure of OPEC to become the vanguard of the
the Third World and to the problems of maintaining unity
among the multifarious Third World actors. Our third
general explanatory set relates to the political mobilization,
organization and coalition formation that the NIEO debate
triggered in the North.

A first point of importance concerns the mobilization of
domestic economic interest groups. The sense of urgency
and threat that prevailed in the industrialized countries in
the aftermath of the oil crises of 1973/4 quickly sensitized
a number of key domestic groups. In particular industry
and commerce perceived the NIEO demands to be threatening
their interests and demanded a greater say in and benefit

from the Third World policy. Some saw unwarranted regulation of the international trading system, others saw cutthroat competition from low-wage labour-intensive industries in the Third World. Although differences existed between the different countries, as a general observation it seems that the effect of the increased mobilization of key domestic interest groups was to increase these groups' participation in governmental decision-making. This has been manifested for example in the appointment of external advisors to delegations to North-South conferences or in the establishment of new contact groups and committees.

A second point of importance concerns the coordination among the governments of the North. Whereas the South, especially at the beginning of the debate, formed a relatively coherent block, the North had difficulty in coordinating the responses. Some countries reacted very strongly to the OPEC actions in 1973 and tried to use counter force to meet the challenge from the South (in particular the USA). The attempt failed, however, since a number of Northern countries chose instead a strategy of accommodation (the EC countries and especially France). It is actually impossible to speak of a Northern response in the initial period. Indeed the different reactions from the Northern countries created a number of opportunities for the South to find support for their demands. This lack of Northern unity was, however, only a temporary breech. The longer the debate went on, the more coherent the Northern responses seemed to become.

This is not without its exceptions. The unity oscillated over time, but certainly also across issues. Right from the start, different supportive groups of developed countries existed in different issue areas. Countries such as Norway, that on commodity issues supported the demands from the South, were among the countries most violently opposed to the Southern demands on other issues, such as cargo-sharing or international shipping. This overall tendency towards oscillation in the unity of the North was a complicating factor in the negotiations, since the preparation of a Northern response in itself became a very involved matter.

The difficulties in shaping common responses to the demands from the South increased the importance of regional divisions. The necessity felt by some countries to respond to the demands in some accommodating manner meant that old ties between the North and the South were used as a basis for small regional North-South discussions. The negotiations on the Lomé conventions between the EC and the former colonies of the EC member countries is the most advanced of these examples, but other forms of debate were started by the USA towards Latin America, by Japan towards the Far East, and by the USSR in relation to her allies in the Third World. In some cases such as Lomé, the result of this was a formal agreement and arrangements that could have been global, but the common result was to underline the division between the different Northern countries. The regional division produced some results for the Third World but also increased the difficulties in reaching results in the global North-South debate.

A final point of interest concerns the role of the Eastern European countries and especially the USSR. At the start of the NIEO debate, these countries almost unconditionally supported the demands from the South. At the same time, however, they did nothing in substance. Consequently, they assumed a position somewhat on the sidelines. Increasingly, however, the Third World rejected the argument of the East that since the present malaise was a product of colonial exploitation, they (the East) had no obligation or responsibility as far as substantial concessions or transfers to the Third World were concerned. The Third World countered this argument by pointing to the OPEC countries that again in the absence of any reponsibility for the underdevelopment of the colonies nonetheless disbursed large amounts of aid and took an active part in the NIEO debate in cooperation with the rest of the Third World. Pressure from the Third World on the East gradually increased. In the UNCTAD a special group was formed to study the question of the relationship between the East and the South and here demands for the active involvement of the East were presented but without any important substantive results. The apparent unwillingness of the East to accommodate to the demands from the South moved the East from its earlier position on the sidelines to one where it was seen to be alongside the West.

These changes in the constellation of key Northern actors had a number of important influences on the outcome of the NIEO debate.

The mobilization of domestic economic interest groups has for the most part been a mobilization of anti-NIEO sentiment. These groups have to some extent transformed the NIEO debate into a domestic political issue. This in turn has obliged governments to adopt a NIEO policy, which in general, reflecting the short-term interest of the domestic economic interest groups, has been supportive of the status quo.

The different initial reactions of the industrialized

countries to the NIEO demands inhibited both outright acceptance and rejection. Over time, however, there has been a movement towards greater unity in the North particularly among the larger states. A further ramification of the variation in attitude among the Northern states is that it has resulted in a prolongation and emasculation of the negotiations. At the same time that NIEO gradually became an accepted subject of international negotiation, the debate itself progressively dissolved from discussion of principles to watered-down compromise agreements, where the wording of the documents became the most important result of the debate.

The fragmentation of the North and the attempt from the North to strike individual deals with the Third World meant that regional divisions became a central part of the North-South debate. On the one hand the effect of this was to divide the South into various groupings that got different deals with different Northern countries, and through this placed pressure on the frail unity of the South. On the other hand, it also placed enormous strains on the attempt to build up a unity of the North. Once again this had the effect on the one hand of prolonging the negotiations and on the other hand of effectively preventing any major operational decisions.

We have already pointed to a number of factors that over time led to a reduction in the Northern perception of the threat from the Third World. An additional factor that encouraged this reduction was the changing position of the USSR. The main consequence of the movement of the USSR from a position on the sidelines to one where it was perceived by the South to be alongside the West was to remove the threat that any East-South alliance would be built. This in turn obviated any necessity of the West to make some substantial concessions in order to preempt a major Soviet expansion into the Third World.

The changing constellation of key Northern actors has had a number of complicating and often countervailing influences on the NIEO debate. The pluralism and diversity of Northern actors has certainly on the one hand inhibited any outright rejection of the NIEO package. On the other hand, it has contributed in no small measure to the general emasculation of the NIEO debate, which once again fits very well the falling curve of the negligible progress.

Principles

The three sets of explanatory factors that we have outlined
thus far are variable in the sense that they could change
over time, i.e. Third World power, for example, can
increase or decrease. Our fourth and final set of explanatory factors, that of principles, is rather more constant.
By principles we refer to a basic set of underlying attitudes and values. While any one policy response is a function of a number of determinants, one extremely important
determinant is that of principle. In this respect any policy
will be seen to reflect a basic set of underlying and enduring principles. The two major principles currently manifested, albeit in varying degrees and mixes, by the major
industrialized countries are liberalism and realism.
    Liberalism can take two forms. The pure case of
liberalism is based on the eighteenth century revolt against
mercantilism. In political terms, pure liberalism is premised on the promotion and protection of the individual's
freedom of choice, which in turn is seen as the prerequisite
or basis of peace and order. Economically, pure liberalism
is manifested in the form of a free market structured internationally by the laws of comparative advantage.
    An enduring problem in classic liberal theory is the
question of how individual freedom can be protected. Thus
politically, many liberals would be willing to tolerate some
degree of state intervention to ensure that the freedom of
any one individual is protected from excesses in the freedom of another. Or again, economically many liberals would
tolerate some degree of intervention or protection, as for
example in the case of infant industries. Such interventions are in one sense illiberal but are tolerated on the
grounds that they serve to foster in the long-run a more
satisfactory achievement of basic liberal objectives. Compensatory liberalism, a second form of liberalism, differs
from the pure variety not in its ultimate objectives but in
that it is prepared to tolerate a greater degree of intervention to achieve those objectives.
    While the hall-marks of liberalism are the pursuit of
interdependence and mutual interest, the critical concerns
of realism are state autonomy and national interest. Economically, realism is manifested in neo-mercantilism. Politically, the statecentric view of realism envisages a hierachi-
cal system of independent sovereign states pursuing and
attempting to maximize their national interests in a context
of zero-sum competition.
    We can now turn to examine how each of the sets of

attitudes and values contained in the liberal and realist principles would structure a response to the type of demands raised by NIEO. As far as the pure liberal position is concerned, it is in strong disagreement both with the rationale of the NIEO demands and with the solutions contained in the demands. As we have already argued the NIEO protagonists saw themselves as being locked in an international division of labour over which they had little control and which was leading to their enduring impoverishment. They were arguing in essence that liberalism was an important, though not sole, contributory factor to their underdevelopment. The liberals on the other hand identify and explain international economic problems not in terms of the over- but the under-development of liberalism. Since the solutions contained in the NIEO demands are essentially logically consistent with their rationale, then it is no surprise to discover that the NIEO solutions are the very antithesis of liberal ones. Virtually every single NIEO demand, involving some degree of intervention, preferential or discriminatory treatment or protection, was prescribing what, according to pure liberal principles, are obstacles to the free working of an international market.

The compensatory liberal position, though not of necessity in accord with the rationale for the NIEO demands, is in much greater sympathy with the solutions offered by NIEO. The Third World is in general underprivileged compared with the North. Simply following an extension of infant industry protection, some substantial concessions could be offered to the South on a temporary basis not for moral reasons but as a way of stimulating and expanding production in the LDCs which in turn would expand international markets. This is not to imply, however, that the compensatory liberals would agree with every demand or every operational implementation.

Viewed from realists principles, the NIEO demands again appear antithetical. The realist deplores the idea that states should surrender any political control. The NIEO demands are seen as being dirigiste and extailing totally unacceptable international intervention in national affairs. Realist beliefs and values are also not in accord with the idea of globalized welfare. The idea that the upper echelons of the international hierarchy of states should make substantial concessions to the lower levels is entirely alien to realist beliefs. Welfare according to realist principles is nationally based and can only be built and defended nationally.

More so than the pure liberal but less so than the

compensatory liberal, the realist could, however, find some
degree of sympathy for certain features of the NIEO package.
Some concessions could be tolerated if some greater gain
could thereby be achieved. Thus minor accommodations
would in fact readily be granted if such accommodations
would for example ensure that the Third World was not
alienated. Or alternatively, unilateral concessions would be
made if a state as a consequence could secure some other
benefit for the national interest. Or again, a state could
concur with some multilateral agreement, which it essentially
deplored, if it perceived that non concurrence could lead to
a loss such as isolation.

All Northern states display varying mixes of liberalism
and realism, as far as their external policies are concerned.
In general the closer a state approximates to pure liberalism
the greater would be the opposition to NIEO; the closer a
state approximates to compensatory liberalism, the greater
the sympathy; an approximation to realism would again
encourage substantial opposition though this would be tem-
pered by a willingness to make some concessions albeit
usually for national opportunistic reasons. Though no one
state represents a pure case, i.e. will usually manifest
elements of all the principles, and though these principles
are not the sole determinant of NIEO responses, these principles nonetheless not only explain why there was a general
antipathy to NIEO from the North but also can explain varia-
tions among states. Thus for example, the Scandinavian
countries and Holland, generally displaying the most marked
degree of compensatory liberalism, were the least hostile;
FRG, the UK and the USA, as generally more ardent adher-
ents to purer liberalism, were rather more hostile; or again
the USSR, as a fairly strong proponent of realism, was also
finally very hostile. Even the Scandinavian countries and
Holland, however, are not without realist elements and commonly opposed certain NIEO items (e.g. Norway on cargo-
sharing or Holland on the sea-bed authority) when they saw
key national interests threatened. Or again the liberal
advocates displayed realist tendencies (especially the USA
and UK) when it become apparent that only token or symbolic accommodations could be made for the greater gain of
not alienating the Third World.

VICTORY IN THE END?

At the start of the 1980s there was general agreement that
although the NIEO debate had produced some small changes

it had failed to produce anything approximating the original
ambitions and goals of the Third World. This agreement on
the state of the present outcome could not however hide a
very substantial disagreement on the longer-term outcome.

Spokesman of the leading protagonist NIEO states continue to assert that final victory will be theirs. A battle may
well have been lost but the war is yet to be won. Thus at
the Eleventh Special Session of the UN, Mishra of India
asserted: 'It is not possible for others to stall for a long
time, That is our strength' or again Benyania of Algeria
claimed 'With the access of two thirds of mankind to control
over its destiny, the present international economic order is
condemned to disappear. Movement towards a new order is
inevitable...' (45) While the major NIEO protagonists certainly do not dispute the current largely moribund state of
the NIEO debate, they also have not surrendered their original goals and ambitions. All that has changed is their
time perspective. The current stalemate and stagnation is
but a temporary hiatus on the road to the final and inevitable victory.

The leaders of the hard-line major states of the North on
the other hand are more inclined to the view that the final
victory is something of the present or past rather than of
the future. While they consider that they themselves may
well have lost a battle, they have nonetheless won the war.
There is among them widespread recognition that the so-
called old order had its problems and came under serious
strain in the early 1970s. Additionally it is accepted that
the old order has changed and will continue to do so and no
doubt new orders will finally appear. What is equally clear
also however is that such change will take place largely
under the control and direction of the North according to
the tried and tested formula of incrementalism. The current
moribund state of the NIEO debate is not a temporary hiatus but the termination of an unacceptable timetable of an
unacceptable set of demands for an unacceptable new order.

Any Northern perception that the war has been won is
probably something of an overstatement. Nyerere is essentially correct when he asserts that povery, justice and exploitation are there to remain on the international agenda.
The Third World has learnt how to mobilize, organize and
make its voice heard. On the other hand, while poverty,
justice and exploitation are unquestionably on the agenda,
any consensus on the degree, causes or solutions are not.
Furthermore, our analysis of the current outcome of the
NIEO debate demonstrates that a very substantial set of
obstacles stands in the way of the type of solutions the NIEO

protagonists would like to enact. The Third World has certainly made its voice heard but it has hardly brought down
the walls of the old order. Thus, while we are not inclined
to agree with the hard-line Northern claim that we have seen
the end of the beginning, we equally cannot agree with the
NIEO protagonists that we have seen, or even glimpsed,
the beginning of the end.

NOTES

1   In describing the response to the Third World demands
    we will focus on the Western countries, as the Eastern
    bloc has played a much more peripheral role in the NIEO
    negotiations. We use the term Northern deliberately
    whenever both groups of industrialized countries are
    included.
2   From 1965 to 1976 Third World exports of manufactures
    increased by approximately a factor of nine. See 'Hand-
    book of International Trade and Development Statistics',
    UNCTAD, 1979, p. 756.
3   See: 'Assessment of the Progress made in the Establish-
    ment of the New International Economic Order and
    Appropriate Action for the Promotion of the Development
    of Developing Countries and International Economic Co-
    operation', Report of the Secretary-General to the UN
    General Assembly of 7 August 1980, A/S-11/5, p. 58.
    This Report is henceforth referred to as the 'UN Assess-
    ment'.
4   Ibid. p. 58. The importance of this development is
    elaborated in 'The Impact of the newly industrialized
    countries on production and trade in manufactures',
    Paris OECD, 1979.
5   'UN Assessment', op. cit., pp. 59-60.
6   Cf. the growing literature on the dynamics of the new
    international division of labour. The basic work is
    F. Froebel, J. Heinrichs and O. Kreye, 'Die Neue Inter-
    national Arbeitsteilung', Reinbek bei Hamburg, Rowohlt
    Taschenbuch Verlag, 1977.
7   This was clearly seen during UNCTAD V in 1979 when
    the parties' positions on this issue were very far apart.
8   At UNIDO III in 1980 the Western countries openly re-
    jected a proposed fund for promotion of industrial re-
    allocation.
9   'UN Assessment', op. cit., p. 24.
10 For more details see 'Development Forum', July-August
    1980, pp. 1 and 2.

11   See, for example, the Opinion expressed by Andres
     Federmann in 'South', October 1980, p. 17. In UN
     language a similar sentiment is expressed more diplo-
     matically in this way: "Experience will show the extent
     to which the nature and size of the Common Fund as
     agreed will provide adequate protection for the many
     financially weak producing countries in the face of
     markets that are dominated by strong oligopolistic
     buyers", 'UN Assessment', op. cit., pp. 25-26.
12   Reported in North-South Monitor, 'Third World Quar-
     terly', July 1981, pp. 410-411.
13   'UN Assessment', op. cit., p. 25.
14   Ibid., p. 41.
15   Ibid., p. 62.
16   South, October 1980, pp. 18-20.
17   They have even tried to raise the target to one per cent
     by 1990.
18   This average figure conceals considerable difference
     among the Western countries. While four countries
     (Denmark, Netherlands, Norway and Sweden) have
     reached the UN target, "the aid performance of most of
     the remaining 13 DAC (Development Assistance Commit-
     tee of the OECD) members deteriorated from 1976 to
     1979", 'World Development Report', The World Bank,
     1980, p. 28. All subsequent references are to this
     edition of the Report.
19   'UN Assessment', op. cit., p. 38. 'In 1979 over three
     quarters of ODA committments by DAC countries were
     for outright grants", 'Development Cooperation 1980
     Review', Paris, OECD, 1980, p. 103. This Review is
     henceforth referred to as 'OECD Review'.
20   The percentage share of bilateral ODA to low-income
     countries has fallen from 47 (in 1970) to 38 (in 1978),
     while the share to middle-income countries have risen
     from 44 to 52 per cent. See: 'World Development
     Report', op. cit., p. 30.
21   'OECD Review', op. cit. p. 104.
22   Ibid., p. 141.
23   OECD countries normally provide from 80 to 95 per
     cent of the resources of these agencies (ibid., p. 139).
24   'World Development Report', op. cit., pp. 30-31. In
     his farewell statement World Bank president Robert
     McNamara said that the International Development
     Association (the softloan branch of the Bank) is on the
     verge of bankruptcy because of delays and cuts in
     US appropriation.
25   UNCTAD resolution 165 (S-IX) adopted in March 1978.

26   In addition the US delegation has even tried to obstruct
     data collection by the UNCTAD secretariat on the imple-
     mentation of the resolution.
27   'UN Assessment', op. cit., p. 39.   OECD has estimated
     that "these actions for all DAC countries cover over $7
     billion of ODA debt and reduce the annual debt service
     burden of the beneficiary countries by over $100 mil-
     lion".   See: 'OECD Review', op. cit., p. 104.
28   'World Development Report', op. cit., p. 31
29   This is illustrated by the agreement between the Fund
     and the conservative Seaga government of Jamaica.
     (For details see report in 'ICDA News', June 1981, p
     p. 4.)
30   These transfers are, however, tied to a country's quota
     in the IMF, not the actual shortfall in export earnings.
31   'UN Assessment', op. cit., p. 40.
32   'IMF Annual Report 1980', op. cit., p. 74.
33   For more details see 'South', November 1980, pp. 5-7.
34   The autonomy of the IMF turned out to be the most con-
     troversial point in the preparations to the global nego-
     tiations.   So far, not even the most intense diplomatic
     manoeuvres have led to any conciliatory move from the
     three "hard-liners", the USA, UK and FRG.   More
     details about this discussion can be found in the 'OECD
     Review', op. cit., pp. 20-22.
35   A favourite description of Third World arguments in
     Western official circles.
36   The failure of the grand plan for reform of the commo-
     dity markets is referred to above.   Concerning debt,
     the LDCs initially wanted this issue-area to be handled
     by a new, independent International Debt Commission.
     They have got no substantial results with regard to the
     institutional set-up, but the UNCTAD secretariat has
     been allowed to provide technical assistance to indivi-
     dual developing debtor countries.
37   The Third World has called for an increase in its share
     of IMF quotas (which determine voting strength by 45
     per cent, but they have got only selective increases for
     eleven individual countries, in particular members of
     OPEC.   See: 'South', November 1980, pp. 5-6.
38   The UN Assessment concludes that "there has been no
     significant change in the voting pattern of the estab-
     lished and most powerful financial and monetary struc-
     tures, and the developing countries have continued to
     have a limited influence on international financial and
     monetary policies.   See 'UN Assessment', op. cit.,
     p. 38.

39   Agreement has been reached on a code of conduct for restrictive business practices, while negotiations continue on transfer of technology and TNC activities in general.

40   An account of this bargaining process can be found in 'South', May 1981, pp. 20-24.

41   'UN Assessment', op. cit., p. 123.

42   See Address by J.K. Nyerere, President of Tanzania, to the Fourth Ministerial Meeting of the Group of 77, in 'Arusha Programme for Collective Self-Reliance', Manilla, UNCTAD, 1979.

43   C.F. Bergsten, 'The Threat from the Third World', 'Foreign Policy', 11, 1973, pp. 102-124.

44   See Hans-Henrik Holm, 'A Banner of Hope? North-South Negotiations and the New International Development Strategy for the Eighties.' 'Cooperationa and Conflict', 16, 4, 1981.

45   Mishra was quoted in the 'Guardian', 24 September, 1980. Benyania is quoted from 'Provisional Verbatim Record of the Fourth Meeting', Eleventh Special Session, A/S-11/PV.4, 1980.

Table 1. Net official development assistance from DAC countries to developing countries and multilateral agencies

Disbursements $ million and per cent of GNP

Countries	1969-71 Average $ m.	as % of GNP	1974 $ m.	as % of GNP	1975 $ m.	as % of GNP	1976 $ m.	as % of GNP	1977 $ m.	as % of GNP	1978 $ m.	as % of GNP	1979 $ m.	as % of GNP
Australia	205	0.59	433	0.55	552	0.65	377	0.41	400	0.42	588	0.55	620	0.52
Austria	12	0.08	60	0.18	79	0.21	50	0.12	108	0.22	154	0.27	127	0.19
Belgium	127	0.49	271	0.51	378	0.59	340	0.51	371	0.46	536	0.55	631	0.56
Canada	314	0.38	716	0.47	880	0.54	887	0.46	991	0.50	1 060	0.52	1 026	0.46
Denmark	63	0.40	168	0.55	205	0.58	214	0.56	258	0.60	388	0.75	448	0.75
Finland	11	0.10	38	0.16	48	0.18	51	0.17	49	0.16	55	0.16	86	0.21
France	1 001	0.67	1 616	0.59	2 093	0.62	2 146	0.62	2 267	0.60	2 705	0.57	3 370	0.59
Germany	638	0.34	1 433	0.37	1 689	0.40	1 593	0.36	1 717	0.33	2 347	0.37	3 350	0.44
Italy	153	0.17	216	0.14	182	0.11	226	0.13	198	0.10	375	0.14	273	0.08
Japan	468	0.24	1 126	0.25	1 148	0.23	1 105	0.20	1 424	0.21	2 215	0.23	2 637	0.26
Netherlands	185	0.57	436	0.63	608	0.75	728	0.83	908	0.86	1 073	0.82	1 404	0.93
New Zealand	14	0.22	39	0.31	66	0.52	53	0.41	53	0.39	55	0.34	61	0.30
Norway	36	0.32	131	0.57	184	0.66	218	0.70	295	0.83	355	0.90	429	0.93
Sweden	132	0.42	402	0.72	566	0.82	608	0.82	779	0.99	783	0.90	956	0.94
Switzerland	29	0.14	68	0.14	104	0.19	112	0.19	119	0.19	173	0.20	207	0.21
United Kingdom	528	0.42	783	0.40	897	0.39	879	0.39	1 103	0.45	1 460	0.47	2 067	0.52
United States	3 214	0.32	3 674	0.26	4 141	0.27	4 360	0.26	4 682	0.25	5 664	0.27	4 684	0.20
Total DAC countries	7 131	0.35	11 610	0.34	13 840	0.36	13 947	0.33	15 722	0.33	19 986	0.35	22 375	0.35

Source: OECD. Development Cooperation, 1980 Review

Table 2. Comparative aid-giving performance in 1979.

Countries (ranked in order of per capita GNP, 1979)	GNP		Total official and private net flows reported		Official Development Assistance						
					Net flow 1979		1978	Net transfer[a]		Grant equivalent[b]	
	$	Rank	% of GNP	Rank	% of GNP	Rank	Rank	% of GNP	Rank	% of GNP	Rank
Switzerland	15 320	1	5.65	1	0.21	13–14	15	0.21	13–14	0.21	13–14
Germany	12 410	2	0.96	11	0.44	10	10	0.41	10	0.46	9
Sweden	12 240	3	1.26	7	0.94	1	1–2	0.94	1	0.94	1
Denmark	11 700	4	1.25	8–9	0.75	4	4	0.75	4	0.87	4
Belgium	11 440	5	2.03	3	0.56	6	6–7	0.56	6	0.54	6–7
Norway	11 290	6	1.64	4	0.93	2–3	1–2	0.93	2	0.93	2
United States	10 740	7–8	0.79	12	0.20	15	12–13	0.18	16	0.19	15
Netherlands	10 740	7–8	1.29	6	0.93	2–3	3	0.91	3	0.92	3
France	10 700	9	1.52	5	0.59	5	5	(0.57)	5	0.60	5
Canada	9 390	10	1.14	10	0.46	9	8	0.46	9	0.45	10
Austria	9 110	11	0.36	17	0.19	16	12–13	0.19	15	0.17	16
Japan	8 730	12	0.75	13	0.26	12	14	0.23	12	0.21	13–14
Finland	8 540	13	0.43	15	0.21	13–14	16	0.21	13–14	0.32	11–12
Australia	8 320	14	0.73	14	0.52	7–8	6–7	0.52	7	0.52	8
United Kingdom	7 080	15	2.83	2	0.52	7–8	9	0.50	8	0.54	6–7
New Zealand	6 390	16	0.38	16	0.30	11	11	0.30	11	0.32	11–12
Italy	5 700	17	1.25	8–9	0.08	17	17	0.08	17	0.10	17
DAC average	9 730		1.14		(0.33)					0.34	

a) Gross disbursements less receipts of both amortization and interest.
b) Grant equivalent of gross disbursements (estimated).

Table 3. Comparative ODA volume performance of major donor groups

	$ million			% of GNP			% of total ODA		
	1975	1978	1979	1975	1978	1979	1975	1978	1979
DAC	13 844	19 982	22 374	0.36	0.35	0.35	66	78	76
OPEC	5 517	4 338	5 197	2.94	1.38	1.44	27	17	18
CMEA (including aid to Cuba, Korea PDR and Viet Nam)	1 437	1 266	1 852	0.13	0.09	0.11	7	5	6
CMEA (excluding aid to Cuba, Korea PDR and Viet Nam)	266	244	560	0.02	0.02	0.03			

Source: OECD. Development Cooperation, 1980 Review.

Table 4. Comparative ODA terms performance of major donor groups

	Percentage of grants in total commitments		Grant element of ODA loans (%)			Overall grant element (%)		
	1977	1978	1977	1978	1979	1977	1978	1979
DAC Countries	72	74	62	62	61	89	90	91
OPEC Countries	73	76	44	50	48	84	88	80
CMEA Countries (including aid to Cuba and Viet Nam)	41	44	52	49	52	71	71	82
CMEA Countries (excluding aid to Cuba and Viet Nam)	13	23	43	37	32	51	52	66

Note: Terms of OPEC countries include estimates. Figures for CMEA countries are rough estimates only.

Source: OECD. Developing Cooperation, 1980 Review.

Table 5. The evolution of CMEA ODA flows to developing countries
Total Net Disbursements

	Including Cuba, Korea PDR, Viet Nam				Excluding Cuba, Korea PDR, Viet Nam			
	1970-1973 average	1974-1977 average	1978	1979	1970-1973 average	1974-1977 average	1978	1979
USSR								
$ million	831	976	914	1 432	226	208	14	282
% of GNP	0.14	0.12	0.10	0.14	0.04	0.03	x	0.03
Eastern Europe[a]								
$ million	240	246	352	420	96	103	210	278
% of GNP	0.10	0.06	0.07	0.07	0.04	0.03	0.04	0.05
Total CMEA								
$ million	1 071	1 222	1 266	1 852	322	311	224	560
% of GNP	0.13	0.10	0.09	0.11	0.04	0.03	0.02	0.03

a) Eastern Europe includes Bulgaria, Czechoslovakia, German Democratic Republik, Hungary, Poland and Romania.

Note: The extremely low figure for USSR aid in 1978 to LDCs other than Cuba, Korea PDR and Viet Nam is due to exceptional large repayments by India for wheat loan obtained in 1973.

Source: OECD. Development Cooperation, 1980 Review.

Table 6. Capital flows and debt of the developing countries: oil importers and oil exporters, 1975-90. (billions of current dollars)

Item	Oil importers					Oil exporters				
	1975	1977	1980	1985	1990	1975	1977	1980	1985	1990
Current account deficit before interest payments[a]	32.9	16.8	42.7	43.5	42.2	6.8	7.8	-11.1	4.0	30.2
	32.9	16.8	42.7	43.5	42.2	6.8	7.8	-11.1	4.0	30.2
Interest payments	6.7	8.1	18.3	35.0	62.0	2.0	4.1	8.8	11.8	17.5
Changes in reserves and short-term debt	-9.1	9.9	-4.4	6.8	23.5	6.2	5.8	20.2	8.4	2.6
Total to be financed	30.6	34.8	56.6	85.2	127.7	15.0	17.7	18.0	24.2	50.2
Financed by medium- and long-term capital										
From public sources	12.5	13.2	21.7	41.1	66.6	5.4	6.0	7.3	11.2	16.6
From private sources	18.1	21.7	34.9	44.0	61.2	9.6	11.7	10.7	13.0	33.6
Private direct investment	4.2	3.9	6.5	9.6	16.4	2.7	2.1	3.5	5.8	8.2
Private loans	13.9	17.7	28.4	34.4	44.7	6.9	9.6	7.2	7.2	25.4
Total net capital flows										
Current dollars	30.6	34.8	56.6	85.2	127.7	15.0	17.7	18.0	24.2	50.2
Constant 1977 dollars	34.2	34.8	40.0	42.1	47.2	16.8	17.7	12.7	12.0	18.5
Outstanding medium- and long-term debt										
Public sources	57.7	77.5	100.4	212.9	397.1	16.2	24.3	48.8	79.6	130.0
Private sources	72.6	108.9	187.1	343.4	558.5	24.7	43.9	66.5	97.5	175.4
Total debt										
Current dollars	130.3	186.4	287.5	556.3	955.6	40.9	68.2	115.3	177.1	305.4
Constant 1977 dollars	146.4	186.4	203.5	275.0	352.9	46.0	68.2	81.6	87.5	112.8
Debt service										
Interest payments	6.7	8.1	18.3	35.0	62.0	2.0	4.1	8.8	11.8	17.5
Debt amortization	12.7	18.9	28.6	65.0	114.2	3.6	6.5	12.2	23.6	40.1
Interest payments as percentage of GNP	0.9	0.8	1.2	1.2	1.3	1.0	1.6	2.7	1.3	1.1
Price deflator	89.3	100.0	141.3	202.3	270.8	89.3	100.0	141.3	202.3	270.8

a Excludes official transfers
Source: World Bank. World Development Report, 1980

Table 7 Direction of merchandise trade, 1970 and 1977

Origin	Oil-exporting developing countries	Oil-importing developing countries Total	Low income	Middle income	All developing countries	Industrialized countries	Capital surplus oil exporters	Centrally planned economies	Unallocated	World	World (millions of current dollars)
							Percentage composition, 1977[a]				
Oil-exporting developing countries	3.9	21.8	1.0	20.8	25.7	66.6	0.5	6.1	1.1	100.0	12,961
Oil-importing developing countries	3.5	17.4	2.5	14.9	20.9	69.0	1.5	7.5	1.1	100.0	39,122
Low-income	4.6	21.7	8.2	13.5	26.3	53.7	4.3	14.6	1.1	100.0	5,779
Middle-income	3.4	16.6	1.5	15.1	20.0	71.7	1.0	6.2	1.1	100.0	33,343
All developing countries	3.6	18.5	2.1	16.3	22.1	68.4	1.2	7.1	1.1	100.0	52,083
Industrialized countries	4.7	18.2	2.1	16.1	22.9	71.0	1.5	3.5	1.1	100.0	215,896
Capital-surplus oil exporters	1.7	20.2	2.9	17.4	21.9	74.4	0.8	1.5	1.5	100.0	11,151
Centrally planned economies	1.7	14.5	1.7	12.9	16.2	21.3	1.0	60.4	1.1	100.0	32,940
World	4.1	18.0	2.1	15.8	22.0	65.4	1.3	10.1	1.1	100.0	312,070
World (millions of current dollars)	12,710	56,019	6,604	49,415	68,729	204,160	4,211	31,400	3,570	312,070	
							Percentage composition, 1977[a]				
Oil-exporting developing countries	2.2	21.5	1.1	20.4	23.7	72.6	0.8	2.8	0.1	100.0	58,391
Oil-importing developing countries	8.4	20.5	2.5	18.1	28.9	61.8	3.1	6.1	0.1	100.0	149,854
Low-income	5.4	21.9	9.4	12.4	27.3	53.6	7.7	11.5	(.)	100.0	13,495
Middle-income	8.7	20.4	1.8	18.6	29.1	62.6	2.7	5.6	0.1	100.0	136,359
All developing countries	6.6	20.8	2.1	18.7	27.4	64.8	2.5	5.2	0.1	100.0	208,245
Industrialized countries	6.7	16.4	1.4	15.0	23.1	65.7	5.6	5.2	0.5	100.0	697,568
Capital-surplus oil exporters	4.3	20.6	1.5	19.1	24.9	69.6	1.2	2.9	1.5	100.0	110,289
Centrally planned economies	2.9	8.8	1.0	7.8	11.7	27.2	3.2	54.5	3.4	100.0	107,523
World	6.1	16.9	1.5	15.4	23.0	62.2	4.3	9.7	0.8	100.0	1,123,625
World (millions of current dollars)	68,149	189,918	16,578	173,340	258,067	699,036	48,665	108,930	8,927	1,123,625	

Source: World Bank. World Developing Report, 1980, p. 100.

ABBREVIATIONS

CIEC	Conference of International Economic Cooperation
CIPEC	Intergovernmental Council of Copper Exporting Countries
CF	Common Fund
CMEA	Council for Mutual Economic Assistance
CNPF	National Centre of French Management
COREPER	Committee of Permanent Representatives
CPE	Centrally Planned Economies
DAC	Development Assistance Committee
DC	Developing Countries
EC	European Community
ECLA	Economic Commission for Latin America
ECOSOC	Committee for Economic and Social Affairs
EEC	European Economic Community
EFTA	European Free Trade Association
EPC	European Political Cooperation
FAO	Food and Agricultural Organization
FRG	Federal Republic of Germany
GATT	General Agreement on Tariffs and Trade
GDP	Gross domestic product
GNP	Gross national product
GSP	General System of Preferences
IBRD	International Bank for Restructuring and Development
ICA	International Commodity Agreements
IDA	International Development Association
IEA	International Energy Agency
IFAD	International Fund for Agricultural Development
IGO	Intergovernmental Organization
IMF	International Monetary Fund
IPC	Integrated Programme for Commodities

ISA	International Seabed Authority
LDC	Least Developed Countries
MFN	Most Favoured Nations
MSAC	Most Seriously Affected Countries
NIEO	New International Economic Order
NORAD	Norwegian Agency for International Development
ODA	Official Development Assistance
OECD	Organization for Economic Cooperation and Development
OPEC	Organization for Petroleum Exporting Countries
SIDA	Swedish International Development Authority
STABEX	Stabilization of export earnings
SWEFUND	Swedish Fund for Industrial Cooperation with Developing Countries
TNC	Transnational corporations
TOT-code	Transfer of Technology-code
UD	Norwegian Ministry of Foreign Affairs
UN	United Nations
UNCLOS	United Nations Conference on Law of the Sea
UNCST	United Nations Conference on Science and Technology
UNCTAD	United Nations Conference on Trade and Development
UNDP	United Nations Development Programme
UNIDO	United Nations Industrial Development Organization

INDEX

Absolute poverty, 151
ACPs, 86
Adjustment fund, 161
Adler-Karlsson, 177
African Bank for Development, 133
African countries, 6, 115, 171
Agricultural goods, 23
American foreign policy, 219, 222
American response, 205, 211
Amuzegar, 189
Arab countries, 123
Arusha Convention, 17, 86
Arusha Programme, 3, 175
Asian countries, 6
Asian Development Bank, 195
Australia, 30
Austria, 22-36
Austrian economy, 28, 30
Austrian response, 23, 34
Austria's aid performance, 25
Austria's foreign policy, 30
Austria's multilateral contribution, 26
Austria's Third World trade, 23

Balance of payments, 10, 12,

Balance of payment (cont.)
18, 29, 50, 69, 70, 71, 77, 79, 107, 108, 135, 140, 192, 197, 228
Bandung Conference, 6
Bargaining power, 115, 138
Bargaining strength, 170
Basic needs, 14, 30, 65, 67, 73, 134
Benyania, 246
Bilateral aid, 26, 38, 40, 55, 66, 67, 69, 70, 75, 151
Bilateral assistance, 65, 66, 116, 150, 201
Bilateral transfers, 150
Bognar, 182
Bogomolov, 174, 177
Brandt report, 238
Bretton Woods, 18, 99, 156, 217, 228, 229, 237, 238
Britain, 37-62, 87, 88, 91, 95, 109, 116, 117, 126, 134, 137, 139, 165
British aid, 37, 39
British commodity response, 50
British development policy, 38, 57
British economy, 49, 50, 51
British foreign economic policy, 45
British foreign policy, 50, 57
Bulgaria, 174

Callaghan, J., 59
Canada, 27
Capital flows, 11
Cargo-sharing, 5, 69, 154, 240, 245
Carrington, 38, 58
Cartelization, 205, 208, 234
Carter administration, 211
Ceausescu, 172
Centrally planned economies, 170, 179
Charter of Economic Rights and Duties, 24, 171
Cheysson, Claude, 198
Chinese influence, 171
CIEC, 88, 89, 94, 124, 126, 232, 237
CMEA, 171, 172, 176, 177, 180, 182
Collective action, 7, 8, 9, 16
Collective self-reliance, 4
Collective power, 16
Colombo Conference, 171
Colonialism, 176
Colonization, 6
Commercialization, 131, 151, 190, 193, 238
Commission, 87, 90, 92, 93, 94, 117
Committee of the Whole, 198
Commodity assistance, 150
Commotidy trade, 4, 124, 125, 224
Common Agricultural Policy, 86
Common Fund, 4, 5, 24, 41, 42, 43, 48, 51, 54, 56, 57, 63, 86, 87, 88, 89, 91, 92, 93, 95, 101, 109, 110, 111, 113, 126, 127, 154, 219, 225, 235
Compensatory financing, 103, 172
Corea, Gamani, 172
CPE aid, 176
CPE-LDC relations, 170, 172, 179

CPE-LDC trade, 181
CPE markets, 173
Czechoslovakia, 174

DAC, 116, 149, 192
Danish aid policy, 65, 67
Danish foreign policy, 63, 71, 72, 73
Danish official development assistance, 66
Danish Third World exports, 69
Danish Third World policy, 63, 71, 78, 80
Danish trade policy, 69
Debt, 4, 10, 39, 65, 98, 103, 104, 105, 115, 116 134, 135, 141, 157, 175, 197, 219, 220, 227, 228, 229, 234, 235, 237
Decolonization, 6
Denmark, 25, 30, 63-84, 88, 91, 237
Development assistance, 22, 25, 67, 150, 189, 191, 195, 196, 226, 227
Development policy, 31, 135
Development strategy, 11, 13
Development Assistance Committee, 17
Development tax, 4
Distribution of power, 52, 53
Diversification of production, 3
Domino theory, 214

Eastern Europe, 170, 177
East-West trade, 175, 178, 181, 183
EC cooperation, 76
ECLA, 10, 12
Economic Declaration, 3, 9
ECOSOC, 44, 108
EEC Treaty, 85, 92, 93, 94, 117

EFTA, 63, 152, 193
Erlander, Tage, 191
Euro-Arab-African-trilogue, 142
European Community, 23, 29, 85-97, 104, 105, 108, 109, 112, 117, 118
European Council, 88, 89, 93, 94
European Monetary System, 71
European Political Cooperation, 86, 93
Export credits, 150, 151, 227 7
Export guaranties, 69
Export quotas, 173, 237
Export stabilization, 110, 112
Extra-governmental pressures, 55

Federal Republic of Germany, 87, 91, 95, 98-121
Financial transfers, 3, 134, 224, 226
Finland, 25, 30
First Development Decade, 216
First UN Development Decade, 11
First Window, 91, 113
Food production, 3
France, 88, 104, 105, 109, 114, 116, 117, 122-147, 240
Free-rider, 68, 116, 148, 164
French economy, 130, 138
French exports, 139
French market, 140
French trade, 139

GATT, 12, 64, 94, 99, 142, 162, 174, 175, 194, 228, 229
General System of Preferences, 8, 17, 23, 86, 117, 142, 174, 226
Genscher, H.D., 118
German foreign economic policy, 98

German economy, 98, 99, 101
German imports, 117
German ODA, 105, 116
German response, 98
Giscard d'Estaing, V., 122, 123, 124, 134
Grant element, 39, 49
Growth rates, 10, 30

Hager, Wolfgang, 101
Hermes, 100
Holzman, 176
Hungary, 173, 174, 175

IDA, 5, 25, 149, 213
IGOs, 52, 53
IMF, 5, 12, 70, 71, 78, 103, 105, 110, 111, 126, 135, 141, 156, 157, 162, 197, 198, 228, 229, 237
IMPOD, 194, 195
Import quotas, 151
Import restrictions, 69
Indexation, 4, 41, 51, 128, 173, 213, 218, 224, 226
Industrialization, 27, 65, 68, 69, 70, 71, 80, 100, 124, 128, 129, 130, 140, 142, 193, 198, 223, 224
Integrated Programme of Commodities, 24, 42, 85, 86, 89, 91, 98, 109, 126, 156, 172, 225
Integration, 92, 138, 143
Inter American Bank, 190, 195
Interdependence, 17, 123, 136, 141, 148, 190, 243
International Commodity Agreements, 87, 89, 112, 126
International communism, 213, 214
International decision making, 3, 5
International Development Strategy, 68

International Energy Agency, 16, 209
International liberalism, 45
International monetary system, 4, 156, 237, 238
International planned e economy, 188
International regimes, 5, 154, 155, 158, 159, 162, 164 165, 228, 230
International Seabed Authority, 157, 229
International trade, 4, 47, 76, 85, 99, 101, 138, 139, 143, 174
Intra-Governmental Organisation, 56
Ireland, 30

Jobert, Michel, 124

Kissinger Plan, 219
Kreisky, B., 27

Latin-American countries, 6, 40
Law of the Seas, 157, 229
LDC exports, 174, 223, 226
LDC imports, 161
Liberalization, 23, 24, 116, 117, 118, 151, 152, 153, 161
Like-minded countries, 30, 116, 159
Lomé Conventions, 86, 92, 128, 240
London Commodity Exchange, 55

McCulloch, 183
Malhassian, 182
Manila, 127, 134, 171, 199
Manzhulo, 176
Marshall Plan, 11, 27, 28, 198, 214
Market access, 224, 226
Market systems, 3, 224

Marten, Neil, 38, 51
Massive transfer of resources, 138, 197, 198, 199
Mediator, 33, 34, 72, 201
Mesteri, Mahmoud, 176
Mishra, Brajesh, 58, 246
Mixed credits, 150, 195, 196, 227
Most seriously affected countries, 24, 25, 133
Moynahan, Daniel, 1
Multifiber Agreement, 152, 194
Multilateral aid, 39, 67, 115, 133, 150, 221
Multilateral capital assistance, 32
Multilateral technical assistance, 32

Neutrality, 22, 30, 72
Non-Aligned Conferences, 8, 10
Non-aligned countries, 3, 9
Non-governmental organizations, 161
Non-tariff barriers, 24, 117
NORAD, 151
Nordli, Oddvar, 150
NORIMPOD, 153
North-South trade, 23
Norway, 114, 126, 127, 148-169, 240, 245
Norwegian aid, 149, 151, 157, 162, 164
Norwegian export industries, 150
Norwegian foreign policy, 149, 159
Norwegian goods, 150
Norwegian imports, 152
Norwegian NIEO policy, 154, 157, 162, 163
Norwegian shipping, 155
Norwegian trade policy, 152
Nyerere, J., 234
Nyerges, 173

Official development assistance, 25, 103, 116, 132,
149, 220
Oil crisis, 123, 124, 139,
205, 208, 209, 211, 212,
216, 239
OPEC, 9, 18, 29, 69, 124,
135, 136, 141, 176, 200,
205, 208, 211, 212, 216,
217, 218, 222, 230, 233,
239, 240

Palme, Olof, 202
Patolichev, N.S., 175, 177
Pearson Report, 11
Political mobilization, 2, 6,
233, 239
Political organization, 7
Prebish, R., 6, 12, 13
Protectionism, 5, 67, 68, 76,
77, 117, 140, 154, 175,
226, 238
Public opinion, 101, 142, 143,
160, 161, 162, 163, 164,
201, 215

Raw material production, 3
Reagan administration, 221
Regional development, 142
Regional development banks,
150, 227
Restrictive business prac-
tice, 5
Restructuring, 125, 129,
154, 205
Revolution, 183
Robles, Garcia, 1
Romania, 171, 172

Seabed Authority, 5, 245
Second Window, 24, 43, 51,
89, 90, 91, 113, 127, 225
Sector-economic interests,
162, 163
Second Development Decade,
16
Shipping, 69, 154, 161, 162,
164, 240

SIDA, 192, 195
Sixth Special Session, 9, 41,
42
Small-state interests, 159
Soviet economy, 181
Soviet foreign aid, 177
Soviet Union, 30, 108, 110,
157, 170-187, 214, 215,
222, 238
South East Asia, 171
South-South, 140
Special Drawing Rights, 4,
18
Special session, 1, 18, 110,
118, 129, 188, 189, 230,
231, 236, 246
STABEX, 86, 110, 127
Stoltenberg, Thorvald, 152
Structural adjustment, 69,
76, 77, 153, 154, 224
Subsidies, 3
Sweden, 25, 30, 104, 114,
116, 117, 126, 127, 152,
156, 188-204, 237
Swedish aid, 192, 197
Swedish assistance, 193
Swedish economic policy, 195
Swedish exports, 195
Swedish interests, 191
Swedish industry, 195, 196
SWEFUND, 195
Switzerland, 25

Technology transfer, 27, 30,
43, 48,   57, 109, 116,
128, 130, 131, 132, 177
Teodorovich, 182
Terms of trade, 12, 128,
182, 216, 226
Textiles, 23, 68, 70, 117,
140, 152, 193
Third Window, 39
Third World Identity, 7, 10
Third World Forum, 210
TNC, 5
Trade policy, 24, 29, 67, 68,
69, 75, 78, 138, 151, 152,
154, 161, 179, 194

Transfer of technology, 43,
  70, 98, 106, 108, 124, 139,
  156, 177
Tying of aid, 69, 116, 150,
  192

UNCLOS III, 157
UNCSTD, 26, 44, 51, 52, 54,
  78, 106, 108, 109
UNCTAD Secretariat, 87, 155
UNDP, 67, 109, 115, 149, 192
UNIDO, 26, 27, 69, 78, 128,
  129, 131, 138, 193, 224,
  231
United States, 104, 107, 108,
  109, 110, 114, 116, 123,
  124, 125, 126, 128, 134,
  137, 140, 180, 205-222
US economy, 216
US exports, 212
US foreign policy, 215
USSR, 174

Wallace, 58
Warsaw pact, 171
Washington Energy Confer-
  ence, 16
West Germany, 126, 128, 134,
  139, 140
World Bank, 12, 17, 25, 67,
  68, 71, 89, 105, 115, 126,
  133, 134, 141, 149, 150,
  195, 197, 213, 227, 228,
  229
World production, 3, 10, 130
World industrial trade, 4
World Trade Organization,
  175, 178, 181, 183
World welfare state, 148

Yaounde Convention, 17, 86
Yugoslavia, 171, 172

LIST OF CONTRIBUTORS

GEORGE C. ABBOTT, Department of International Economic Studies, University of Glasgow.

HELGE OLE BERGESEN, Fridtjoh Nansen Foundation, Oslo.

JOACHIM BETZ, Institute of Political Science, University of Tübingen.

HANS HENRIK HOLM, Institute of Political Science, Aarhus University.

MICHAEL KREILE, Institute of Political Science, University of Heidelberg.

COLIN LAWSON, School of Humanities and Social Science, University of Bath.

ROBERT D. McKINLAY, Department of Politics, University of Lancaster.

MAHINDRA NARAINE, Department of Politics, University of Lancaster.

BIRGITTA NYGREN, Secretariat of Future Studies/Ministries of Foreign Affairs and Commerce, Stockholm.

MARIE-CLAUDE SMOUTS, Centre d'Etudes et de Recherches Internationales, Foundation Nationale des Sciences Politiques, Paris.

ANSELM SKUHRA, Institute of Political Science, University of Salzburg.

UDO STEFFENS, Institute of Political Science, Technische Hochschule, Darmstadt.